Kwame Kwei-Armah

Plays: 1

Elmina's Kitchen, Fix Up, Statement of Regret, Let There Be Love

Elmina's Kitchen: 'This is an angry, provocative, vital play, one that demands change in society while recognising that there are no easy solutions, and is passionately political while understanding that the best way to communicate with people is to keep them entertained.' *Guardian*

Fix Up: 'What is striking about [Kwei-Armah's] richly eloquent new play is that it deals with a subject that has specific racial resonances but a wider application: the sacrifice of historical identity to the insatiable demands of brute commerce . . . Kwei-Armah builds a philosophical argument out of a practical problem.' *Guardian*

Statement of Regret: 'The play is unashamedly political, driven by dialectic, and bravely provocative: it brings sensitive questions from and about the black community in Britain . . . to the stage. It focuses on the continuing legacy of the slave trade and how best to overcome it. It champions debate and celebrates discussion, is honest, quizzical and daring.' *Financial Times*

Let There Be Love: 'Initially, [the play] looks like an amusing study of racial and generational tolerance, in which a cantankerous old Caribbean Londoner establishes a rapport with his young, Polish cleaner that he can't find with his two daughters. But it ranges far wider and deeper than that, decisively transcending issues of race. In a series of surprising turns, *Let There Be Love* delves into domestic violence and illness, as well as gender and sexuality, dignity and death, without ever losing its sense of humour.' *Evening Standard*

Kwame Kwei-Armah won the Peggy Ramsay award for his first play, *Bitter Herb* (1998), which was subsequently put on by the Bristol Old Vic, where he also became writer-in-residence. He followed this up with the musical *Blues Brother, Soul Sister* which toured the UK in 2001. He co-wrote the musical *Big Nose* (an adaptation of *Cyrano*) which was performed at the Belgrade Theatre, Coventry, in 1999. In 2003 the National Theatre produced the critically acclaimed *Elmina's Kitchen* for which in 2004 he won the *Evening Standard* Charles Wintour Award for Most Promising Playwright, and was nominated for a Laurence Olivier Award for Best New Play 2003. *Elmina's Kitchen* has since been produced and aired on Radio 3 and BBC4. His next two plays, *Fix Up* and *Statement of Regret*, were produced by the National Theatre in 2004 and 2007. He directed his most recent play, *Let There Be Love*, when it premiered at the Tricycle Theatre, London, in 2008. He received an honorary doctorate from the Open University in 2008.

KWAME KWEI-ARMAH

Plays: 1

Elmina's Kitchen
Fix Up
Statement of Regret
Let There Be Love

with an introduction by the author

Methuen Drama

METHUEN DRAMA CONTEMPORARY DRAMATISTS

1 3 5 7 9 10 8 6 4 2

This collection first published in Great Britain in 2009
by Methuen Drama

Methuen Drama
A & C Black Publishers Limited
36 Soho Square
London W1D 3QY
www.acblack.com

Elmina's Kitchen first published by Methuen Drama in 2003
Copyright © 2003 Kwame Kwei-Armah
Fix Up first published by Methuen Publishing in 2004
Revised in this volume. Copyright © 2004, 2009 Kwame Kwei-Armah
Statement of Regret first published by Methuen Drama in 2007
Copyright © 2007, 2009 Kwame Kwei-Armah
Let There Be Love first published by Methuen Drama in this volume
Copyright © 2009 Kwame Kwei-Armah

Introduction © 2009 Kwame Kwei-Armah

Kwame Kwei-Armah has asserted his rights
under the Copyright, Designs and Patents Act, 1988,
to be identified as the author of these works

ISBN: 978 1 4081 1560 2

A CIP catalogue record for this book is available from the British Library

Typeset by Country Setting, Kingsdown, Kent CT14 8ES
Printed and bound in Great Britain by
CPI Cox & Wyman, Reading, RG1 8EX

Contents

Chronology   vii

Introduction   ix

ELMINA'S KITCHEN   1

FIX UP   97

STATEMENT OF REGRET   167

LET THERE BE LOVE   257

Kwame Kwei-Armah
Chronology

1998   *Bitter Herb* (winner of the Peggy Ramsay Award)
        premieres at the Bristol Old Vic, directed by Andy
        Hay.

1999   *Big Nose*, co-authored and directed by Chris Monks,
        premieres at the Belgrade Theatre, Coventry.

2001   *Blues Brother, Soul Sister* is produced by the Bristol
        Old Vic; national tour directed by Andy Hay.

2003   *Elmina's Kitchen* premieres at the Cottesloe,
        National Theatre, directed by Angus Jackson.
        Wins the *Evening Standard* Charles Wintour Award
        for Most Promising Playwright, nominated for
        an Olivier Award and for a BAFTA (Best New
        Writer). The play was produced as a film for
        BBC4 Drama (2003) and BBC Radio 3 (2004),
        and transferred to London's Garrick Theatre,
        becoming the first play by an African Caribbean
        playwright to be produced in the West End.

2004   *Fix Up* premieres at the Cottesloe, National
        Theatre, directed by Angus Jackson.

2007   *Statement of Regret* premieres at the Cottesloe,
        National Theatre, directed by Jeremy Herrin.

2008   *Let There Be Love* premieres at the Tricycle Theatre,
        London, directed by the author, and returns for
        a second run in the summer of the same year.
        Television drama *Walter's War* is produced by
        BBC4.

2009   *Statement of Regret* produced by BBC Radio 3.

Introduction

While writing a new play I play a game with myself. I pretend that all of the plays I have written to date do not exist. The successes and the failures, the narrative arcs and themes, all must be banished to a place that cannot easily be reached in the vain hope of fooling myself that whatever I am writing at present is not connected to or part of a world I have ever visited before. Of course this is nonsense, for more than anything else I long to connect the dots, to find the link between each play and the circumstances I find myself in mentally or spiritually, but it is something I must do.

I have just got to the end of a new play (you never get to the end but you know what I mean, right?) and as I write this have no idea whether it will be accepted or not, produced or designated to the bottom drawer forever. But as these few days, the grace period between completion and submission, are the last days of peace I will have until I hear back from the theatre, it is the perfect time for me to speak of the narratives that have brought me to this juncture.

The existence of these four plays and notably the triptych produced by the National Theatre – *Elmina's Kitchen*, *Fix Up* and *Statement of Regret* – changed the trajectory of my life. *Let There Be Love* solidified me in another way, but I shall return to that later.

Elmina's Kitchen

I was driving home one evening to the flat in Hackney where I then lived, when I drove past a gleaming metallic green new BMW wrapped around a lamppost. When I got home I saw on the news that there had been a shooting in Hackney – then dubbed Murder Mile for the number of black-on-black shootings that had occurred over the previous few years. They then cut away to the green BMW and the newscaster reported that two men had been fatally shot: one died immediately, the other who tried to crawl away from the vehicle died later in hospital. It had all the hallmarks of another black-on-black attack. This pained me to my core.

I had grown up in a Britain where it was white youths that attacked my community; when I saw another black youth I would nod a kind of acknowledgement, I would feel safer in the knowledge that if I were to be attacked there was someone close by to help me. Now, young blacks were more afraid of being attacked by someone who shared the hue than by an extreme right-wing National Front member, or, slightly later, BNP skinhead.

It had been ingrained in me as a child by my brilliant mother that whatever occupation I found myself in, serving the greater community through that occupation had to be a goal, an aim. Anything less was selfishness. But how could I serve – discuss this new blight that had taken hold of our young – through my chosen profession, that of the artist? That night before I slept I wrote the first scene of *Elmina's Kitchen*. Actually it wasn't the very first scene that is in the script – as often happens that scene didn't make the final script – but the idea of writing, of seeking to look beyond headlines to ask fundamental questions of our young men, was born: why were they not trying hard enough to overcome their circumstances, and why was society not trying hard enough to remove the circumstances they had to transcend?

I handed the script in to Jack Bradley, the then literary manager of the National Theatre, and he in turn handed it to the then new artistic director of the National Theatre, Nicholas Hytner. Nick liked it and programmed it into his first season. It went on to be a huge success. I will never forget the attention this theatrical superstar gave me and how he placed a team of brilliant people around me to help nurture the development of both the script and myself – support he has never stopped giving.

After the success of *Elmina* the pressure was on, not from anyone other than myself, to repeat that success, to be not a one-hit wonder but instead create a canon of work that could withstand the vagaries of flavour-of-the-monthism. I was offered lots of screenplays to write about gangs and the like, but, always one to buck against a limiting stereotype, I was determined to not be the chronicler of the underclass, to not be the one who writes about young black males in the pejorative until my day in the sun was gone. I decided to write a triptych of plays chronicling the black British experience as I saw it at the beginning of the 'noughties'. Whether they were critically successful or not would be secondary to the achievement of having something that my great-grandchildren could read and say, 'That was my ancestor's view of the Britain he found at the turn of the century.'

Fix Up

My wonderful agent Sean Gascoine had given me a book of African American slave narratives as my opening night present for *Elmina*. I opened it up one night many months later and the play *Fix Up* was born. The words of the enslaved were so strong, so potent so personal. Like most people, regardless of whether or not they have degrees, I am mainly self-educated and I gained much of my knowledge from the independent black bookstores that were in existence during what I call the modern Black Renaissance – that time in the nineties when intellectual pursuits were the dominant feature of black youth. This was the time when the greatest hip-hop band of all time, Public Enemy, ruled the airwaves (well, the stations and clubs I used to frequent anyway), when Spike Lee's movies opened up with a 'where's my forty acres and a mule?', days when the history that had been long hidden from the children of the African diaspora was coming to light and invigorating a generation to aim higher, learn more, teach thyself to know thyself. Now these tremendous community resources – the black bookstores – were dying out, and with them, I believed, the knowledge and wisdom those stores were set up to impart. A community without knowledge of itself, its history, soon self-destructs because the present isn't big, strong or robust enough to sustain the needs of fully rounded human beings.

I had written *Elmina* in the spirit – dialogue-wise at least – of David Mamet: hard, fast, corrupt. I decided that I wanted to create a more lyrical prose, one that could hold the magic that I felt when I read the first page of the slave narratives; one that I felt when I saw the plays of my 'wrighting' role model August Wilson. Its journey to the stage was not an easy one. I rewrote and rewrote, and threw out and discarded so many times, and it was only the foresight of Nicholas Hytner and the tenacity of my director Angus Jackson and dramaturg Nick Drake that saved me from completely destroying my original vision. I learnt more lessons during that process than from the rest of my career put together. And although the least performed of my plays thus far, it is still one of my favourites because it spoke to me of many things. It was my attempt to not be contained, to not allow myself to be something I was not; it was my attempt to give voice to the generation that was almost voiceless, save for the poetry of Linton Kwesi Johnson – the generation of those now in their fifties who came over to Britain as children with their parents from the Caribbean; the generation that walked the streets of London when it was cold; the ones who existed before we discovered the disgracefully high level of discrimination in the police force and schools and everyday life. How they survived, mentally and spiritually, was a story I wanted to tell, that I continually want to tell. I also wanted to look at the issues of being 'mixed raced' or 'bicultural' in a world that divides itself often into straight black and white. *Fix Up* would be the last new play of mine that my mother would see, and at the end of the final performance she thanked me for telling that story. That of itself was worth more than every prize in the world. It *was* every prize in the world.

Statement of Regret

I then attempted part three of the triptych. It was to be set in the church and be a thumping big gospel musical. I wrote three different versions and none of them worked. Then I opened the black newspaper, *The New Nation*, one morning during late 2006 to see the headline, Tony Blair's 'STATEMENT OF REGRET' over the British involvement in the slave trade. The fact that Britain *was* the slave trade until it decided to be the trade's policeman hit me hard. That the word 'sorry' could not be said hit me even harder. For the first time in my life I had a title before the play.

I decided to set the play in the world of a black think tank. I wanted to explore the themes of reparation for the slave trade – not for slavery itself, but for the deculturalisation of the African Caribbean, the process, to paraphrase a speech in the play, whereby the African had his language, religion and culture taken from him/her to make them beasts of burden. A process that would lead to generations of Africans – no, African Caribbeans – not knowing where they originated from or what their original language might have been. For centuries a people had been made almost cultureless. I didn't want it to be blacks shouting at whites, 'Look what you've done to me!' That's boring. So to highlight the deculturalisation I placed the argument between two 'black peoples': one of direct African descent, the other Afro-Caribbean. I wanted to look at 'grief': grief for the loss of a culture, grief for the loss of family, grief for the pains of living second-class lives in first-world settings. Could one be reparated for that? I have since adapted the play for radio – 'Obama-ed' it some might say – so there are two endings: one that was staged at the National, the other for BBC Radio 3. I'm happy with them both.

Let There Be Love

Let There Be Love is the first play of my own that I directed, and is quite frankly my tribute to my mother. Like most of the middle classes in London mid-noughties, your builder or cleaner, or both, were Polish. Actually they could have been from anywhere in Eastern Europe, but just as every West Indian was Jamaican when I was growing up, every Eastern European person was Polish. I found myself becoming almost like a teacher of Britishness for them. My builder especially would ask me how to pay this and that bill – and more importantly *when* to pay it – and what the wording on certain letters, or comments he would receive from customers, meant. I would hear them both speak of only planning to be in Britain for five years and then they'd return home to Poland as 'kings' – a direct repeat of what I would hear my

West Indian elders say when I was a child. Ironically, though, I began to hear those same people speak despairingly of the new immigrants, in almost exactly the same way we were spoken of as West Indians. When I sat down to write the play, what came out more than anything for me was my desire to record how quickly we forget: how the impulse to feel threatened by the next group to arrive in society overrode memories of the discrimination and pain we had ourselves suffered. Although all the above scared me, I also wanted to write about how much warmer, how much easier, the country had become for immigrants, mostly due to the battles my parents' generation – the *Windrush* pioneer generation – had fought and won.

I had received some pretty scathing reviews in some quarters for *Statement of Regret*. Coming directly after that, *Let There Be Love* was a type of healing for me, not in terms of the way it was reviewed (as I don't read reviews of my own plays or those of playwrights I know), but simply because it was there so that I could get back in the saddle immediately. It was there to help me remember why I write.

I strive to make the plays I write as good as possible because only then can the subjects I wish to raise people's consciousness of, only then can the thing that ultimately changes people, truly start its process. I write to be catalyst for a debate.

I hope you enjoy the plays. More importantly, I hope you talk, fight and argue about them.

Kwame Kwei-Armah
May 2009

Elmina's Kitchen

Elmina's Kitchen was first presented in the Cottesloe auditorium of the National Theatre, London, on 29 May 2003. The cast was as follows:

Digger	Shaun Parkes
Deli	Paterson Joseph
Anastasia	Dona Croll
Ashley	Emmanuel Idowu
Baygee	Oscar James
Clifton	George Harris

Director Angus Jackson
Designer Bunny Christie
Lighting designer Hartley T.A. Kemp
Music Neil McArthur
Sound designer Neil Alexander
Company voice work Patsy Rodenburg
Dialect coach Claudette Williams
Musicians Steve Russell, Juldeh Camaram, Atongo Zimba
Original songs Kwame Kwei-Armah, Neil McArthur,
    George Harris, Oscar James

Characters

Digger
Deli
Anastasia
Ashley, *Deli's son*
Baygee
Clifton

Act One

Prologue

The stage is in darkness. A single spotlight slowly reveals a costumed man, standing absolutely still with a gurkel (a one-string African guitar famed for possessing the power to draw out spirits) in his hands. His head moves sharply as if smelling something distasteful. The music starts. It is a slow lament-sounding concoction of American blues and traditional African music.

The man then covers the length and breadth of the stage flicking handfuls of powder on to the playing area. The music ends.

Blackout.

Scene One

It's Tuesday, mid-afternoon. It's raining. We are in Elmina's Kitchen, a one-notch-above-tacky West Indian takeaway restaurant in 'Murder Mile' Hackney. The walls are littered with 'Dance Hall' advertisements and Whey and Nephew-type posters. Amid the Budweiser series of posters celebrating African-American heroes there is a big sign saying 'NO DRUGS ARE PERMITTED ON THESE PREMISES. RESPECT.' *The TV that is attached to the left wall closest to the counter is blaring out the ragga tune 'Sufferer' by Bounty Killer. To the right is a rack of spirits. There is a telephone on the counter. Behind the counter are two wooden swing doors that lead to the kitchen. Above that is a huge picture of a middle-aged West Indian woman, Elmina,* **Deli***'s mother. Next to that is a framed laminated poster that reads, 'Life is beauty, admire it. Life is costly, care for it. Life is wealth, keep it. Life is love, enjoy it. Life is a dream, realise it. Life is a challenge, meet it. Life is a duty, serve it. Life is a game, play it. Life is a mystery, know it. Life is an opportunity, benefit from it. Life is a promise, fulfil it.'*

Standing behind the counter is **Deli** *(thirty-four), a happy spirit. He is a born struggler and optimist, but today he is a little restless. Although* *slightly overweight, we can see that he once possessed a fit, athletic body. His personality is slightly soft at the core. He has his head buried deep in a letter while mouthing the words to the song being played on the TV. 'Born as a sufferer, grow up as a sufferer, struggle as a sufferer, fe mek it as a sufferer, fight as a sufferer, survive as a sufferer, move amongst the ghetto ah most ah dem ah sufferer ah!', etc., etc.*

When he raises his head we see that he has a big bruise above his eye and a few cuts on his forehead.

Sitting on a stool close to the counter is **Digger** *(mid-thirties). He is very powerfully built and looks every bit the 'bad man' that he is. His hair is plaited in two neat sets of cane rows which meet each other at the top of his head. At the ends of the cane rows are multicoloured ribbons, the kind traditionally seen in young girls' hair.* **Digger** *is from Grenada but came to England aged fourteen. His clothes are not flash but are brand-name street clothes. The Chopper bicycle that we see chained outside the restaurant is his.* **Digger***'s accent swings from his native Grenadian to hard-core Jamaican to authentic black London. He has his hands-free adapter permanently plugged into his ear. He is busy reading the* Daily Mirror.

Digger *(to himself but loud)*   You mudder arse!

Deli *glances up at* **Digger** *and then to the picture of his mother.*

Deli *(as if on autopilot)*   How many times I got to tell you about language like that in here, Digger?

He returns to the letter. **Digger** *raises his head from his paper momentarily and gently kisses his teeth in* **Deli***'s direction. He's got to get back to the article.* **Deli** *finishes reading the letter, screws it up and throws it in the bin. Suddenly* **Digger** *shouts out.*

Digger *(in disbelief)*   Blood CLATT.

Deli *(irritated)*   Digger!

Digger   What?

Deli   Ah you me ah talk too yuh na!

Digger *(vexed)*   You can't see dat I reading som'ting?

He ignores **Deli** *and carries on reading.*

Deli   Man, you're ignorant!

Digger *doesn't like being called ignorant.*

Digger (*half playful*)   Char! You only lucky I don't want eat wid dem drug-selling niggas down Yum Yums, why I don't boo you down and tek my business dere. Gimme fritter an a Ginness punch.

Deli   Please!

Digger   What's wrong wid you today?

Deli   Cos I ask you to say please something must be wrong with me? See my point? You're ignorant.

He brings the fritter and the punch he has poured out over to **Digger**.

Deli   Two pound twenty-five. Please.

Digger (*checking his pockets*)   Give me a squeeze na?

Deli (*almost laughing*)   Squeeze? You *own* more money than anyone I know.

Digger   But dat's my business, Deli.

Deli   Just gimme me fucking money.

Digger   See you. You coming jus' like your cousin Sofie, a rhated Englishman.

Deli *pauses for a moment, confused.*

Deli   Please explain to me how my female cousin, can be a white male?

Digger   You know what I mean, she love too much blasted Englishman. (*Shaking his head.*) You British blacks, boy.

He shows him a picture of her in the paper.

Every time she dey in the paper, she have a rhated white man on she hand. Wha' appen! Ghetto willy too big fe her or what?

Deli   What the hell that has to do with putting your mean hand in your pocket to pay for your fritters? It's low-life dregs like you that probably send her dere.

Digger (*taking umbrage*)   Low what? See me and you, we go fall out one day, you know! I not no low nothin'. I's a legitimate businessman!

Deli   You forget I know where the butcher knife is!

Digger *pulls out his gun and points it at* **Deli**.

Digger   Yeah, but what's that gonna do against my tech nine, motherfucker?

Deli (*vexed*)   Don't fuck about, Digger, how you gonna be pulling that ting out in here? . . .

Digger   Sorry! Sorry! . . .

The phone rings.

Deli   What happen if a customer walk in now? I done told you about that x amount a times. Damn. Hello! Elmina's Kitchen, takeaway and delivery, how can I help you? . . . Chicken? We have jerk chicken, curried chicken, fried chicken, brown chicken, stew chicken and our new vibe is sweet and sour chicken. Yeah, West Indian style . . . Yeah, yeah . . . Where'd you live, bra? Berringham Road, seen, gonna be forty-five minutes, you alright wid dat? . . . What's your name? Badder youth? Seen, Badder, that'll be five pounds fifty cash handed over to my delivery boy before he takes the food out of the heated rear box, yeah? Nice.

Digger *who has returned to the paper, looks up at* **Deli** *and shakes his head.*

Digger   Da'is why you nigger people go fail every time. How you go tell a hungry man he have to wait forty-five minutes for he food?

Deli (*shouting from the kitchen*)   You can't run a business on lies.

Digger   You think a Indian man would do that? That's why the black man will always be down. He don't know how to analyse his environment.

Deli   What graffiti wall did you get that from, Digger?

Digger   Your mudder's. Sorry!

He bites into his fritter. He grimaces.

Bombo! Deli, your cooking is shit! How can a man fuck up a fritter?

Deli (*smiling*)   Don't watch that, Dougie reach and you know his cooking is baddd!

Digger   What! He's gonna sit down in the kitchen and cook? Ha ha!

The phone rings.

Deli   Elmina's Kitchen, takeaway and delivery, how can I help you? . . . Sweet and sour chicken? . . . Where'd you live, bra? . . .

He looks up at **Digger** *and hesitates for a moment.*

Deli   Well, that'll be . . . that'll be the next one out. Yeah, yeah, respect.

Digger *laughs at him.*

Digger   See, I told yu you was coming like dem English man. Fork-tongued motherfucker.

Deli (*feigning ignorance*)   What? Man, since I've put that sweet and sour shit on the menu the phone's been off the hook.

Digger   I don't mean to be disrespectful but your shop is never, has never and I doubt will ever be, off the hook.

Deli   Some things shouldn't be measured in financial terms.

Digger   A business is one of those thing that should!

Deli (*kisses his teeth*)   Digger, fuck off.

Digger   Oh, it's alright for you to use all manner of
Viking exple, exples, swear word, but as soon as a
motherfucker uses language of our heritage you start to cuss.
Dat is what I talking about when I cuss you British blacks.

Deli *kisses his teeth and ignores* **Digger**. **Digger***'s phone rings. He
takes out three. He finds the right one. He switches his accent to hard-
core Jamaican.*

Digger   Yeah, yeah? Tricky wha you say, rude bwoy? . . .
Seen . . . Seen . . . Na!!! Wha you ah say? . . . Alright . . .
usual tings ah go run . . . seen . . . tie him up wait for me . . .
Tricky, don't be a pussy and get trigger happy, wait for me,
you hear? Alright, what is it, three now? I'll see you 'bout
four thirty. Later . . .

He ends the call.

I gotta get myself some new blood. Tricky stewpid!

Deli   Thought you was a lone operator?

Digger   I subcontract on a job-by-job basis. Eh, you know
who I had business with de odder day? Spikey!

Deli (*not really interested*)   Spikey who?

Digger   Spikey, who own the hair shop down by
Stamford Hill lights.

Deli (*suddenly interested*)   What Roy's from across the road
big mouth friend with the hair? You lie?

Digger   Oh ho! You interested now?

Deli   Who Spikey did owe money?

Digger   Me!

Deli   Before you, fool?

Digger   Matic posse.

Deli   I knew that motherfucker had to be dealing. How else could he move from one fucking blow-dryer and Sat'day girl to employing twelve fit woman in under nine months?

Digger   I thought you doesn't watch odder people tings?

Deli   Shut up. How much was he down for?

Digger   Nothin' real big. Twenty.

Deli   Twenty?

Digger   Well, he owe Matic dem fifteen and once I put my fee pon top . . .

Deli   . . . Twenty? Damn.

Digger   When I put de gun by he head, you know what he do?

Deli   What?

Digger   He offer me him fifteen-year-old daughter?

Deli   To do what wid?

Digger   To fuck of course.

Deli (*outraged*)   You lie?

Digger   I buck him with me pistol. Who the hell you take me for, Rodent?

Deli   Rodent?

Digger   The Yardie bwoy that rape all them people dem pickney when he was collecting. Motherfucker gave the trade a bad name.

Deli   Ras! He pay yuh you money yet?

Digger   I told him I'd kill his family across the whole world. He had my money to me in five days.

Deli   So that's why the shop's closed!

Digger   I give him an extra lick cos me did hear he was an informer.

Deli   Yeah? Fucking bitch. Should'a give him two.

The men sing together.

Deli/Digger   Man fe dead lick a shot inna informer man hend.

Enter **Ashley**, **Deli***'s son (nineteen), hooded street clothes, headphones. He has his hair in two bunches. Trousers falling off the arse. Has no respect for anyone older than himself except for* **Digger***. He walks in slowly talking on the phone.*

Deli   Yo! Ashley, what took you so long? How you let the man cut up your head so? Look like Zorro.

The men laugh together. **Ashley** *kisses his teeth, grabs the TV remote off the counter, changes the channel to MTV base and attempts to sit down.*

Deli   What you sitting down for? Can't you see there's ting waiting here to get delivered?

Ashley *looks at his dad's cut head.*

Ashley (*nonchalantly*)   It's raining out there, you know! Give me a second to catch my breath.

Deli   You wanna catch you arse out street and deliver the people dem food.

Ashley   Nigger needs to chill, boy!

Deli   Hey, I ain't no nigger with you.

Ashley (*to himself almost*)   No you're not, what they calling you on street now? Deli the sissy punk.

Deli   What?

Ashley   How am I supposed to walk the street an look my bredrens in the eye when mans all grip up my dad by his throat and you didn't deal wid it?

Digger (*still confused*)   What?

Deli *doesn't answer.* **Ashley** *does.*

Ashley   Roy from over dere coarse up my dad . . .

Deli   Coarse up who? . . .

Ashley   . . . and he didn't even lift a finger to defence. Can you believe that?

Digger   You let Roy da coolie coarse you up?

Ashley (*under breath but loud enough to be heard*)   It's a good thing uncle Dougie's coming home that's my word . . .

Deli   He never coarse me nothin'. We had a little someting . . . and I decided not to deal wid it THERE and THEN.

The guys stare at him in amazement.

Digger   Rasclaat!

Deli (*to* **Ashley**)   Me will deal wid him right! What?! I can't see me fucking brodder! Is pass me must pass him in the jail van? (*Beat.*) Did you buy the banner ting for your uncle?

Deli's *explanation has meant nothing to him.* **Ashley** *slams a big roll of banner tape on counter and pushes it towards his father.*

Deli   Thank you.

Ashley *looks at the address he has to deliver to.*

Ashley   Berrington Road? I ain't delivering no cold food there. Trust me. You better heat it up dread or no can do!

Deli (*sharp and fast*)   Who you talking to like that? Don't mek me have to lick you down you know! Your mouth too quick these days.

Ashley *pushes out his chest.* **Deli** *catches himself, pulls back and takes the container back into the kitchen, kissing his teeth.* **Ashley** *nods* *his head to* **Digger** *who just about acknowledges him.* **Ashley** *pauses for a moment then approaches* **Digger**.

Ashley   So, yes my don, what a gwan?

Digger (*back to reading his paper*)   Just cool ya.

Ashley   You still busting the TT?

Digger (*short*)   Yep.

Ashley   Sweet but when I get my dollars, mine's a BM boy. You done know!

Digger *does not reply.*

Ashley (*checking to see that his dad can't hear*)   Listen, I kinda wanna talk some tings through wid you, you na mean?

Digger   No, I don't know what you mean.

Ashley (*taken aback but bounces back*)   Seen, seen. You're hooked up and dat, and mans needs to get hold of proper tings, not no air pistols runnings, you get me? So I wondered if . . .

Digger (*firmly*)   No.

Ashley   No what?

Digger   No.

Ashley (*with attitude*)   What what? Mans ain't looking a free tings, you know!

Digger   Yes you is. Don't ever be forward enough to ask me about tings like that again, seen?

Ashley   Seen.

Enter **Deli**. *Hands food to* **Ashley**.

Deli   Take it na! And hurry come back. You gotta to help me sort the room for your uncle.

Ashley *does but he's staring at* **Digger** *as he exits.* **Digger** *takes the remote and puts it back on to the old school music channel.*

Digger   Dem blasted young children duh' have no
respect. You know, some parts ah de country fucking big
man like you and me 'fraid to come out dey yard because
young punks like him wanna shot dem down to get stripes?
Not me a rass!

Deli stares at the door that **Ashley** *just exited with great concern in
his eyes.*

Deli   What! . . .

Enter **Baygee**, *a hyper lively old Bajan man in his sixties who often
speaks at a hundred miles an hour. He's the last of West Indian door-to-
door salesmen. Defying logic he is carrying about twenty different designer
bags. He is wearing a three-piece suit with trilby hat to match that have
all seen better days. We can see his long grey hair sticking out of the
sides. He rushes into the restaurant.*

Baygee   Hey, Delroy, give me a quick shot of Clark's and
have one you yourself, I win ten pounds on the lottery
today. What James Brown say? (*Sings.*) I feel good,
dadadada, I knew that I would now.

Deli   You still playing that stupidness?

Baygee   Be happy for a fella na! You know how many
years I giving them people me money and never get fart
back?

Deli   Congratulations, Baygee.

Baygee   Thank you. I have some niceeeeeeee new clothes
for the children this week, you know, Deli. (*He searches to find
the right bag.*) Tracksuits, jeans, baggy trouser that show dey
underpants, nice tings, boy. I even have a Donna Karen Los
Angeles dress for the wife . . .

Deli   New York.

Baygee   She on holiday?

Deli   Donna Karen New Y . . . Forget it. And it's the ex-
wife, Baygee.

Baygee (*smiles*)   Even more reason why you should buy it.
Anyway take a look through, I coming back. Just popping to
see Ms Mary on Abbots Road.

He decks the shot of rum in one.

Deli (*knowing full well*)   She have something for you?

Baygee (*trying to front*)   She owe me twenty pound.

Digger (*teasing him*)   I'll buy that debt off you for fifteen
pound.

Baygee   White boy, I wouldn't sell you my stepmodder
piss, and she been dead twenty years, God bless her soul.
Give me one more, Deli.

*He selects the bags he's going to walk with and makes for the door. He
looks at the picture of Elmina and turns back to* **Deli**.

Baygee   Oh God, how many times I have to tell you?
I love that you have you modder up there but you need to
have one of yourself too. You could have been one of the
greatest, boy. Clifton took me to see him fight once and
I said, Cliff, he could be one of the greats, you know. He
smiled and said, I know. Put up the picture, boy.

Deli   Soon, Baygee. Soon. Your usual curry goat and rice?

Baygee   Who cook?

Deli   Me!

Baygee   Na, just line me up a patty and a Guinness
punch. In fact, make that two Guinness punch. I go need a
little energy when I leave Ms Mary's. I gone.

He's gone.

Digger   You British blacks, boy.

Deli   And I don't know why you gots to be dissing us all
the time, you been here since you was blasted fourteen,
you're as 'British' as the rest of us.

Digger (*shoots out*)   Never! I was born in Grenada and I've lived in jailhouse all over the world. I know who the fuck I am, don't you ever include me in all you stupidness.

Deli   Five years in a New York jail don't make you a citizen of the world, motherfucker.

Deli *starts to tidy up.* **Digger** *takes the remote control for the TV and points it towards the screen attempting to change the channel. It doesn't work.*

Digger   How you get this thing on the news again?

Deli   You got to watch the news every time it's on? Square then tick.

Digger   What happens up there today, happens on the streets tomorrow.

The news channel is on. **Digger** *is really concentrating.*

We hear the chime that accompanies the opening of the shop's door. The boys look up. Enter **Anastasia** (*forty-two*). *Although dressed soberly, we can see that she has the kind of body that most men of colour fantasise about. Big hips and butt, slim waist and full, full breasts. There is something incredibly sexual about her presence. Beneath the very well applied 'make-up' we can see that she must once have been a real beauty. There is an insecurity, a soft sadness about her even though she attempts to hide this with a veneer of coarse West Indian confidence. Although black British, she too swings into authentic, full-attitude Jamaican at the drop of a hat. She speaks with confidence if not a little attitude.*

Anastasia *scans the shop quickly then pauses for a second. Then, as if she is somehow rooted to the spot, looks around again but this time slower, more deliberate, as if trying to see something that is not visible, something that is hiding. Subtly, she inhales slowly and then exhales. She snaps out of it and smiles genuinely at* **Deli**. *She has a bag in her hands.*

Anastasia (*firm and confident*)   Hi! I come to apply for the job in the window.

Deli/Digger   Really!

Anastasia   No, I just like opening me mouth and talking stupidness!

The boys clock each other.

Deli   Right, um, you have any experience?

Anastasia, *full of natural sexiness, walks and puts her bag on the counter. She takes out a Pyrex dish of macaroni pie and steps back.*

Anastasia   Macaroni pie. I cooked it yesterday, but next morning food is always the sweetest.

Digger (*half under his breath*)   Mind she obea you, boy!

Deli   Shut up, Digger! (*To* **Anastasia**.) So you've worked in an West Indian restaurant before?

Anastasia (*almost winking*)   No. But I figure it's not beyond me!

Deli (*a little surprised*)   What makes you would want to work here?

Anastasia   The truth? You're in serious trouble my bredren! Anyone that names his restaurant Elmina's Kitchen is in need of help. The good news! It's the help that I can give . . .

Deli   Elmina's my mother's name!

Digger   Ras!

Deli   And your name is?

Anastasia   Anastasia, it's the name of a princess. Brudder, you can't have a picture of a woman on the wall and the place look so! But what really makes me wanna work here! You is the best-looking man I have seen in a very long time.

Digger *looks up.*

Deli (*taken aback*)   Really?

Anastasia   No, but I knew that would sweet you. So how about you taste my macaroni pie na?

Deli   Are you smoking rock?

Anastasia (*shakes her head*)   No, I don't do drugs and I don't drink.

Deli   . . . Cos, girl, you got brass balls coming in here and tell me about my mudder! People have dead for less.

Digger   True!

Beat.

Anastasia (*seriously*)   Forgive me, I have a warped sense of humour.

Pause.

Deli *takes off the top of the Pyrex dish.* **Anastasia** *takes a pre-package plastic spoon from her bag and hands it to* **Deli**. *She also takes her book out and clenches it like a Bible. It is* The Celestine Prophecy.

Anastasia   Don't you want to heat it up?

Deli *shakes his head. He tastes the pie.* **Digger** *shakes his head.*

Deli   Ummmm, that's good . . . wicked in fact. Wow. You got anything else in there?

Anastasia   I have a goat ready for stewing.

Deli (*gets serious*)   Well, it's a full-time post we have here. It may not look busy now but it can get real rushed at lunchtimes.

Digger *coughs.*

Deli   And we have a reputation in the area for excellence.

Anastasia   So, you offering me the job?

Deli   Why, don't you want it?

Anastasia   You know what I mailed my son last night? I tell him that me walk into a restaurant named after a slave castle but couldn't see the castle.

Deli *doesn't quite know how to respond.*

Digger (*exclaims*)   Rasclaat!

Deli (*ignoring*)   So, when can you start?

Anastasia   Whenever.

Deli   Thursday? . . .

Anastasia (*before it's come out of his mouth*)   . . . Thursday? Fine.

She gathers her things and gets up to leave.

Do you read?

Deli   What do you mean?

Anastasia   How you does feed your mind if you don't read? Typical man.

Deli   I haven't mentioned pay?

Anastasia   It's gonna be more than I'm earning now, right!

He nods. She exits.

Digger (*getting out of his seat*)   That's a rasclatt madwoman! How you could employ dat?

Deli (*ignoring*)   Digger, shut up, man.

Digger (*sitting back down*)   Rhated madwoman.

Lights down.

During the blackout we hear the voice of the **Newsreader**.

Newsreader   The headlines. As the case of John and Peter Goodyear enters its fifth day at the Old Bailey the brothers go on record saying they murdered their parents 'for the hell of it'. We talk to Denton Philips, the Jamaican

gangster, or 'Yardie', brought into Britain by the
Metropolitan Police to supposedly help in the fight against
crime. And thirty-five million pounds of personal assets were
seized from celebrated Ranter frontman, William Forsheve,
in the biggest pension scandal to hit the private sector in a
decade. (*Music.*) Scenes of astonishment at the Old Bailey
today as a spokesman for the two brothers . . .

The lights slowly come up to reveal:

Scene Two

Baygee, **Digger** *watching the TV. The fourth screw is in. They
have glasses of rum in their hand.* **Anastasia** *and* **Deli** *are putting
the finishing touches to the 'Welcome Home' decorations for Dougie while
watching the TV when they can. The freshly painted banner reads 'Yes,
dread, you reach! Respect due!'* **Anastasia** *steps down from a chair
and heads towards the kitchen. The restaurant looks a little cleaner.
Nothing serious but it looks better.*

Digger   Thirty-five million, you know!

Baygee (*conversationally*)   My father use to say when a black
man tief one man cry, when the European dem tief, whole
continents bawl. (*Holding up the rum glass to* **Deli**.) Give me
one last quick one.

Deli *heads behind the counter to do it.*

Deli   No problem. (*Referring to banners.*) What you think,
Baygee?

Baygee   Look good.

Digger   How's a man suppose to enjoy his food when all
he can smell is paint to bloodclaat?

Anastasia (*referring to decorations*)   Yes, dread, you reach,
now there's a fitting welcome for a black man. 'Bout
welcome home.

Deli (*smiling at her*)   OK, you were right.

Anastasia   My God, these tablecloth, Renk! . . . You worse than my son. If I don't change the bedclothes he'll sleep on the same ting for a year!

Digger *and* **Baygee** *clock each other.* **Digger** *puts out his hand.*

Digger   One week before he sex that! Twenty pound.

Deli *hears and looks up at* **Digger** *disapprovingly.* **Baygee** *ignores him.*

Baygee   What time you brodder reaching?

Deli (*kisses his teeth*)   Ahh you know Dougie, he said today *sometime* but I'll believe it when I see him.

He smiles, excited at the prospect.

Baygee   You shouldn't make the boy find he own way home, you should'da pick him up from the gates?

Deli (*flash of anger*)   Alone, is how he wants to come out.

Digger   Yo! Gal, gimme me a next dumpling.

Anastasia (*flash of temper*)   Is who you talking to so? Cos believe, it better not be me.

Digger *is slightly taken aback.* **Deli** *jumps straight in.*

Deli   I bet a hundred pound it's informer business that catch that thirty-five million man.

Digger   Your money would be better spent teaching you staff how to talk to people. (*Changing back to subject at hand.*) Informer, yes!!

Deli   Better you shot me before you ask me fe do that.

Anastasia *stares at* **Deli**, *disappointed. He recoils slightly.*

Digger   Dem man dere, you don't even waste bullet pon dem. (*Imitating stabbing.*) Just jook jook jook him till he dead.

Anastasia   Take it that's why they call you Digger?

Digger   Yep. It tells people who the fuck *I* am and what I do! Ask any nigger in the street and they'll tell you! Digger's like one of them African names. It's got meaning. Remember that!

Anastasia *gets the dumpling from the heated cabinet. She brushes past* **Deli** – *their bodies touch momentarily –* **Deli** *steps back, and looks away.*

Baygee (*annoyed at* **Digger**'s *boasting*)   What you do, young white bwoy, is buy and sell black souls!

Digger   I buy and sell debts. Not no cheap-arse fake designer clothes, like some motherfuckers I know.

Baygee   Don't test me, young man. I lash a man last week and he is still falling down!

Deli   Baygee, cool na!

Baygee   Once upon a time, businessmen like me were the only street salesmen our community had. Now look what they got! You may frighten all them others round here, I don't 'fraid you young bad-johns. I hate you, but God blimey, I don't 'fraid you.

Digger (*about to get vexed*)   Wha?!!!

Anastasia *jumps in.*

Anastasia   Digger! Your dumpling! And here (*slams down a glass of rum*), cool your spirits na!

Beat while the men cool down. **Deli** *clocks that* **Anastasia** *saved the moment. He smiles at her.*

The phone rings. **Deli** *picks it up.*

Deli   Hello Elmina's Kitchen, takeaway and delivery, how can I help you? . . . Ashley, what you phoning me on the business line for? Call me on the mobile.

He puts down the phone. **Anastasia** *looks to* **Deli**. **Deli** *smiles, half apologising for his ignorance. His mobile rings.*

Deli   Yes, who's calling? . . . (*Gets serious.*) Yeah, mate, your uncle's been here an hour already . . . Upstairs . . . (*Vexed.*) Tell him what? . . . I'm not telling him nothing . . . No! I don't know if we'll be here when you finally decide to arrive!

He puts down the phone. **Anastasia** *exhales, shaking her head.*

Deli   Ani, I ain't seen the boy in three days, his uncle is due out and he ain't got the manners to be here first thing in the morning to greet him! Let the bitch stew.

Anastasia *doesn't comment but you can see that she disagrees.*

Anastasia   But he's a bwoy, Deli, dem do tings so.

Deli   Thanks. Think we're all done here? I'm gonna go and get ready.

Anastasia   What's wrong with what you've got on?

Deli   Need to put on something that hides the weight, mate.

Anastasia   You look good to me.

Anastasia *smiles.* **Deli** *stops for the briefest of moments and then carries on. As he steps through the swing doors* **Digger** *picks up the TV remote and switches the TV on to the horseracing channel.* **Anastasia** *(who has just picked up her book) automatically turns to the TV screen.* **Deli**, *however, knew* **Digger** *would do this and pops his head back round the swing doors. He clocks that* **Anastasia** *is paying a lot of attention to the horses.*

Anastasia   Gwan!

She turns away from the TV screen when she hears **Deli**'s *voice.*

Deli (*ignorant*)   Take the horse gambling off, Digger. Ladbroke's is up the bloody road. How many times do I have to tell you?

Digger *turns it back on to MTV base, looks at* **Anastasia** *and indicates to* **Deli**.

Digger   Him luck salt.

Baygee   Turn that ting down, boy.

Digger *takes out a packet of cigarettes and offers one to* **Anastasia**. *She picks up her book and reluctantly accepts. She steps from behind the counter. He lights it for her.*

Digger   Your face is very familiar to me. We meet in a bashment or something?

Anastasia   Bashment? (*Touch of bitterness.*) All the nice dance close up or full up wid pickney. I don't rave.

Digger   You don't drink, you don't rave. Wait, wait, I get it, I get it. I see you wid Bobbler and dem, don't it?

Anastasia   I don't move wid no crack crew!

Digger   Then how you know it's crack dey does run?

Anastasia (*stutters a little*)   Everybody know dat! (*Recovering, goes on the front foot.*) Wait, what you trying to say? Me look like one straygay street gal to you?

Digger   You's a feisty thing, innit? That's the way me like them. Ride better when them have a little spirit. What you say, Baygee?

Baygee   Why you don't leave the woman alone?

Digger   Wha?! I just getting to know Deli gal.

Anastasia (*aggressively*)   Who tell you that I was Deli's gal?

Digger   No one.

Anastasia   Young bwoy, I doubt if you could ah handle it. Excuse!

Anastasia *stubs the cigarette out semi-hiding the ashtray and exits through the swing door into the kitchen, picking up a pen in the process.*

Baygee (*prodding* **Digger**)   Eh, I see a couple of wild Yard boys driving up a one-way street yesterday. When a man show them the sign, the youth don't just take out he gun and threaten to kill him!

Digger *doesn't reply.*

Baygee   Figure it must be one of the new set of Yardies that eating up Hackney. They giving children BMWs, who could compete with that, eh? Hmm! People should always read street signs, don't you think, Digger? I gone. Tell Deli I'll pass back and pay on my way back from Mrs Alexander's house.

He exits with his bags. **Deli** *enters the restaurant dressed in black shirt and pants. He even has a black tie on but not done up. He rolls his head like a boxer preparing for a fight.* **Digger** *looks at him.* **Anastasia** *comes out after* **Deli***, she looks approvingly at him.*

Digger   Bloodclatt, who dead? Where you going dress up so?

Deli   I ain't dress up, just wanna look good for my bra, innit? I spouse up the place, so wah! I can't spouse up meself?

Anastasia   Yes, man, you looks goooooods. Hold up.

She straightens **Deli***'s tie so that it is hanging around his chest.* **Deli** *is not comfortable with her doing this.*

Anastasia (*straight, almost motherly*)   Now you look 'ready'.

Digger   Na na, you right, man should meet his brodder the right way and dat and it's nice that you clean up the place for him, but if you'd have come to me, I'd have give you the money to do it up proper, you know big picture of Haile Selassie, next to yuh modder, proper bamboo furniture, dim lighting and such!

Deli   Thanks but if I ever want to do that, I'll go to the bank.

Digger *bursts out laughing.*

Deli   What you laughing at?

Digger   What bank is going to give you money, nigger?

Deli   One that could recognise I've been a businessman from morning . . .

Digger   . . . And one that ignores your black skin?

Deli   Ahhhhh fuck that old school shit, Digger. That was some old eighties shit you talking.

Anastasia *goes to the kitchen. Enter* **Ashley**. *His hair has been done. Neat cane rows. He's aware he looks good. He's vexed.*

Deli   So you decide to show up?

Ashley   I can't believe it. See, Dad, I told you you shoulda deal wid that Roy.

Deli   That subject's dead, Ashley.

Ashley   They've not only gone and bought the Chini restaurant shop next to theirs.

Digger *looks away.* **Anastasia** *clocks this.*

Deli   What's the matter wid that?

Ashley (*surprised*)   You ain't read the note, have you?

He produces it out of his back pocket.

'Sorry for the temporary closure, reopening soon as Roy's West Indian restaurant.' They're taking the piss out of you.

Ashley *stares at* **Deli** *with hate in his eyes,* **Digger** *looks away.* **Deli** *rolls his head, clicks his neck. We can see the rage in his eyes. He clocks* **Anastasia** *and tries to cover it.*

Deli   Hey, it's a free world, man, people can do what they want.

Ashley   He takes away your pride, then your livelihood, and all you can do is stand dere like a fish? You've lost it, blood.

Deli (*flash of temper*)   I'm not no blood wid you.

Ashley   Regrettably, that's exactly what you are.

Anastasia *exits to the kitchen.*

Ashley Char! Where's Uncle D?

Deli He ain't here yet.

Ashley I thought you said . . .

Deli (*quickly*) . . . Don't worry about what I said. You ain't seen your uncle in seven years and the day he's due out you can't be bothered to get your arse here to greet him . . .

Ashley I had runnings . . .

Deli Runnings is more important than being here for your uncle?

Ashley *does not reply.*

Deli So, it's not just me that lets the family down is it?

Beat. **Ashley***'s face drops.* **Anastasia** *walks into the kitchen.* **Deli** *feels a little guilty so tries to change the subject a bit.*

Deli You see your child today?

Ashley Yep!

Deli (*gives him a twenty-pound note*) Good. Give it to the mother this evening. Tell her thanks?

Ashley I don't need it actually, Dad.

Deli Oh yeah?

Ashley Yeah.

Deli *snatches it back.*

Deli Seen.

Anastasia *comes out with a tray of food. While speaking, she fills up the cabinet.*

Deli Anastasia, you've met my son Ashley, right?

She pauses for a second. It is as if all of a sudden her breath has become very heavy for a beat.

Anastasia   What a good-looking boy you have, Deli. No we haven't met, nice to meet you, Ashley.

Ashley (*looking her up and down*)   Wha appen?

Turns to his dad. Sotto voce.

So what, you sex it yet?

Deli (*angered*)   Don't be stupid and have some respect.

Anastasia   Deli, I put on the pan ready to fry the plantain but I can't find any.

Deli   Oh shit!

Ashley   What?

Deli   I don't done forget to re-order the blasted plantain!

Ashley   How you gonna forget that? That's Uncle D's favourite.

Deli   I know that! Shit! Gotta run to the supermarket.

He runs to get his black jacket.

Ashley   Don't be long, you know!

Deli, *with jacket on, moves past* **Ashley**.

Deli   Ani, I'll be back in ten? Later, Digger.

Digger   Later.

As **Deli** *exits the phone rings. As* **Anastasia** *is closer* **Ashley** *indicates that she should answer it.*

Anastasia   I don't know what to say!

Ashley   You're taking an order not speeching da queen! Answer it then!

While **Anastasia** *is on the phone* **Ashley** *pours himself a brandy and begins to build up a spliff.*

Anastasia   Hello, Elmina's West Indian food shop –

Ashley   – Kitchen, takeaway and delivery!

Anastasia   Takeaway and delivery, how can I help you?
No, he's out at present, you can probably catch him on his
mobile, OK.

Ashley   Who was that?

Anastasia   The prison service.

Ashley (*smiles*)   Uncle Dougie's the original warrior boy.
He's probably been put back in solitary.

Anastasia *suddenly remembers.*

Anastasia   Lard Jesus, the pan.

She dashes back through the swing doors.

Ashley *looks at* **Digger***'s glass.*

Ashley   You want a top-up?

Digger   Yeah. Mek it a brandy though. In fact, while you
dere give me one of dem Chana ting that girl just done
bring out.

Ashley *takes a Chana out of the cabinet and pours out the drink, then
hands it to him.* **Digger** *already has a ten-pound note in his hand
ready to pay.*

Ashley   Na, man. Dis one's on da house.

Digger   Did your father authorise you to give anyone
anyting on da house?

Ashley (*pure admiration*)   No, but you ain't any old anyone.

Digger   Did your father authorise you to give anyone
anyting on da house?

Ashley   No.

Digger *stares at him.*

Ashley   OK. That'll be four fifty.

*He puts the money in the till but spends just a little bit too long looking
at its contents.* **Digger** *looks up at him. He quickly closes the till and*

gives **Digger** *his change.* **Ashley** *then picks up the remote control for the TV.*

Ashley You watching this?

Digger *shakes his head.* **Ashley** *changes it to VH1 music channel. There's a kicking garage video playing.* **Ashley** *starts 'chatting' with the tune. He's looking at the reflection of himself while he dances and chats.*

Ashley Hold the mic while I flex, I'm a lyrical architect with the number-one set. Player haters get bang so what if dey get a back han' or else man will get jiggy, hear what! Man a pack him nine milli.

Digger *finishes his food and gets up to leave.*

Ashley Digger!

Digger Yow!

Ashley Could I speak to you about som'um?

Digger I'm busy.

Ashley You don't look busy!

Digger Looks can be deceiving.

Ashley I know you don't like me . . .

Digger *doesn't answer.*

Ashley But that's all good, cos you don't have to like people to do business wid dem, right?

Digger I don't buy stolen phones.

Ashley Very funny, but I ain't no pussy street punk.

Digger Ah so?

Ashley Ah so. No disrespect, this shit (*the restaurant*) is all good for my dad, but me, I wanna do big tings with my life, bredren. But mans needs a little leg-up.

Digger Really?

Ashley *looks around to check that* **Anastasia** *is not about to enter. She is not.*

Ashley   I was kinda wondering if mans could run wid you? Give you little back-up and dat?

Digger   Wha appen you ears dem beat up? I don't deal wid boys.

Ashley (*flash of temper*)   I ain't no fucking boy.

Digger *moves like the wind towards* **Ashley** *and punches him full in the face.* **Ashley** *hits the deck, blood flowing from his mouth.*

Digger   What did you say to me?

Beat.

Ashley (*whispers*)   I ain't no boy.

Digger   No! Did you use a Viking expletive when talking to me?

Ashley *is confused.*

Ashley (*staying on the ground*)   No . . . Yes . . . What's dat?

Digger (*cool*)   And you wanna be a bad man? Go back to school, youth, and learn. You can't just walk into dis bad man t'ing, you gotta learn the whole science of it. You step into that arena and you better be able to dance wid death till it mek you dizzy. You need to have thought about, have played wid and have learnt all of the possible terrible and torturous ways that death could arrive. And then ask yourself are you ready to do that and more to someone that you know. Have you done that, youth?

Ashley (*wiping the blood away from his mouth and finding his balls*) I stepped to you, haven't I?

Digger   Seen.

He sees **Anastasia** *enter. She stares at* **Digger** *with hate. His phone rings.*

Digger (*overjoyed*)   Bloodclattttttttttt. Is when you reach? Haaaaaaa. Where you dere? Dem let you in the country? Bloodclatttttttt.

He exits. When **Ashley** *turns and sees* **Anastasia** *he is momentarily taken aback.*

Ashley   How long have you been there?

She doesn't answer.

(*Trying to flex his manhood.*) Don't you understand English?

Anastasia (*motherly*)   I just reach.

She moves towards **Ashley** *to help him up. As if to hold him. As she kneels down, he jumps up.*

Ashley   What you doing? Get off.

She steps back.

You talk anything of this and you're dead!

Anastasia   How old are you?

Ashley   Nineteen. Why? You looking for a fit young tings to wok?

Anastasia (*pointed*)   When my son was nineteen you think he would talk to a big woman like dat?

She moves away. Enter **Deli**, *with plantain box under one arm and his mobile in his hand. His face is drained of all life. He stands unable to move for a moment.*

Anastasia   Wha' wrong wid you?

Deli (*quietly to himself*)   They've killed Dougie. The man was practically home and they done kil . . . kill him. (*Holding his head.*) Ahhhhh.

Ashley *jumps up to comfort his father.* **Deli** *pushes him off.*

Deli (*screams*)   Oh God, dem catch me again. I could kill a bloodclaat man tonight.

Lights down.

As the lights go down we hear a haunting eight-bar refrain played on the gurkel.

Scene Three

Day. We are in the restaurant. **Anastasia** *is stacking the heated cabinets with food with one hand and reading a book.* **Ashley** *is on the phone taking an order. Seated with* **Digger** *and* **Baygee** *is* **Clifton** *(sixty-three, but looks mid-fifties). He is a large man with a mouth full of gold teeth. Dressed in a very flash three-piece suit, his cashmere coat is over the back of a chair. His suitcase is visible. He is a boastful man who defines himself very much by how much attention he gets from those in his immediate surroundings. There is a slight shake in his left hand from time to time. With his catchphrase 'you see',* **Clifton** *uses his eastern Caribbean accent to full effect when storytelling. He is mid-story when we join the scene.*

Ashley   It'll be with you in twenty minutes. (*To* **Clifton**.) Carry on.

He hands order to **Anastasia**. *She enters the kitchen.*

Clifton   . . . Well, you see, this man was at least six foot . . .

Ashley   Six foot . . .

Clifton   . . . five. And in dem days dere that was a giant . . .

Ashley   In any day, boy . . .

Baygee   Clifton, every time you tell that story, the man has to grow two inches? . . .

Clifton   Shut up and let me tell the youth the story.

Ashley   Yeah, Baygee, let the man tell the story na.

Clifton   So, like I saying, he say to me, 'Who tell you you could speak to my woman? You want a cut arse?' Well, it so happen that them days was when the Teddy boys weren't making joke, and man had to have some defence . . .

Baygee   That's right!

Clifton   . . . So I gently brush back me coat and show him my blade. One big arse heng man ting, and I said in a low Robert Mitcham drawl, 'If you is me fadder. Do it na! Let we see who is the man and who is child.' And I just leave that in the air hanging. Well, I see a flash in he eye as if he was going to rush me, *you see*, cos the eye betrays an untrained man. I go to grab me ting but something deep inside me, and I swear to this day it was the voice of my old mudder, say, 'Wait till he mek he move.' Well, let me tell you it was that voice save me old mudder having heart attack when she hear Clifton come to England to get hang. Cos he look at me but the monkey must have realised that this would have been his last night on earth cos he just let out a little 'Ha' and walk off. Not another word.

Ashley   Gwan.

Clifton   But you know what the real funny thing was about that evening? When it all done, tell me where the woman was?

Ashley   All over you!

Clifton   Gone. Nowhere to be seen. The two stewpid black men would have finish their lives over a woman that didn't give a coconut leaf about either of dem.

Baygee   Huh, dem was the days when they use to feel you bottom to see if you had a tail. Clifton, you remember what Mary Lou do you?

Clifton   Yes, but that's another story for another time.

Anastasia *with her usual look of concern in her eyes comes out with the order and places it in front of* **Ashley**. *He ignores it.*

Ashley   Raaaaaaaaa, you got stories, man, you're smooth.

Clifton   Me, na. I coarse like saltfish skin. But I believe in living life to the full, and it is only possible to live as long as life intoxicates us. As soon as we sober again, we see it all as a delusion, a stupid delusion, and death provides the only alternative.

He decks his rum in one.

You at college, right?

Ashley *nods.*

Clifton   Who said that?

Ashley   I don't know.

Clifton   Baygee? Come on, you had the benefits of West Indian education, which European writer said that?

Baygee   Is me you asking?

Clifton (*sizing up* **Digger**)   Young fellow? Or should I say 'bad man'. You know the answer?

Digger (*cool and mellow*)   No I don't know who said that, do you?

Clifton   Now, you see, there's a clever man. Flip the script, turn the tables. The truth is I don't know either, but it sound pretty good, don't it?

Digger*'s phone goes off. He answers.*

Digger   Yow! . . .

Anastasia (*annoyed at being the only one not asked*)   Tolstoy!

Clifton (*shocked*)   What?

Anastasia   Tolstoy. The minor Russian aristocrat . . .

Clifton, *who knew all along, doesn't like being upstaged. He automatically goes into verbal slap-down mode. The speeches overlap.*

Clifton   . . . who is reputed to be Gandhi's direct
inspiration. And without Gandhi, you have no Martin
Luther, and without MLK you have no civil rights, and
without civil rights you have no equal rights which means
women, blacks, none of us would be standing on the soil we
do today.

Digger   Seen . . . Seen . . . Don't fuck about, yu hear, star!
Me will kill a man dead fe dat . . . Stone dead . . . Me soon
come . . . Hold it right ya dere so . . . Move an inch and
coffin lid have fe close.

Digger *leaves some money on the counter and begins to leave hurriedly.*
Anastasia*'s eyes follow him.*

Digger (*kisses his teeth*)   People just can't do what they
suppose to do in this world, can they?

Ashley   I can!

Digger *stops and stares at* **Ashley** *for a moment. Almost
instinctively, he's about to tell* **Ashley** *to come with him, but he doesn't.*
Anastasia *stares at* **Ashley***.*

Anastasia   Ashley!

He turns to her momentarily.

Ashley   What?

Digger   Mr C. Later.

Clifton *clocks this interaction.* **Ashley** *runs to the door and watches*
Digger*. After a beat he turns to* **Clifton***.*

Ashley   Sorry, carry on. I like to hear you, you're proper
clever.

Clifton (*takes in* **Digger** *leaving*)   What's the point in being
clever and none of you children take you foot? One end up
a bloody thief, the next a brok-hand boxer. Tell me what I
did to deserve that, eh? Where me brains go, Baygee?

Baygee   Life don't go the way we want it.

Clifton (*decking his glass of rum*)   You don't lie, partner, you
don't lie. Maybe you'll be the one that'll take me mind, eh,
junior?

Deli *walked in near the end of the conversation with a box under his
arm, but was not seen.*

Deli   Maybe he will, but that'll be because his father was
around to nurture and support him.

Clifton *turns to* **Baygee** *embarrassed.*

Clifton   Oh God.

His hand begins to shake slightly. He calms it.

Hello son.

Deli *checks* **Ashley** *who is watching him closely.*

Deli   Hello, Clifton.

Clifton *and* **Baygee** *clock each other.*

Clifton   I come to pay me respects to you and help bury
me first-born.

Deli   Is that so?

Clifton   I didn't mean nothin' by –

Deli   – Ashley, did you give your grandfather something
to eat?

Ashley (*he's never seen his father treat anyone like this*)   Yeah.

Deli   Good. Then, Clifton, your respects are accepted and
thank you for your visit.

He opens the door for **Clifton** *to leave.*

Clifton (*calm and cool*)   Oh, I haven't quite finished my
food. You wouldn't put a man out on an empty belly, would
you?

Deli *closes the door.*

Clifton   So I hear I'm a great-grandfather? (*Jesting.*) Bonjey! How you let the child age me so? (*Beat.*) The place don't look all dat but I hear you're doing OK? That's good!

Deli (*pointed*)   Bad luck is always just around the corner.

Clifton   Must be doing well to have bought two acres of land home!

Silence. **Clifton** *clocks that this is not public information.*

Deli   Like I said, man never knows what's around the corner.

Clifton (*changing the subject. To all*)   Eh! You know the first man I see when I reach Hackney?

Baygee   Who?

Clifton   Macknee the old Scottish man.

Baygee   Oh ho!

Clifton   I laugh till I couldn't laugh again. You see, I knew this was going to be a good trip when I saw that mean-nose bastard in a wheelchair, drunk, raggedy, throwing himself in front of people car shouting abuse.

Ashley (*shocked*)   You know the old drunken Scottish man, Grandad?

Clifton   Me use to rent a room from him. If I think hard, you fadder may have been conceived dere.

Ashley   Boyeeee, he's off his head, dread. Bare swearing and ramming people's vechs with his wheelchair. Man's due to get spark!

Anastasia   The man in a wheelchair, have some pity on him na.

Baygee   The bitch can walk. Sorry. (*To* **Anastasia**.) I mean, there's nuttin wrong with his leg.

Clifton   Is all the wickedness he do people that haunting him.

Baygee   If he was West Indian I'd say somebody wok obea him.

Clifton   Is only black people that know witchcraft?

Baygee *shrugs.*

Clifton   The most witchcraft is practise by the white man. How do the arse you think he managed to take Africa from we. That white man –

Deli *explodes, 0–60.*

Deli   . . . Don't bring none of your white this and dat in here, Clifton. I don't want to hear that.

Baygee   That's no way to speak to your father, Deli.

Deli (*trying to hold it down*)   Baygee, please!

*He clocks **Anastasia**'s response.*

Clifton   No, the boy's right. In his place, his word is *the* word.

Beat.

Baygee   Clifton, come let we go over to the betting shop na? The old boys in there they go shit when they see you.

Beat.

Clifton   I coming, I coming. Baygee, you mind if my son and I have a few minutes?

Baygee   Of course.

He steps to the back of the restaurant.

Clifton   I know your brother meant a lot to you. I'm sorry. But this is the way of the world.

Deli *stares at him blankly.*

Clifton   You see, death is around us everywhere.

Deli   Ah ha.

Beat.

Clifton I need somewhere to stay just until the funeral finish.

Beat.

I was wondering if . . . Until I see the doctor for me hand, and attend the funeral . . .

Deli *still doesn't reply.*

Clifton I wouldn't burden you. A sofa will do. Two weeks max.

He stares right into **Deli***'s eyes.* **Deli** *thinks. He sees* **Clifton***'s hand shake. Silence.*

Deli I can't have you stay here. This is Elmina's place. I'll call Ashley's mother and see if she'll put you up in the spare room. But once Dougie's buried I want you to leave, Clifton.

Clifton *looks at Elmina's picture and picks up his suitcase.*

Clifton I'll be in the Black Dog across the road. When you ready, send for me. (*Taking in* **Deli**.) Baygee, come na! The boys go say, 'Big time Clifton, what you doing back in England, boy?' And I go tell them the Queen send for me. You mind if I leave my suitcase here?

Baygee How you could ask the child that? Of course he don't. Come, boy.

Clifton I coming. I coming.

Baygee Stop coming and come.

They leave. **Ashley** *takes the food to deliver off the counter and looks at his father before leaving. As if paralysed,* **Deli** *stands rooted on the spot.* **Deli** *looks up to the picture of his mother. He is disappointed in himself for not outrightly refusing* **Clifton***.*

Deli (*whispers to Elmina*) I tried.

Anastasia Your pops is a character eee!

Deli Before I knew myself, I knew I was Clifton's child.

Anastasia   They fuck you up, your mum and dad.

Deli   That's what Digger says about women.

Anastasia   You think that too?

He shrugs.

(*Innocently.*) Do you get on with Ashley's mother?

Deli   I'd rather not talk about her actually.

Anastasia   OK.

Silence.

How did the meeting go?

Deli   'To find the information needed to start the case would be' – how did they put it? – 'cost prohibitive' was the common phrase. Everybody knows your last day in prison you keep you fucking head down. But Dougie, no! He was a troublemaker, Anastasia, that's why no one wants to take the case, no one that I could afford right now anyway.

Anastasia   He left you money, right?

Deli   Sorry?

Anastasia   Dougie left you a whole heap ah money, right, everybody knows dat.

Deli *doesn't answer.*

Anastasia   Even if you have to spend you last cent, find someone. You can't mek people kill you family and left it so! There must be somewhere else you could go?

Deli *flashes a steely glance.*

Deli (*flash of anger*)   No, there is not somewhere else I can go, I have been everywhere, alright?

Beat.

Anastasia   You know that tone you just employed, you're sure that's the choice you wanna stick with?

Deli   Pardon?

Anastasia   Cos I don't know what kind of women you are use to but, baby, I don't let men speak to me like that.

Awkward silence.

Deli   Sorry.

Anastasia   Apology accepted.

Beat.

She runs over to her bag and gets out her Acts of Faith. *She rips out a page.*

Deli   What you doing?

She sticks it to the counter.

You don't find there's enough posters on the wall? What's that, Anastasia?

Anastasia   It's a page I don't need any more.

She enters into the kitchen through the swing doors, whistling. **Deli,** *intrigued, gets up and reads the page. Shaking his head, he laughs while reading it.*

Deli *(kissing his teeth)*   What rubbish . . . rubbish.

Anastasia *pops her head over the swing doors. The speeches tumble over each other.*

Anastasia *(surprised)*   Why's it rubbish?

Deli *walks away.*

Deli *(taking the piss)*   'In every disaster lies a lesson' . . .

Anastasia   It's true . . .

Deli   . . . 'If you can truly learn that lesson' . . .

Anastasia *(increasingly frustrated)*   . . . I know it in my own life . . .

Deli   . . . blah blah blah . . .

Anastasia (*vexed now*)   . . . It ain't no blah blah blah, this is, this is, life-healing stuff . . .

Deli   . . . Healing? What you healing for? . . .

Anastasia (*firm and straight*)   . . . So when the good tings come along you're ready?

Deli (*vexed*)   Good tings don't happen to me, Anastasia . . .

Anastasia   What stupidness . . .

Deli   . . . Ah my life me ah talk 'bout you na! And you know what me discover? Man is not suppose to want. I wanted, I could have been da don, and what happen? Bam, it get mash. I wanted to, I fucking worked hard to be there with Ashley and his mum! Bam, it get mash. I wanted my brother home, here with me and what happen? One step from the fucking gate, bam, he get mash. Don't tell me about my life.

Anastasia (*bitter*)   Oh you's one feeling sorrow for yourself, motherfucker?

Deli   What? . . .

Anastasia   You have things others dream of. This place . . .

Deli   . . . This place! Tell me what's so great about this place? I have a handful of customers who spend five pound a shot and talk nonsense all day! What did you say I have again?

Anastasia   You have you child. 'Anyting better than having you child –' How could anyting good happen to you when you don't look after the shit you have.

Beat.

Deli (*angry*)   And how am I suppose to do that?

Anastasia (*growls with passion, close up to his face*)   You supposed to clean up your environment, Deli. This restaurant stinks. People walk in here, they smell Digger and walk straight back out. I've seen it. But you, my friend, you're comfortable with the stench of death around you?

Deli   There's nothing wrong with Digger that a couple of years' intense hard labour wouldn't put right.

Anastasia   If you're gonna joke forget it. You mek me tired.

Deli   You know that tone you just used with me? Do you always talk to your bosses like that? Cos I ain't use to my employees taking to me like that!

Anastasia   You know what? You're right.

Anastasia *walks to get her coat.*

Deli   Where you going?

Anastasia *(screams, visibly upset)*   Why are my men too weak to raise their head above the fucking water. I don't want to be around another loser, Deli! I lose too much in my life already.

She's putting on her coat.

Deli   It's cos Digger's in here that them other punks don't come looking for money.

Anastasia *(stops)*   What money?

Deli   Ah, so there's something's you don't know, Oprah? Protection money.

Anastasia   You pay protection money?

Deli   No, that's the point. So Digger helps me, OK!

Anastasia *(tired)*   Whatever, Deli, whatever!

Coat in hand she makes to leave. **Deli** *thinks for a moment.*

Deli   Hold up na!

She carries on walking.

Do you like plantain?

Anastasia (*stops, unsure where he is heading*)   Ummm! Sure!

Deli   Well, wait na!

He enters the kitchen leaving her outside now. He laughs.

Huh! Look up there, what do you see?

Anastasia   Ummmmm, picture of your mother?

Deli   That was the last person to talk to me like that and still have dem head.

Beat.

'We have entered a stranger's dream, and for trespassing he has rewarded us with his worse nightmare' is what my father use to say about living in England.

Anastasia   He come back here though, innit?

Deli *enters with two 'plantain burgers' and hands one to* **Anastasia**.

Deli   Da da! You ever had a plantain burger before?

Anastasia   No!

Deli   Here, try this. Breast of chicken, sitting on crisp lettuce with three slices of succulent plantain, all in a sesame toasted bun.

Anastasia   I hope you're not trying to obea me!

They laugh. She takes a bite.

Anastasia   Ummmmmmmmmmm!

Deli   Good, huh?

Anastasia   Yeah, almost as good as my macaroni pie!

Beat.

Deli   About a week before Clifton left, right, I was about ten and it was around midnight, I had the munchies bad. So I went downstairs and looked in the pot. There was one piece of juicy-looking chicken. But I didn't fancy that by itself so I opened the fridge door and there it was, a plantain. So I took it out and commenced to fry. (*Laughing at*

the remembrance.) And it came out alright. I jammed that
chicken in a bun and threw the burnt-up plantain on top ah
it and boyyyyy that ting taste gooooood. I was so digging on
that bun, I had forgotten to switch off the frying pan. And
yeah, it went up. Blacked up the whole kitchen. Mum and
Dad heard me scream and ran down. Eventually, Dad put
out the pan. My mum was just pleased that I had survived
but first thing my dad did when the smoke had cleared was
open the chicken pot. When he saw it had gone he ran
upstairs and got his belt boy and beat my claat. He said it
was because I nearly burnt down the kitchen, but I know it
was because of the chicken breast.

Anastasia *laughs.*

Deli   I haven't made it since then.

Anastasia (*excited*)   Deli, you's a fool. You know you have
the answer right here, you know?

Deli   What?

Anastasia (*excited*)   Blouse and skirts, West Indian fast
food! That's wicked. You sell dis and do up a place likkle bit
and different mans would come into your restaurant. I take
back all I said, damn, I knew I liked you for a reason.

She throws her arms around him. He's unsure how to react.

Deli   You can't take back! . . .

Anastasia   . . . Yes I can! . . .

Deli   . . . No you can't . . .

Anastasia (*close to his face*)   . . . Yes I can . . .

*She kisses him. He kisses her back. After a few beats, though, he violently
stops and pulls away.*

Deli   Na, na. Sorry.

Anastasia (*searching for his eyes, trying to convince*)   It's OK . . .
I liked it.

He walks to the other side of the counter. **Anastasia** *steps back, a little rejected.*

Anastasia   What's wrong?

Deli *doesn't respond.* **Anastasia** *walks to him, gently puts her hand on his face again.*

Anastasia *(without emotion)*   I'll do the wanting.

Deli *(vexed, moves away)*   No, I can't do this. You're not a bore-through gal, Ani.

Anastasia   Well then, don't just bore through.

Deli   I ain't got nothing else to offer you right now.

She doesn't reply.

(Angry.) The boys are betting on when I'm gonna fuck you, Anastasia! Ashley's betting.

Anastasia   I don't watch what other people think.

She slowly pulls **Deli***'s head to face her and kisses him gently on the mouth. He kisses her back. Just as the shop bell rings he pulls back, holds her face in his hands and stares at her carefully.*

Enter **Digger***. He looks well vexed. Frustrated,* **Anastasia** *walks and stands near the swing doors to the kitchen.* **Deli** *is unsure what* **Digger** *has seen.*

Deli *(embarrassed, says the first thing that comes into his head)* Hey! You're back?

Digger *(snaps back)*   What kind of question is that? Of course I'm back. Give me a cocoa tea.

Anastasia *exits to the kitchen, shaking her head. Silence.*

Digger *(convincing himself)*   Me have fe talk it. Me just have fe talk it. I'm not vex, you nah, I'm vex na pussyclaat. I just had to deal with tricky. The fool na just switch pon me!

Deli *is not really that interested. He looks in the direction of the kitchen.*

Deli   Switch?

Digger   Switch, that's what I fucking said, innit? Switch! He na go collect money that is mine, and give it to Renton crew as a 'gift-offering'.

Deli   Wha?

Digger   Yes, gift, so that they would accept him inna dem crew! My fucking money! What the fuck is happening around here? I had to mark him str –

Deli (*holding his hand in the air to stop* **Digger**)   Yo! Digger –

Digger   – Don't cut me in mid-flow! You na hear what the advert say – it's good to talk. Me, I need to get this off my chest. Anyway, when me finally hunt down Tricky I tek out my blade – the long one with the bend on the top – and me slice –

Deli   – Digger, don't pollute up my vibes wid dem talk dey – !

Digger (*exclaims*)   . . . Pollute?! Deli, you went to prison for GBH, on three men and their dogs. How de fuck I gonna pollute you?

Deli (*losing it a little*)   A restaurant is not the place to discuss fucking murder.

Digger   Where else me suppose to talk about it? On the street?

Deli   Digs, right now I don't care, just not in here, not today.

Digger   I didn't murder him, I just cu –

Deli (*shouts*)   Digger! You can't hear me? I said I don't want to hear about it. If you can't hear me, man, come out!

Digger (*disbelief switches to cold*)   What? Of your restaurant?

Deli (*a little defensively*)   I ain't saying that, Digger, I'm just saying, what if someone walked into the place and overheard this kind of talk? They'd have heard all your bizness. You didn't even check, you just come in and start fe talk. Suppose 5.0 was in here?

Digger   But they ain't! Nobody comes inside here.

Deli (*losing it a bit*)   Well maybe that's the problem. Look, I don't want no dirty talk inside yere, take from that what you want.

Beat.

Digger   Well, I shocked, Deli. When you does call me ignorant I don't like it but I take it, but now my talk is not good enough for you and your restaurant? Me that sit down in here for a lifetime, is not good enough? . . .

Deli (*tired*)   . . . I didn't say that, Digger.

Digger   Seen, so you, like all them other niggers round here, switching on me?

Anastasia *comes to the swing door.* **Deli** *looks to her.* **Digger** *looks to her.*

Deli   Let me get some more cocoa from the back.

Deli *and* **Anastasia** *clock each other for a moment before exiting into the back, leaving* **Digger** *in the restaurant alone.*

Digger (*vexed, to himself*)   Keep your fucking tea. Ah wha de?!

Ashley *enters.*

Ashley   Yes! Digger!

Digger *turns to* **Ashley**. *He pauses for a moment. Looks to see if* **Deli**'*s about. He's not.*

Digger (*slow but over-friendly*)   Yes, Ashley, what gwan?

The lights slowly fade.

Act Two

The lights are down. We hear the voices of all the characters sing a slow blues called 'You Gotta Move'. While they are singing the lights slowly rise so that we can just about make out the figures. Facing upstage, the characters are at Dougie's funeral. Set to the side is a lone female figure in traditional African headgear playing the gurkel.

All
  You may be rich
  You may be poor
  You may be young
  You may be old
  But when the Lord gets ready you ga'da move
  You may be black
  You may be white
  You may be wrong
  You may be right
  But when the Lord gets ready you ga'da move
  You ga'da move
  You ga'da move
  You ga'da move child
  You ga'da move
  And when the Lord gets ready you go'da move
  And when the Lord gets ready you go'da move

The lights fade during the final chorus.

Scene One

Restaurant. Night, three weeks later.

Lights snap up on a refurbished restaurant. It looks good. The newly painted walls no longer have any posters. And the stools have been replaced by new Ikea-type modern ones. The only thing that remains is the picture of Elmina above the swing doors. And the TV, which is on. Above Elmina's picture, however, is a new sign that reads, 'ELMINA'S PLANTAIN HUT'. On the back wall is a picture of Dougie with the

*words 'Dougie Andrews, 1959–2003 RIP. They have just had the
opening-night party.* **Deli** *is closing the door behind the last
customer/party attendee.* **Anastasia** *is clearing away the glasses and
plates of food.* **Baygee** *and* **Clifton**, *who are very tipsy, are sitting at
the counter.* **Baygee** *is playing his guitar and* **Clifton** *is singing
loudly to the calypso rhythm being played. As he sings his eyes follow*
Anastasia. **Deli** *is in buoyant mood.*

Clifton (*sings*)
  Jooking, jooking, jooking
  Gal her you bottom do so much stunt
  Jooking, jooking, jooking
  Let we try disting from de front
  Jooking, jooking, jooking
  I hope it's good seed you does lay
  Jooking, jooking till de break of day.

Deli   Clifton, stop dat na, man.

*He shouts to the customers who have just left. He is in new businessman
mode.*

Bye, thanks for coming. Don't forget for each ten burgers
ordered you get the eleventh free . . . OK . . . Thanks again.

Clifton *mocks him to* **Baygee**.

Clifton (*sings*)   For each ten burgers ordered you get the
eleventh free! (*Speaks.*) Black people buying ten ah anyting,
eh, Baygee?

Ashley (*swigging from champagne bottle, looks at his watch nervously*)
Right, that's the family ting done!

Deli (*friendly*)   So what, you can't help me clean up the
place?

Ashley   What?!

Anastasia   Thank you for helping, Ashley, tonight,
Ashley.

Ashley *doesn't quite know how to react, so quickly smiles.*

Deli *turns to* **Clifton**.

Deli   And I hope you're proud of yourself?

Clifton   What happen to you?

Deli   The need for you to get on the table, start singing blasted rude calypsos and running the blasted customers was what. It was supposed to be an upmarket launch.

Beside herself, **Anastasia** *laughs under her breath.*

Clifton (*taking the piss*)   Upmarket launch? It was a party! And when man have party people suppose to dance, not stand up and chat. What de arse this generation coming to?

Deli   It's the opening of a new West Indian restaurant, Clifton, not a blasted shebeen!

Clifton   There was nothing West Indian about it. You have a master calypsonian sitting right here, you know, and would you let him play? NO! We had to mek coup in the name of culture and take matters into we own hand.

Deli (*matter-of-fact*)   No disrespect, Baygee, but that was not the image we (*looking at* **Anastasia**), I, want people to connect with this restaurant. It's a new vibes we ah deal in right now.

Anastasia   Listen, the man from the council pre-ordered a month's delivery of plantain burgers for black history month and paid upfront. We should be proud ah we ourselves. West Indian fast food reach.

Just as she is about to hug him, he steps back, takes the bottle of champagne away from **Ashley** *and returns to* **Anastasia** *with a glass.*

Clifton   If you ask me, fast and West Indian is a contradiction in terms.

Deli (*to* **Anastasia**)   Here.

Anastasia (*pointed*)   I've had too much already. Any more and you'll have to carry me home on your back.

Deli   Drink the drink na. Tonight is well special, it's also my bir . . .

Baygee *changes to an old-time kinky reggae rhythm.* **Clifton** *instantly recognises it, stands on the stool and starts to sing at the top of his voice.*

Clifton (*sings*)
   Soldering ah wha de young gal want, soldering.
   Welding ah what de young gal want, welding.

Deli   Jesus!

Ashley (*nervously checks his mobile*)   Gwan, Grandad.

Deli   Clifton, will you stop you noise?

Clifton *stops momentarily.*

Clifton   What de arse do this, boy?

Kisses his teeth.

Anastasia   Maybe you should call your dad and Baygee a taxi!

Clifton *is offended by* **Anastasia**'s *comment.*

Clifton   What you trying to say, I is drunk?

Deli   Finish up you drinks, Clifton, home time.

Clifton   Answer me this! Can a drunk man extemporise?

Anastasia   I don't know, Clifton.

Clifton (*concentrating hard*)   Well, think about it. See! You can't answer because, the answer would be contri, contradictory to your current thesis.

Anastasia *laughs.*

Clifton   Baygee! Prepare me a rhythm.

Deli   Oh man!

Baygee *starts to play an old-time calypso rhythm.*

Clifton   You ready? You ready? Young boy, give me a subject quick while the rhythm hot! Quick!

Anastasia *pours herself a drink.*

Ashley   Um, um football! Football!

Clifton   Here we go. They use to call me culture master. Be prepared to get teach. (*Sings.*)

> History is a funny thing,
> History is a funny thing,
> Listen to me, people,
> Cos is about football me ah sing.
> Clive Best the greatest
> Baller West Ham ever had,
> But from the stands they'd shout each game,
> Go home you black bastard.

Deli   Oh here we go!

Clifton (*sings*)
> Oh England, what a wonderful land,
> In England what you must understand,
> Is whatever you do, wherever you rise,
> Please realise, you could never disguise
> You's a black man in a cold cold land.

Deli   That isn't about football! It's you on your high horse again.

Clifton (*vexed*)   Did you hear the word football?

Deli   Yeah . . .

Clifton (*turning to* **Ashley**)   . . . Did you hear the name of a footballer?

Ashley   Yes.

Clifton   Den it was about football, wasn't it?!

Ashley   Grandad, you give me jokes, boy!

Deli   I'm going to put the rubbish outside and I'm calling you a taxi, Clifton.

Anastasia   I'll help you!

Deli (*softly*)   You ain't paid for dem kinda work dere, girl.

Anastasia *exhales quietly.*

Clifton   Sweet gal, give me a subject na!

Anastasia   Um, love.

Clifton   That easy, man. Something hard.

Anastasia   OK. Trust!

Clifton   Alright, you ready now? Slow down the rhythm, Baygee.

Baygee   Oh God, man, you's a dictator!

He slows down the rhythm. **Clifton** *sings.*

Clifton
I look at you, you have eyes that I could trust,
The way you look me up and down on da number
   seven bus . . .

Baygee (*disgusted*)   Number seven bus?

Clifton (*quickly*)   Shut up. (*Continues to sing.*)

I think you is a lady,
But I don't know maybe,
Tonight if you'll give yourself to me.
(*Chorus:*) Give it to me.

Baygee (*sings back-up*)
Give it to me.

Clifton
Give it to me.

Baygee
Give it to me.

Clifton
Nice and soft, soft and hard, give it to me.

Baygee
  Give it to me.

Clifton
  Give it to me.

Baygee
  Give it to me.

Clifton
  Cos tonight you'll live you fantasies.

He ends kissing **Anastasia***'s hand.* **Ashley** *applauds.*

Anastasia   Clifton, that was rubbish, but you're brilliant!

Clifton *turns to* **Baygee***.*

Clifton   Don't stop, boy, eh, eh, you losing you touch!

He grabs **Anastasia** *by the hand to dance with him.*

Anastasia   No, no!

Clifton   Get up, girl.

She gets up.

Baygee, sing one of them love song you use to play when we was young na!

Baygee *starts to sing.*

Baygee   Darling, I can feel you sweet aroma, *etc. etc.*

While **Baygee** *is singing* **Anastasia** *makes to leave, but* **Clifton** *pulls her close to him. They slow-rub.*

Anastasia   You're very strong for a, a, a older man.

Clifton *smiles.*

Clifton   Iccceeettch! It's been a long time.

Anastasia   Since you danced with a woman?

Clifton   Since *you* danced with a man. I can tell a woman's history by simply touching her. See, when I *grabbed* you, you flexed vex but now that I hold you softly, you don't know what to do with yourself, do you?

Anastasia   You are very sure of yourself!

Clifton   Am I wrong? Or am I wrong?

Beat.

Anastasia (*matter-of-fact*)   Actually, you're not. I haven't had . . . let a man touch me with tenderness for a lifetime.

Clifton   Why?

Anastasia   Cos men kill things.

Clifton (*ignoring*)   What about my son, hasn't he touched you with, how you say, tenderness?

Anastasia   I don't think your son is interested in me that way. I'm a bit old for him, Clifton.

She loses her balance. **Clifton** *holds her.*

Anastasia   Oh!

Clifton   Whereas I, on the other hand, *like* a sprightly young thing?

Anastasia *stands and then steps away from him.*

Enter **Digger**. *He pops his head round the door. As soon as* **Ashley** *sees him he drops the champagne glass he has in his hand. Everyone clocks this, except* **Clifton** *who is still deadly focused on* **Anastasia**.

Digger   So all you have big-time party and nobody doe invite me?

Clifton   Eh, eh, Digger, where you been, I thought you was dead!

Digger (*cold*)   Wha! You miss me?

Ashley *moves out.*

Ashley   Laters, people.

He touches **Digger** *with his fist very casually.* **Digger** *nods back again very casually.* **Ashley***'s gone.*

Anastasia   Ashley, where you go(*ing?* . . .)

Enter **Deli** *from the back.*

Deli   Ashley!

He sees **Digger***. He is slightly taken aback.*

Deli   Yo! Digger. Good to see you, man. What gwan?

Digger (*very cool*)   Just cool, yu nah! Hmmmm, all you fix up the place good.

Deli   Thanks. Want a burger or something?

Digger   Nah. Dem fast ting dere just give a man wind. Innit, Clifton? . . .

Clifton   . . . You doe lie, you doe lie.

Deli   I could probably cut up some chicken, stew it up and put it in a bun or something?

Digger   Nah, man, I wouldn't want you to mess up you new kitchen and dat. Anyway, just passing, yuh na! Later.

Clifton   Digger, where you going!? You don't hear me sing yet?

Digger   When business calls, Clifton!

Digger*'s gone.*

Deli   Where's Ashley?

Anastasia   He just popped out.

Deli (*contained anger*)   Jesus.

Deli *picks up his mobile and speed-dials.*

Anastasia   Deli, come and dance man, deal wid de rubbish later.

It's engaged. **Deli** *kisses his teeth.*

Deli (*still elsewhere, cold*)   . . . I don't have time for that! I don't, Clifton, your taxi's gonna be about five minutes. Gonna have to share one with Baygee, they're running low!

He exits.

Anastasia   Clifton, something look wrong wid me? Excuse.

She leaves for the toilet. **Clifton** *sits next to* **Baygee**. **Baygee** *is looking at the swing doors, thinking of* **Deli**.

Clifton   You see she, dirty gal that!

Baygee   What you talking about, man?

Clifton   You don't see how she push up she hot tings pon me!

Baygee (*with a drunk man's directness, still strumming*)   You too nasty! I know you, you know! Take you eyes off the man woman.

Clifton (*all innocence*)   Is not the boy woman yet. Anyway, there's only two woman in the world I wouldn't trouble, me modder and me sister. And both ah dem dead.

Baygee *cuts his eyes at him.*

Baygee   I find since you come back that boy turn cold, you know.

Clifton (*kissing his teeth*)   Man should be glad not mad to see him fadder. In my day . . .

His hand is shaking.

Baygee   . . . Eighteen years is a whole heap ah time . . .

Clifton   . . . Too fucking soft. What happen between his mother and me is between his mother and me. He's a fucking divorced man, he should know that.

Baygee (*goes into performance*)   That's why I never marry, you know. I like a cat, I hunt alone, eat alone and the only time I want to be stroked is when I giving 'thunder'.

Clifton   Alas, a good philosophy, but too late for me.

Baygee   What is really wrong wid you, Clifton?

Clifton   Ah, a little sugar, little pain in me foot dem. Nothing I can't lick.

Baygee   Yeah?

Clifton   Personally, I blame the white man.

Baygee   Oh gosh, how you reach there, boy?

Clifton   Is true. People who feel discriminated against, you see, have higher blood pressure, die earlier, have more heart disease and die of cancer in higher numbers. Dem prove it. There's a test case in America right now that women bringing against men.

Baygee (*not really interested*)   So you sick bad?

Clifton   Baygee, a batman's can be called out several ways. Caught in the slips, clean bowl like a fool swinging for a huge six . . .

Baygee   . . . That's the way I want to go . . .

Clifton   . . . or he can get LBW'd. But it's not until the umpire raise he finger so, that you leave the crease. An he don't even look in my direction yet. Heaven go have to wait, boy.

He raises his glass. The men finish off their drinks. **Baygee** *plays the guitar. We hear the toilet flush.*

Baygee (*sings*)   Here's to life, joy and prosperity, may I be in mid-stroke when death call on me.

(*Speaks.*) Wooooooooooow! How that ting does just spring up on you so. The other day man was in full action when all of ah sudden me feel like me have to piss.

Clifton   You should'a let it out! She wouldn't ah know.

Baygee   Shut up, man. You too damn nasty.

Baygee *runs to the toilet.* **Anastasia** *enters. She has a rejuvenated sensual air about her.* **Clifton** *puts his head in his hands and lets out a slight groan. She stops when she hears this.*

Anastasia   I know that sound.

Clifton *looks up, surprised.*

Clifton   You do?

Anastasia   You don't fool me, Clifton. I can hear the pain.

Clifton   . . . Pain? . . .

Anastasia   . . . Of losing your first-born . . .

Clifton   It's the cramp in me foot actually. The diabetes does bring it on terrible.

Anastasia   Oh!

Clifton   But I'm glad you're concerned. Listen, I'm a direct man. You look good and I look great. What you say we keep each other company tonight? It's a long time since I really talk to a woman, maybe you show me how to grieve?

She understands loud and clear what he is trying to say.

We hear the loud tooting of the minicab.

Baygee *enters the room doing up his flies.*

Baygee   Ah, lovely! The only thing that can compare to sex! A good leggo water.

Enter **Deli**, *with a very dirty heavy carrier bag. He puts it under the counter.*

Deli   That will be your cab, gentlemen. Ani, you have to jump in with the guys, they're out of cabs.

Anastasia   It's OK! Do you want me to wait till you finish what you doing and you can drop me?

Deli   No, I can't do that. Get in the cab.

Anastasia *stares at him hard.*

Anastasia   Fine, I will. Clifton, you ready?

Clifton *jumps up.*

Clifton   Right, let's not keep the driver waiting. Your carriage awaits you, madam.

She quickly puts on her coat. She doesn't look at **Deli***. She exits.*
Baygee *has finished packing away his guitar and has his coat on.*

Baygee   Deli, sometimes when tings staring you in the face you must take it you know. I gone!

Clifton *and* **Baygee** *exit.*

Deli *spots* **Anastasia***'s* Acts of Faith *book. He runs to the door. We hear the car door slam and the cab drive off.* **Deli** *walks back in. Book in hand, he switches off the TV, gets the keys out of his pocket and is about to lock the door when* **Ashley** *barges in.*

Deli   What the arse!

Ashley   Sorry, Dad, I didn't see you there.

Ashley *is making his way through to the kitchen. He is slightly hyped.*
Deli *searches for something to speak to him about. Before* **Ashley** *disappears behind the swing doors it comes.*

Deli   Hey, Ash, what date is it today?

Ashley   Oh shit, it's your birthday!

Deli   Yeah.

Ashley   Oh shit, sorry, Dad.

Deli   It's all good. The event tonight was my party. That's why I was glad that even though you've not been around much lately, you were around tonight.

Ashley   Yeah, well, um . . .

Deli   Come, let we break some bread together na, just you and me!

Ashley   Well, I kinda wanted to go up . . .

Deli   Stay there, I'll get us a piece of chicken each.

Ashley   Let me get it. (*Wanting to go and wash his hands.*)

Deli   Na, man, you'll only make a mess.

Ashley (*shrugging shoulders*)   Alright.

Ashley *sits by the counter. He picks up some napkins and wipes his bloody hands.* **Deli** *exits with the chicken. He puts it in the microwave.*

Deli (*entering, genuine question*)   Hey, Ashley, do you read? You know, like for fun?

Ashley   Why am I going to that?

Deli   Feed your mind maybe?

Ashley   They make all the good books into films, innit?!

Deli   Seen!

Ashley (*laughing*)   I ain't never seen you pick up a book. Oh, except *now*, yeah, you reading all bred of self-help manuals like you's a blasted white man!

Deli   Reading's for whites? I'm trying to open up my mind to different tings, what's wrong with that?

Ashley   If that's your ting, nothing, man.

The bell on the microwave indicates the chicken is heated. **Ashley** *makes to get up, but* **Deli** *moves off first.*

Deli (*exiting*)   I'll get it.

Ashley *doesn't quite get why he's being served in this way.*

Deli (*entering*)   So where was I? Oh yeah, you said there was nothing wrong with education.

He gives **Ashley** *the food.*

Ashley   Happy birthday, old man.

Deli   Thank you.

He pulls out the dirty carrier bag from beneath the counter.

Then why did I find all of your college books in the rubbish?

Deli *puts the bag next to* **Ashley**. **Ashley** *stops eating.*

Beat.

Deli *won't say another word.*

Ashley   Char! I ain't got it for this.

He gets up to leave. **Deli** *instinctively pushes him back into the chair. He backs off, but only a little.*

Deli   Why are your college books in the bin, Ashley?

Ashley   You know what? They're there, cos I put them em there!

Deli (*calm*)   Don't be rude.

Ashley (*shouts*)   I ain't got time for college!

Deli   You don't have time? What do you have time for? Fucking Machino and garage raves?

Ashley   Don't come doing this whole good caring dad number right now! . . .

Deli   . . . I've never asked you about college before now? . . .

Ashley   . . . I stand corrected, you did ask me about college, when you wanted me to take a day off to run fucking food errands . . .

Deli (*vexed*)   . . . Who you swearing at, boy . . . ?

Ashley   . . . Forget this. College does not fit into the plan I have for my life. You want to keep selling your little plantain burgers, good luck to you, may you always be happy. Me, I'm a man.

Deli *loses it. He raises his hand to hit him but pulls back at the last moment.*

Ashley   Go on na!

Deli You'd like that, wouldn't you? Yes, you'd like me to punch your lights out, so you could walk street and say, 'See, see, I told you man dad weren't no punk.'

Ashley Why would I say that? You are a punk.

Deli Don't you push me!

Ashley And what? . . .

Deli . . . And *what*? . . .

Ashley . . . Yeah, what you gonna do, with your old self?

Deli . . . Take you the hell out . . . (*He pulls back.*)

Ashley (*laughs*) . . . You're joking bredren. You can't touch me! . . . I'll deck you before you can raise your hand star.

Beat.

Deli (*trying to defuse*) And how you gonna put your hand on your father and think that you gonna live good?

Ashley Man lives how he can.

Deli Ah so?

Suddenly he springs forward and grabs **Ashley***'s arm before he can move. He twists it behind* **Ashley***'s back.*

Do it then! If your name is man, put your hand on me! . . .

Ashley . . . Ahhhhhhh . . .

Deli . . . No, not ahhhhh, put your hand on me!

Ashley . . . Get off . . .

Deli (*firm*) You know what I read in one of those 'white' books the other day? The true sign of intelligence is how man deals with the problems of his environment . . . (*Shouts.*) I don't want to live like this, Ashley, it ain't fun . . .

Ashley . . . Get offfffffffff, you're hurting me . . .

Deli (*from his heart*)   . . . I'm trying, I'm trying to change shit around here, but you ain't on line, bra! Where you are trying to head, it's a dead ting, a dark place, it don't go nowhere.

He releases the grip. Emotionally exhausted, he throws his hands in the air in near surrender. **Ashley** *is silent for a moment while he adjusts to the new freedom from pain.*

Ashley (*screams*)   Don't you ever touch me again! Do you hear me? Put your hand on me ever again, father or no father, you're a dead man. Do you hear me?

Deli   Calm down, Ashley. Calm . . .

He notices blood on his own hands. He scans **Ashley** *and sees that it has come from cuts on his hands. One cut is still bleeding.*

Deli   What happened to your hands?

Ashley *pulls his hands away.*

Ashley (*slightly taken aback*)   Ummmmm, cut them, innit.

Deli   Don't take the piss.

We hear the sounds of approaching sirens. **Ashley** *becomes alert.* **Deli** *notices his nervousness even though he is shielding it well. We hear them pull up.*

Deli   Are you – you're charlied to rass! (*Beat.*) What the fuck is going on, Ashley?

Ashley (*losing it*)   Then don't ask me nuttin. What the hell you think this is?

Deli   I don't know, son. That is why I'm asking you?

He goes to the door and looks outside.

Bloodclaat, ah Rose's place dat ah burn so?

Surprised, he turns to **Ashley**. *After a beat* **Deli** *runs to get his coat to go out and help. We hear more fire engines pulling up.*

Deli   We'll come back to this!

Ashley (*shouts*) You know what I don't like about you? You don't do nothin but sit back and let the world fuck you over. Not me, dread!

Ashley *exits.*

Deli You coming or what?

But **Ashley** *has gone. He looks around for a beat and then rushes out.*

Lights down.

Scene Two

Restaurant. Day.

Deli *is sitting by the counter, he looks a little dazed, unsettled. After a beat or so* **Anastasia** *runs in a little flustered.*

Anastasia Sooooo sorry I'm late . . .

Deli (*snaps back*) No problem . . . I heard traffic was bad.

Anastasia (*ignoring him*) . . . I overslept like a fool. It must have been the champagne! Eh, what gwaning across the street? When dat burn, last night?

Deli Look so. Man, Roy's in Homerton, x amount of burns. Rose's life work gone. That's why you got to live life while you can, boy!

There's silence for a bit.

Hey, Ani, you're quiet today?

Anastasia Am I? Just a little tired.

Deli *shakes his head in understanding. He wants to say something but can't quite find the right words. Eventually it comes out.*

Deli I cleared out Dougie's room in the flat today, you yuh!

Anastasia Positive move, well done.

Silence.

Deli   Ani, how old did you say your son was again?

Anastasia   Nineteen.

Deli   Look at that, huh, we must have been doing it at the same time.

Enter **Clifton**, *with an extra spring in his walk.* **Anastasia** *moves swiftly back into the kitchen.*

Clifton   Bonjour, good morning good morning good morning. And how is everybody this bright fine morning? Well, noontime?

Deli   Someone woke up on the right side of bed!

Clifton   Oh yes, I had a very good night's sleep.

Deli   Lucky you.

Clifton   Yes, lucky me indeed. Anybody dead across de road?

Deli   No!

Clifton   Dem is Indian, innit? Insurance man.

Deli   Clifton . . .

Clifton   . . . Anyone in the labast? I wanna bust a piss!

Deli   No.

Clifton *exits to the toilet.* **Anastasia** *enters with a new batch of burgers and fries.* **Deli** *steals a few of the chips. She starts to put the burgers and fries in their takeaway bags.*

Deli *(struggles through this)*   Ani, I was thinking, as the business expands we gonna be kinda busy. If you wanna, you could stay in the flat upstairs you know! Save you getting bus in to work every day and dat?

Anastasia *looks up at* **Deli**, *surprised and pleased.*

While **Deli** *is speaking,* **Clifton** *re-enters but is unseen by the other two. His face drops when* **Deli** *mentions the flat.*

Anastasia (*genuine sadness*)   Oh Deli . . .

Deli (*jumps in*)   . . . You don't have to worry, I ain't using this as an excuse to jump you bones or nothing . . .

Anastasia (*straight and fast*)   . . . Why not? I'm a woman, Deli.

Deli (*struggling*)   . . . Of course you're a woman, Ani, a beautiful one, but . . .

Anastasia   But what? You know what, I got to think this through!

Deli (*covering defeat*)   OK! . . . But the offer's there if you want it.

Anastasia (*looks lovingly at **Deli***)   Thanks, I'll think about it!

Deli   Cool.

Clifton *makes a bold entrance.*

Clifton   Baygee don't reach yet?

Deli (*pissed*)   He won't be here for at least another hour, you want something to eat?

They clock each other momentarily.

Clifton   What! That stupidness you have there?

Deli (*not surprised*)   Alright, I got some rice and peas upstairs from Sunday.

Clifton   How all you English people does eat three-day-old food I will never know. You could never be strong like my generation.

Deli   Yeah yeah yeah.

Anastasia   I'll go and get it for you!

Deli   No, it's alright.

He exits. **Clifton** *comes and stands close to* **Anastasia**. *She moves away.*

Anastasia (*firm, fast, whispered and very violent*)   What de arse you doing? I told you not to follow me in so quickly, what the hell you think it look like?

Clifton (*not whispered*)   It look like we had something nice last night!

Anastasia   Let me tell you, what happened last night was . . .

Clifton   . . . Beautiful? . . .

Anastasia   . . . Horrendous would be closer. It was a mistake that's not going to happen again.

Clifton   Um-hum!

Anastasia   Now, can we, no, I want us to keep this between me and you.

Clifton   Um-hum.

Anastasia (*struggles*)   This, it could . . . really mash up . . . Deli and . . .

Clifton   . . . And what is it that you and my son have today that you didn't have when you whining on top of me last night?

Anastasia (*angry, looks over her shoulder*)   We never had sex!

Clifton   Damn well near as. I wonder if it could be the offer of a ready-made family that is making this conversation have an air of desperation.

Anastasia (*stutters a bit*)   What you mean by dat? I don't need no family.

Clifton   . . . Oh I think you do.

Anastasia   I have my family an believe I'm not desperate for nothin', I'd just prefer if we keep it . . . to weselves.

Clifton   And from this arrangement I get what?

Anastasia   What could I possibly give you?

Beat while he thinks.

Clifton What you didn't last night?! But in fact you know what? I've changed my mind about that. You, young lady, have a disproportionate amount of influence over my son, and I don't like it. So I tell you what I want, I want you to leave. Leave this place before I tell Deli what you taste like, and believe, he'll put you out on your arse before I've finished.

Anastasia I beg your pardon?

Clifton *grips her tightly.*

Clifton My son don't need his heart broken by a dirty gal who'll lay down with any man that hold her the right way.

Anastasia (*outraged*) Who you calling dirty gal, you bomberclaat rude.

She's about to slap him. He squeezes her arm tighter.

Clifton . . . You think you found yourself a little sucker in Deli, eh? You stick around long enough you'll share the big money he get from he brodder? Ah ah! Too many in line for that, my friend.

Anastasia *forces herself away from* **Clifton**.

Anastasia You're a, a, *wicked* man.

Clifton Oh, you ain't seen nothing yet! Trust me!

We hear **Deli** *enter from the kitchen. He comes through the swing doors into the shop. He is carrying* **Clifton**'s *plate of food.*

Deli Here. I'm not doing this again, you know. You eat what's in the restaurant from now on, or nothing at all.

Clifton *shifts the plate away.*

Clifton If it's so you going to talk to me over a little piece of food, best you keep it.

Deli OK! Don't eat it then.

Clifton Gimme the food.

Anastasia   Deli, I got to run over to the internet shop for five minutes. I really need to −

Deli   . . . It's not there any more . . .

Deli *can see that she is upset.*

Is the council order ready?

Anastasia (*dashing out*)   Yeah, it's on the counter.

She leaves, bumping into **Ashley** *at the door. He is really dressed like a street hoodlum. She doesn't say sorry but carries on running.* **Ashley** *has a stronger stand about him, a more fixed hardness.*

Ashley   What's this world coming to, your woman bumps into me and can't even say excuse!

Deli   Don't . . . (*He catches himself.*) Listen, Ashley, about last night . . .

Ashley   Don't watch dat, I've come to get my clothes.

Deli   Why?

Ashley   How you gonna ask big man his business?

Ashley *accidentally on purpose drops his car keys on the floor. And walks on. He picks up his keys and waves them in the air singing.*

Ashley   Who am I, the gal dem love, zim zimmer, who's got the keys to a bimmer.

Deli   Whose car you thieve boy?

Ashley   I ain't thieve nothing, I bought it bra!

Deli   You bought a car?

Ashley   Yep. Cash money!

Deli (*laughing*)   What car is that?

Ashley   A bimmer . . .

Deli   A BMW!? . . .

Ashley   Yep.

Beat.

Deli   Huh! You insurance it?

Ashley   I would have, but I ran out of money!

Deli   Ohhh! So that's why you're here flashing keys!

Ashley   I ain't here asking you for nothing star. You ain't got nothing that I can't get!

Deli   You always gots to be rude innit? Drag us back!

Ashley   No old man, it's bear forward motion *I* deal in.

Deli *stares at him hard.*

Ashley   Actually you know what? You're right I was rude. Hear what! Let me tek you for ride, old man, let me show you *my* world. You na mean?

Deli   Your world?

Ashley   Yeah!

Deli   You're joking aren't you?

Ashley   Sorry?

Deli   Look at you, you little monkey. Dressed up like a fucking circus clown! You want me to partake in that?

Ashley (*aside to* **Deli**)   What boy! That is poetry!

Deli   Where you get the money Ashley?

Ashley's *phone rings. He checks the number but doesn't answer.*

Ashley   That's long talk.

Deli   Dere's nothing long about it. It's an easy question, where'd you get the money?

Ashley   Some things, when you do em right, life rewards you.

Deli   . . . life rewards you? Where the fuck (*you get that shit from*)?

Ashley I'm living proof of it.

Clifton *is about to intervene but* **Deli** *stares him down, at the same time continuing with* **Ashley**.

Deli Do you honestly expect me to come in your car and sanction your nastiness?

Ashley (*angry*) No, I expect you to be happy for me, happy at my progress. What I don't expect, want or need, is you fronting your jealousy with petty excuses!

Deli (*even angrier*) Jealousy? I'm a hard-working man who's survived because I don't watch other people's tings. What makes you think I'd be envious of your stupid car, I haven't even seen it?

Ashley (*overjoyed*) Wait till you do, it's crisp!

Deli It can be as crisp as it wants. I want nothing to do with you and your nastiness. Come out that world, Ashley.

Beat.

Ashley (*laughs*) You're a punk, Dad. I was giving you a chance. A chance to let the whole area know that ooooh you're Ashley's father and so we roll! But no, you want to stay small, insignificant, weak. You, you disgust me. I'll be back for my clothes.

He turns to leave. His phone rings. He answers this time with his bluetooth headset.

(*Deliberately.*) Yo! Yes, Digs . . . ? Soon come, yeah, soon come.

Deli*'s face drops at the mention of* **Digger***'s name.* **Ashley** *exits the shop.* **Clifton** *looks at* **Deli**.

Clifton You should have at least looked at the car.

Deli *stares back at him with contempt.*

Lights down.

Scene Three

Restaurant.

The news item is playing as the lights come up.

Deli *walks into the restaurant from the kitchen. He has a huge knife in his hand. He places it under the counter. He then walks back into the kitchen and comes on with a metal baseball bat. He places that behind the front door out of sight.*

Newsreader   This is not just one isolated incident. Last month Catherine Henderson, an accident and emergency consultant at Homerton Hospital, called for staff with experience from cities such as New York and Johannesburg to join her team because NHS workers were simply not equipped to deal with the flood of gunshot wounds pouring into the department.

Deli *switches the channel back to MTV or whatever music channel he can find. As he is flicking through he passes the God channel. An American preacher is screaming out.*

Preacher   It shouldn't be no surprise our inner cities are burning up. It is the sinnnnnns of the *fathers* bearing down on our youth.

Deli *kisses his teeth and finds the music channel. Playing is the ragga video to 'Satan Strong'. As if stiff, he moves his fists, almost warming-up style, and punches the air.*

Enter **Anastasia**. *She has a bag over her shoulder.* **Deli** *sees her and stops. He clocks the bag. He smiles.*

Deli (*surprised*)   Hey!

Anastasia   Hey!

She doesn't move from the door. Pain is etched all over her face.

Deli (*pointing to bag*)   I didn't think you were coming back. You want some help with that?

He makes to the door to pick up the bag. **Anastasia** *puts up her hand to stop him.*

Anastasia   No!

He stops.

Deli   Ani, I've been thinking that maybe I should just talk straight. What I meant this afternoon was . . .

She moves to a table and opens the bag. She begins to take out some clothes. The first thing is an Averix leather jacket.

Anastasia *(ignoring him)*   . . . This belonged to Marvin, my son. I know kids don't like wearing other people's clothes but I figured Ashley might like this . . .

Deli *is unsure why she is doing this.*

Deli   That's a wicked jacket, doesn't Marvin still *(wanna wear that)* . . .

Anastasia   . . . Unless you think it's bad luck to give him dead clothes?

Deli *stops in his tracks. He stares at her at first not understanding, then understanding. There's a long pause while they speak to each other without words.* **Anastasia** *finally answers the question* **Deli** *has been trying to articulate.*

Anastasia   Long.

Deli   Why . . . ?

Anastasia   I'm sorry. Tell Ashley that I hope it fits and, um . . .

Deli   You're leaving?

Anastasia *nods her reply. Their speeches overlap till they reach an emotional climax.*

Deli   Don't!

Anastasia   If you hit the canvas one more time brother, you ain't getting back up. I will hurt you, Deli . . .

Deli   Is this because I asked you to move in with me? . . .

Anastasia (*flash of anger*)   No. It's because the stink around this place is getting stronger and I got to run (*before it takes me down*).

Deli   But I cleaned up the place, Anastasia!

The horn is honked.

Anastasia (*looking out*)   I better go. That's my cab.

Deli (*frustrated, it stumbles out*)   I could, shoulda, woulda coulda right now but you know what? You got to give a brother time to turn shit around, to talk what's in his heart. You can't just walk so!

Anastasia (*tender but hard*)   Sometimes you should listen to people when they say they're no good for you. It might be the truth.

The car horn honks again. She doesn't move.

Deli (*pulling himself together*)   Right.

Anastasia   Hope Ashley likes the jacket.

She leaves. **Deli** *stands still for a moment. He doesn't quite know what to do with himself. He starts to pace up and down the restaurant, fretting, frustration building. To hold back the tears he starts swing-punching the air. We hear the car drive off. He doesn't notice that* **Clifton** *has entered the shop and is watching him. Eventually he falls on to one of the stools, head in hands.*

Clifton   It's all right, son.

Deli *springs up.*

Deli   Clifton! What you doing?

Clifton   It's all right. Do you want me to give you a little time to yourself?

Pause.

Deli   No.

Pause. **Clifton** *smiles to himself.*

Clifton   No woman no cry.

Deli   . . . I liked her . . . She could have taught me . . . things.

Clifton   Yes she could have, but listen to your father when I say she wasn't for you. She was using you for lifeboat, child.

Deli (*with a little attitude*)   And how do you know that?

Clifton   I'm a man of the world . . .

Deli   Oh and I'm not? You know what? Go away! I don't need you to stand above me gloating.

Clifton   Now wait a minute, I'm trying to be sympathetic and you're insulting me? . . .

Deli   I don't want your sympathy, Clifton . . .

Clifton   . . . I'm not giving you my sympathy, Deli, I'm giving you some fatherly advice . . .

Deli   . . . Well, I don't want it! Not from the man that ran left my mother for some Irish woman.

Clifton   Oh! Well, it had to come out sometime.

Deli   Yeah, I hear that after you spend out all your money on her, she run leave you for a younger model! You think we didn't hear? We heard and we laughed.

Clifton   Well, it's good to know that the gossip express is still going strong . . .

Deli   Don't mamaguy me, Clifton. Your money ran dry. You mug me mother and now you're trying to mug me.

Clifton   I didn't thieve nothing from your mother!

Deli   Yes you did. You build big house with swimming pool off my mother's savings.

Clifton   Your mother and I split the proceeds of the house . . .

Deli   . . . that my mother put the deposit down on, that she paid the mortgage on when you spend out the money down the pub and the bookies or running next woman?

Clifton   I put down my wage packet every week on your mother's table . . .

Deli   And then thief it right back.

Clifton (*snaps*)   . . . You're a grown man, for Christ's sake, stop acting like a child and use you mind. Your mother going to tell you both sides of the story?

Deli   There is no other side to the story.

Clifton   Yes, I did leave, but why, Delroy? . . .

Deli   Irish pussy!

Clifton   I didn't have to leave my home for pussy.

Deli   Really?

Clifton (*calmly*)   If I hadn't left, Delroy, I would have died. Your mother suffocated me, child. She suffocated me . . .

Deli   . . . My mother was a brilliant woman . . .

Clifton   Yes she was. Too brilliant for me. And boy, she never let me forget it. Way I talked was too rough, way I spoke was too loud. The way I walked, the way I ate. Jesus, living with that woman was like being in an airless room. It drew all of the life from me.

Deli   . . . That's fucking rubbish, she loved you like –

Clifton   No she didn't. She was stuck with me.

This stops **Deli** *momentarily.*

Your mother was not interested in me, or any other man. You ever see her with anyone new after I left?

Deli   Raising two children on one income doesn't leave much time to fraternise with the opposite sex.

Clifton   Sex! Don't let me start, your mother hated sex . . .

Deli (*puts his fingers in his ears*)   . . . Don't wanna hear this!

Clifton   She never loved me. Not the way a wife should. And let me tell you, you and Anastasia would have walked down the same street.

Deli   Rubbish, Anastasia was the only decent thing around me.

Clifton   Decent!? That gal asked me to fuck her last night because I threatened to expose her dirty nasty ways to you. How decent was that?

Beat.

Deli (*stunned*)   What did you do?

Clifton   I fucked her to prove I was right. She was a thieving little whore who was only after you and Dougie money.

Deli   No she wasn't!

Clifton   I smelt her the moment I walked in here.

Deli *runs at his father.*

Deli   How could you do that?

Clifton   Was she your woman?

Deli   No. But you must have known?

Clifton   Which is exactly why I had to prove her to be the woman I knew she was. She was here to thieve your money. Like all of them. You don't need people like that around you, Delroy, you need people around that love you.

Deli *looks at him. Enter* **Digger***. He's in a bad mood. He brings his Chopper bike into the restaurant.*

Digger   Boyyyyy, I just done nearly kick up this fucking ambulance man. I'm driving in my car and I hear the siren so I wait for the right spot to pull over. Instead of the man wait, he swings in front of me and then cuts across my front. The fucking man doh just clip me wing! So I jump out and instead the man say sorry, he come open up his big mouth and come call me an ignorant idiot. You know I don't like that people call me that already. I had to threaten him. You been watching too much fucking 'Casualty', mate. I'll punch down your claat. When he saw that, he calmed himself and just freed up his insurance details. Fucking chip my new TT, you know, shouldda shoot him clatt.

Clifton   Wasn't there someone in the back waiting to reach the hospital?

Digger   I don't give a bombo! Deli, give me a roti.

Deli   We don't do roti no more, Digger.

Digger   Oh yeah, me forget.

Deli *throws a glance at the baseball bat behind the door.*

Deli   Eh! The police came round about the Roy ting today.

Digger   Oh yeah? What you tell them?

Deli   What Rose told me.

Digger   Which was?

Deli   That some Yardie men in mask asking for protection money burnt down the place, after beating the hell out of Roy.

Digger   Really? She told the police that?

Deli   I told her she should. How else we gonna rid this place of such vermin.

Digger   I wouldn't have thought that would do her much good. Nobody likes an informer. Not even you.

Beat.

From what I hear she refused a reasonable deal.

Deli   Did you get my son help you in your nastiness, Digger?

Digger What you talking about? Don't be stupid.

Deli I don't believe you. How much odder dirty youth out there you gonna recruit, you gonna take my son? I don't want you anywhere near anything of mine again, Digger. My son, myself, my shop.

Digger You don't? . . . You should think about that. Particularly after the recent events.

Deli You threatening me?

Digger No. Just reminding you of who protects who! Shit's gonna change, Deli, dey run tings now. They was going to send a next man to talk to you but I said, true say that you and me go back, that I would do it and negotiate the best price for all involved.

Deli The best price?

Digger Best price.

Deli After I already pay rates, tax and employees' insurance, Renton crew want me to pay protection money?

Digger Yep. I might could a get you less but ah, pay you do.

Deli What appen, Digger? How you gonna go and join them lowlives?

Digger Watch you mouth, Deli.

Deli Ha, well, run tell your new employees that no. Not me.

Digger Don't be stupid. You don't want dem kinda friction dere.

Deli I been here ten years, Digger, what makes you think I'm gonna start paying some 'off the boat' bloody Yard boy money that I don't have?

Digger   Because they said so. It's not like you can't afford
it. Everybody knows that Dougie left you a whole heap ah
money.

Deli   Dougie never left me shit. You know what? Tell
them they can come burn down my place, before they get a
red cent from me, that they can fuck off.

Digger   I ain't gonna tell them that, Deli.

Deli   That's your business.

Digger   No, this is. Once I say you have to pay, you pay,
Deli, or else I look bad.

Deli   So it's money you want, well, here, Digger, have
some money.

He empties out his pockets and throws the coins at **Digger**.

Digger   Ah wha de bloodclaat!

Clifton   Delroy . . .

Digger   Deli, calm and settle youself before I have to.

Deli   Take the money, Digger.

He throws more money that he has found by the till.

Clifton   Deli, calm the hell down.

Deli   Take the money na!

He grabs hold of the till and rips it out of the counter and throws it at
Digger.

Take the blood money.

Digger   Deli!

Digger *goes to pull his gun out but before he can get it out* **Deli** *is at
his throat with the big knife.*

Deli   Do it na! See if you could shoot me before I cut your
bloody throat!

Digger Deli, you're behaving like an arse. Calm down and move the knife from my throat unless you plan to use it this very minute.

Deli Digger, you used my son, you used my blood, to do my neighbour. You knew the first place the police were gonna come to was here.

Digger He wanted to defend your manhood. Is not me!

Deli My son doesn't have to defend me, Digger.

Digger Take the knife from my throat, Deli.

He doesn't.

Clifton Delroy, use your mind. Take the knife from the man throat.

Digger I told him no. But all you got on the street is your rep, bro, and my youth wants rep.

Deli I see you close to Ashley again, Digger, and I will kill you.

He takes the knife away.

And take back your stinking BMW!

Digger *stands up.*

Digger That's a very silly ting you jus' do. (*Beat.*) I hope you can defend that.

Digger *exits, staring* **Deli** *out.*

Clifton Was that wise?

Deli *stares at* **Clifton** *and then backs out towards* **Digger**.

Lights down.

An intense gurkel melody plays until:

Scene Four

Restaurant. Day.

Baygee *is sitting with a half-eaten plantain burger in front of him. He is mid-story to* **Clifton** *who is in the kitchen area.*

Baygee   Now you know Charlie! Twenty years he dere in this country and doe miss a day work. But that afternoon, out of the blue, he head start to hurt him bad. He beg the manager not to send him home but they order him, so he go. Well, is just by chance I meet him on the street, vex he vex. I say, Charlie boy, go home and enjoy the missus. Huh, well, is den he start to tell me ting. Apparently, before Thelma would give him anyting he had to agree to put out the bins and wash de wares and all breed ah stupidness!

Clifton   What?

Enter an aproned **Clifton** *with a tray of plantain burgers. He starts restacking the shelves.*

Baygee   Yes, blackmailing de man before she get him he tings, and even then he say, no matter what he tell her, all she doing is laying stiff so dreaming ah Trinidad. Not even a little (*he imitates a female groan of pleasure*) ahhhhh to sweet him.

Clifton   Is he that wrong, he should a grip woman long! Me I would a . . .

Baygee   Wait hear de story na! So I give him a few sweet boy tips and I send he on he way. De next time I see the man, is not in burial ground!

Clifton   You lie?

Baygee   Well, the story go that when he reach home flowers in hand and ting, he hear one set a noise from upstairs. Well, he say somebody break in and must be beating he wife. So he run into the kitchen grab one big knife and creep up de stairs so as to catch the criminal in the act . . .

Clifton   Surprise him yes . . .

Baygee   When he bust into the room, tell me what he see?

Clifton   The wife beating the man?

Baygee   Thelma head stick out the window leg cock up so, and a man half he age woking it hard from behind.

Clifton   You lie?

Baygee   I look like I lie? . . .

Clifton   What he kill de man?

Baygee   Well, he sister tell me that the wife tell she, that he just look at her, and then he look at this young stallion dat making Thelma shout ting he doe hear in he life and he heart just give up so, bang, he drop and dead.

Clifton   Just so? . . .

Baygee   Just so.

Clifton   Bonjay! Ha! Well is so he had to dead. Me old man use to say, if you have to drown you can't burn.

Baygee *downs the rum in front of him in one and salutes* **Clifton**.

Baygee   He don't lie, Clifton, he don't lie.

Enter **Deli**. *He doesn't greet either of the men. He is in a world of his own.*

Clifton   Where the France you been, boy?

Deli *looks at* **Clifton** *but doesn't reply.* **Clifton** *addresses* **Baygee** *at first.*

Clifton (*to* **Baygee**)   But look me crosses na! Delroy, you going deaf? I had to set up the shop by myself, you know. Where you been?

Deli   In a meeting.

Clifton   Meeting, what kind of meeting?

Deli   I said a meeting, OK!

Clifton   You don't know we have a business to run here. None of the things going to be ready for lunchtime, you know?

Deli   Clifton, Clifton please. We miss lunch, we miss lunch.

Baygee *looks up at the two men, checks his watch and decides it's time to leave. He takes one last shot of Clark's and slams the glass on the table and stands to go.*

Baygee (*laughs*)   Gentlemen, I promised I'd drop something before twelve o'clock.

Clifton   I go have you food ready. What time you passing back?

Baygee   No, it's OK, dey just reach back from Trinidad. She go have a little home food for me.

Clifton   Who is that?

Baygee   Ms Thelma. I gone.

He exits and leaves the shop. There's silence for a bit.

Clifton   You's still a suspect?

Deli   You see Ashley this morning?

Clifton   No! (*Beat.*) I feel rather proud, you know. We seem to be running this ting well. Don't you think?

Deli   We?

Clifton   Yes, it wouldn't be unfair to say we. In fact, you know what I was thinking? You should let me move into the flat with you, son, that way we'd always be ready!

Deli   Clifton, I'm selling this place.

Clifton   Because them Yardies want a little money from you? It's better you pay them than you run away. Men don't run, son.

Deli (*fed up with everyone questioning his manhood*)   So what do they do, Clifton?

Clifton   They stay at the crease till the umpire's hand go so. (*Pointing up and out.*) Running is never the answer.

Deli   I'm not running.

Clifton   I thought you had more brains than that, man!

Beat.

Where you going if you sell this place?

Deli   I don't know. Somewhere far.

Clifton   You going to take Ashley?

Deli   I want to.

Clifton   What about me?

Deli   What about you, Clifton?

Clifton   Aren't you going to need someone to help you run the business?

Deli   Who said anything about a business?

Clifton   What else you go do? Who's going to employ someone that has no qualifications, spent a year in jail and ran away from the one positive thing he has achieved in his life. Where's your respect?

Deli   Respect for what?

Clifton   Ashley, me.

Deli   You?

Clifton   Yes actually, me. As your father you owe me respect. The respect that says, 'Daddy I know you're not well, as your son I'll take care of you till you're strong again.'

Deli   Clifton, this is the wrong time for us to be having this debate.

Clifton (*losing it*)   No, this is exactly the right time to be having it. As a child, did I ever let you walk the street raggedy?

Deli   No, but . . .

Clifton   Exactly!

Deli   That was about you, you and your children always had to be the smartest in the street!

Clifton   Exactly, I looked after you . . .

Deli   To a point.

Clifton (*to himself*)   Once and man, twice a child. Jesus. Your generation curse. You British blacks pick up worse and leave best. Instead ah you pick up the Englishman thirst for knowledge and learning you pick up his nasty habit of dumping their old people in some stinking hole for them to rot when they are at the prime of their wisdom.

Deli   Clifton, is you that said when the doctors give you the all-clear that you going home . . .

Clifton   . . . I lied. I don't have nowhere to go, Delroy.

Deli   What do you want me to do? I can't help you, Clifton, believe me, I don't have nothing!

Clifton   You and your brother bought some land home! You got money hidden away, I know. Let's go home together na? Open a little something in town. Show them bitches that Clifton can bounce back. Clifton have something. He children amount to something. You know they does laugh at me home? Yes. Your own uncle laughs at me. 'Look,' he does say, every time he sees his daughter in the paper hug up with a next white man, 'she doing well, innit? By the way, Dougie come out of jail yet.' Laughing at my seed. Let we go home show them that my seed is something. We are somebody.

Deli   Clifton, listen to me, you are not going to want to be where I am, believe me.

Clifton (*loses it*)   Don't say that!

He begins to throw over the chairs and tables.

What have I got to show for my life, Delroy? Parkinson's! What do I have to do, beg you? Fight you for it?

Deli Calm down.

Clifton No, you fucking calm down. Calm down? Calm down? Come and make me na, think the old man can't knock you down.

He starts swinging his fists in the air. **Deli** *stares at him, bewildered. He loses steam eventually, falling to the floor.*

Ashley *enters. He stares at* **Clifton** *on the floor and the messed-up restaurant. He doesn't say a word. Eventually, he goes to help* **Clifton** *stand up.* **Clifton** *shrugs him off and picks himself up.*

Clifton Get off me. All you generation curse. You go rot, mark my words.

He leaves the restaurant. **Ashley** *stares at his grandfather leaving.*

Beat.

Ashley Where's he going?

Deli I don't know.

Ashley (*cool and deadly*) I hear you was down the police station this morning?

Deli Yeah, how you know that?

Ashley What did they want?

Deli More details of your whereabouts when Rose's place was burn.

Ashley What did you tell them?

Deli What I have before, that you were here with me. Why?

Ashley You sure?

Deli Yeah!

Ashley *walks up and hugs his dad.*

Ashley Thanks, Dad.

Deli (*slightly taken aback*) It's alright.

Ashley You know I was only looking out for you?

Deli *pushes him off.*

Deli No, you were looking out for yourself. But it's my fault. Should have got you out of here years ago. But I didn't have the resource, the wherewithal . . .

Ashley . . . What you talking about?

Deli They know it was you. They know it was Digger. It's only a matter of time. If Roy dies they coming to get you, son, no matter what.

Ashley *is about to say something but* **Deli** *stops him.*

Deli Ah . . . Now I know you's a big man and dat but it's up to me to protect you the best way I know how. If I was to say that I've arranged a place away from here for us, what would you say?

Ashley I'd say why?

Deli *struggles to find the words. Eventually.*

Deli OK. I did go to the police station today but it wasn't about you entirely.

Ashley No?

Deli No. I went because I've struck a deal. You . . . for Digger.

Ashley (*shocked to his core*) Noooo! You can't have done dat? You're many things but you're not an informer, Dad.

Deli I knew Digger was bad but, son, he's terrible.

Ashley He does what he has to do to survive.

Deli Don't talk shit to me. What do you want me to do, son, protect Digger and throw you to the wolves? This is about your survival, you better know.

Ashley (*sickened*)   You didn't have to inform, Dad. Where you ever going to go in the world and not have to look over your shoulder?

Deli   That's not better than being in prison?

Ashley   Is still prison, just bigger cells.

Deli   Well, I've been in a cell, son, and it is not very nice. Each generation is suppose to top the previous one. If I have to die on the street to get you out of that dere runnings, wouldn't I be doing my job?

Ashley   I don't believe you did this?

Deli   I did, now listen to me. The police are going to arrest Digger today, but they're only gonna be able to hold him for forty-eight hours. After he's released, he's gonna know that I shopped him, then he's going to come right here and deal with me.

Ashley   You're damn right he will!

Deli   But if you speak to the police and say that you'll testify that Digger told you to do all that happened that night, we will get fifty grand and a safe house out of the country. Coupled with the money I already have, when we ready we could fly back home and live the lives of kings.

Ashley   Hackney's home.

Deli   It won't be when Digger gets out. What? He's gonna have an informer's son in his crew?

Ashley (*realisation*)   You did that on purpose?

Deli   Yes I did.

Ashley (*screams*)   I don't believe you.

Enter **Digger**.

Digger   You better do! Didn't I tell you your father would do this. Didn't I?

Deli *stands. A little afraid but ready whatever comes next.*

Digger   How did you think you were going to get away wid dis? Wha, you think you could just pull knife on me, inform pon me and me would let you get 'way?

Deli   Man has to tek his chances in life, you get me, don't you, Digger?

Digger   I get you, but what about your son? What have you done to your child, Deli? Branded him for life. Ashley, the informer's boy.

Deli *stares him out.*

Digger   What did you think was going to happen, Delroy?

Deli   Stop all the long chat, Digger, if you come to deal wid me let's get it on like men.

Digger *pulls out a packet of crack rocks and throws them on the floor. He then removes another bag from his pocket. It is pure cocaine. He opens it and, as if releasing magic dust from his hand, throws a handful at* **Deli***.*

Digger   Um-um. It's not me that's gonna deal with you. You don't know what we do to informers these days, do you? Well . . .

He turns to **Ashley***.*

My youth. Deal wid this properly and you go straight to the big league. Rep is everything, and yours is gonna be huge after this.

Ashley *slowly takes out his gun.* **Deli** *just stares at him.*

Ashley   You let me down, Dad.

Digger   OK, let's do the solicitor's work for him. Put one in the roof, shows we had a struggle.

Ashley *shoots the gun off in the air.*

Deli   You ready for this life, Ashley?

Digger   Alright, now point the gun at your punk-arsed dad. The one that gets beat up and does nothing, has his business near taken away and does nothing, but then informs on a brother man to the other man for what? A piddling fifty grand! I could ah give you that! Is this the type of people we need in our midst? Weak-hearted, unfocused informers? No, I don't think so. Do you, Ashley?

Ashley's *hands are shaking a little. After a beat.*

Ashley   Digger, I don't think . . .

Digger (*screams at him*)   Is this the type of people we need in our midst?

Ashley   No.

Digger   OK then, raise the gun, point it.

Ashley *does.*

Digger   Good. Is your finger on the trigger?

Ashley   Yes.

Digger   Good.

Digger *pulls out his gun and shoots* **Ashley** *dead.*

Deli   Noooooooooooooooooooooooooooooo.

Digger *looks to* **Deli**.

Digger   Yes. Ah so dis war run!

He exits.

Deli *kneels, still, by his dead son. After a few beats he rises, takes the jacket that* **Anastasia** *left for* **Ashley** *and covers his body and head. With one final glance around, he stares at the picture of his mother, then walks out of the restaurant. The violent ragga tune plays as we fade to black.*

Fix Up

Fix Up was first presented in the Cottesloe auditorium of the National Theatre, London, on 16 December 2004. The cast was as follows:

Brother Kiyi	Jeffery Kissoon
Carl	Mo Sesay
Kwesi	Steve Toussaint
Norma	Claire Benedict
Alice	Nina Sosanya

Director Angus Jackson
Designer Bunny Christie
Lighting Designer Neil Austin
Music Neil McArthur
Sound Designer Gareth Fry

Characters

Brother Kiyi (*pronounced 'Key'*), *an old fifty-five, with greying unkept locks. Owner of the Fix Up bookstore.*

Carl, *thirty-five. A local care-in-the-community delivery boy.*

Kwesi, *thirty-two. A militant black activist who uses a room upstairs in the shop.*

Norma, *fifty. Kiyi's long-time best friend.*

Alice, *thirty-four. A beautiful but troubled visitor to the store.*

Non-Present Characters

Marcus Garvey, *Jamaican-born leader of the UNIA back-to-Africa movement in America, early 1920s. Seen as the godfather of Black nationalism.*

James Baldwin, *celebrated outspoken New York novelist, essay writer and playwright.*

Claude McKay, *celebrated poet of the 'Harlem Renaissance'.*

Scene One

Fix Up bookstore.

It's Thursday, late afternoon in early October – Black History month. Outside is well cold! We are in 'Fix Up', a small, old-school, 'Black conscious' bookstore. The place is much too small to hold the many shelves and bookcases that jam and squeeze up next to each other. However, although at first sight the shop looks chaotic, with no subject labels or even indicators, to the trained eye it is perfectly arranged. Starting at the shelf closest to the door each subject is in alphabetical order, subdivided by genres, again in alphabetical order, followed by the authors, again in painstaking alphabetical order. Sitting nobly on each and every bookshelf, almost as closely stacked together as the books, are African statues and carvings of giraffes, busts of great leaders, perfectly formed couples entwined, Ashanti stools, sculptured walking sticks, etc. Various Kentes and African cloths are hung on what little wall space there is left. Hanging from the ceiling in a less ordered fashion are a few dusty-looking male and female African outfits. Written over the door and above **Brother Kiyi***'s till enclosure is a sign reading* 'CLOSING DOWN SALE'. *It is well old and dusty. On the floor, however, is a big black bin. The sign above that reads:* 'HELP KEEP US OPEN – ANY DONATION WELCOME'.

Playing a little too loudly is a speech by the early Black leader Marcus Garvey. It is an old 1920s recording. As with all recordings of that day it's slightly speeded up, but through the hiss we can hear the words clearly enough. Although his Jamaican accent is clear, we can hear Marcus is over-articulating in a 'Trumanesque' style.

Carl*, thirty-five, happy by nature, enters through the front door. He is a care-in-the-community patient.*

Carl   Owiiii, 'cuse us, mate, you sell rat-poison in here?

Brother Kiyi *is still out of sight, but we hear his anger. He has a refined but noticeable West Indian accent.* **Carl** *hides behind a shelf.*

Brother Kiyi   No! I do not sell rat-poison. Rat-poison, is sold in the shop three doors down on the left. You'll find it behind the Halal meat refrigerator and to the right of the 'well cheap airfares to the subcontinent' counter.

Now standing, **Brother Kiyi** *can't see the hidden* **Carl.** **Brother Kiyi** *is dressed in an African-shaped Kente shirt on top of a thick woolly polo-neck with jeans. He has very long, greying locks. They are not hanging but twirled on top of his head almost like a turban.*

Brother Kiyi   Hello! Hello!

Carl *is still hidden.*

Carl (*using cockney accent*)   No, I was definitely told the Fix Up bookstore sold a whole load of rat-poison . . .

Brother Kiyi   What? . . .

Carl   Filling de yout' dem hea, hea, head, wid rubbish!

Brother Kiyi   You see you? When is stupidness you talking you don't have no stammer dough!

Carl   I love it! You get so *ig, ignorant* when your vex.

Brother Kiyi   Ignorant? How many times do I have to tell you, I am not ignorant! Ignorant is when you are not aware, I, on the contrary *am* aware –

Carl   – of the rightful place I hold in hi, hi, history –

Brother Kiyi   – because unlike the overwhelming majority of my people –

Carl   – I read –

Brother Kiyi   – digest and make manifest –

Carl   – the greatness of our heritage.

Brother Kiyi (*a positive acclamation*)   Iiiiiitchsss!

Carl   Wish I never said it now!

Brother Kiyi   Oh dash!

He runs back to his desk, picks up the phone.

Hello, hello, yes! I'm terribly sorry, I've found it now . . . The order reference number is . . .

He stands with an very old-fashioned telephone in his hands. **Carl** *is looking at the books.*

Brother Kiyi   WA 23767. Brother Kiyi, Fix Up bookstore, Tottenham N15. No, Brother is not my Christian name! The name on the order sheet should simply say . . . You know what? I have been waiting three weeks for what should have been here within ten days! Have you ever faced a crowd that's waiting for their history to arrive? . . . No, it has not been delivered!

Carl *has wheeled his trolley into view. He tries to point to the boxes on it, but can't catch* **Brother Kiyi***'s eye.*

Brother Kiyi   My friend, I am the only person that works here.

Carl *waves this time. Still no attention is being given to him.*

Brother Kiyi   If a parcel from DHL had been delivered today . . .

We can see that the boxes have 'DHL' written all over them.

Carl *starts to point to the boxes in an over-the-top manner.*

Brother Kiyi   It could only have been delivered to me!

Carl (*shouts*)   Brother Kiyi!

Brother Kiyi   Excuse me. (*Barks.*) What?

Carl   Are these dem?

Brother Kiyi *looks at the logo blazoned all over the books. He goes back to the phone.*

Brother Kiyi   Madam, I may have to call you back!

He puts down the phone.

Carl. What are you doing with my delivery of . . . (*He calms himself.*) With my delivery?

Carl   The brother was unloading his van, and that's my job innit? Delivery! I saw it was for you, signed for it and bought them in. Bloody stinking parking warden was just about to give the man a ticket, you know? Delivering, you know, and was still gonna ticket him, you know.

Brother Kiyi   I figure I know, Carl.

Carl   Shotters for them.

Brother Kiyi *looks up sharply.*

Brother Kiyi   I don't believe he deserves to get shot for doing his job.

Carl   You've changed your tune. When they introduced the red lines you said they were murdering you and dem deserve death!

Brother Kiyi   Well, that was . . .

Carl   When Mr Mustafar bought the freehold you said fire pon the weak hearts that didn't back you up . . . and when . . .

Brother Kiyi   Yes, I get the message . . . (*Changes the subject to get out of it.*) That still no excuse for you to not tell me they reach!

Carl   I tried to, but you know what you're like when you're focused on one ting. You shut out the rest of the world.

Brother Kiyi *comes swiftly towards the boxes. He approaches them with reverence.*

Brother Kiyi   That's cos man is only suppose to do one ting at a time.

Carl   What you talking about? When I'm with my gal, I does be stroking (*hip actions*) and feeling. (*Tuning in a radio for the breast action.*) It feels perfectly natural to be doing those two tings at the same time!

Brother Kiyi   You never stutter when you're talking nastiness. (*Indicates the boxes.*) Help me na!

Enter **Kwesi**, *thirty-two, good-looking.* **Brother Kiyi** *likes* **Kwesi**, *mainly because of his militant Black stance. He has a big box in his arms.*

He makes his way to the back of the store almost as if he doesn't want to say hello to **Brother Kiyi** *and* **Carl**.

Brother Kiyi   Tende Mwari, Brother Kwesi.

Kwesi   Tende Mwari.

Brother Kiyi   They reach, you know, they reach! History, my friend, reach!

Kwesi   Great!

Brother Kiyi   You've three friends upstairs waiting for you.

Kwesi   Thanks.

Brother Kiyi   Somalians? I don't know much about their history. What happen to Jamal, Eric and Ade?

Kwesi (*still trying to get away*)   . . . Need people around you with backbone, know what I'm saying?

Brother Kiyi   Know what you're saying? I am surrounded by the most spineless punks this town has ever seen!

Kwesi   That's Babylon. Later.

Brother Kiyi *looks at the box in his hands.*

Brother Kiyi   Big box?!

Kwesi   Computer from home.

He leaves.

Carl *notices the slave narratives.*

Carl   How much did they set you back?

Brother Kiyi   All I have . . . I feel like a *child* in a . . . (*Questioning his own lack of eloquence.*) Words, what are they, huh?!

He pulls out another book from the box. Carefully opens it and looks through. He pulls another book from the box. He does this again and again.

Brother Kiyi   You know what these are? Forget Booker T, forget Langston Hughes! These are the great voices of we past. Twenty-four volumes of truth!

Carl *decides to pick one up and read the title for himself. He struggles with the words.*

Brother Kiyi   Careful!

Carl   'Sla-slave nar-ra-tive . . . '

Brother Kiyi   That's right, 'narrative' . . .

Carl   'Collection of her Majes . . . '

Brother Kiyi   'Her Majesty's . . . '

Carl   'Colonial voices.'

Brother Kiyi   Well done!

Carl   Yeah! What's all that about then?

Brother Kiyi   In 1899 a group of social anthropologists went across the entire West Indies – British, French, Spanish, Dutch – and interviewed the last remaining beings that were enslaved. Two thousand three hundred Africans that were between the ages of five and twenty-five when slavery was abolished. Most of them old like 'so-um! But this is bondage, brother . . .

Carl *raises his eyebrows and smiles at the word 'bondage'.*

Carl   'Bondage', oh yeah?

Brother Kiyi   Come on now, don't be stupid.

Carl*'s face returns to studious enquirer.*

Brother Kiyi   This is the institution that brought us here, Carl, spoken about, written down in their own words, their dialect. That's always been the problem with slavery, see . . . We've been able to witness other people talking about *their* genocide, but ours, well ours has been confined to saccharine American sagas or puerile political statements by people who don't give a blast about we!

Carl   I don't know what the fuck you're talking about.

Brother Kiyi *(catches himself about to preach)*   At last, this is the human connection, Carl. Maybe if more of the youth could hear, see where they've come from, they'd have a little bit more respect for where they are.

Carl   Seen. Look, gotta go, all this deep talk is making me sick. Mr Dongal, from the Halal butcher's, wants me to run down to the abattoirs with him. First time. Neat, huh?

Brother Kiyi   We'll do your reading when you come back then.

Carl (*sings to himself as he leaves*)
    The main reason me like it from behind
    You can reach under me belly rub me clit same time!

Enter **Norma**.

Norma   What nastiness is that?

Carl   Sorry, Aunty Norma.

Norma   Stop that 'aunty' ting. People will think we is family.

Carl   But we are family! The African family. What Marcus say, every black man is an African, innit, Brother Kiyi?

Brother Kiyi   Exactly, Carl.

Norma   I'm not related to no crack addict!

Brother Kiyi   Norma!

Carl   Former! . . .

Norma   Hard love, Kiyi, hard love.

Carl   Later.

He exits.

Norma   Every time I see that boy on the street is a next white woman he chasing. You don't see the amount of half-caste pickney ah run de street already.

Brother Kiyi *ignores her.*

Brother Kiyi   Um ha!

Norma   So they reach?

Brother Kiyi   Yeah man.

Norma   Good, good.

Brother Kiyi *undoes his locks and shakes them out.* **Norma** *looks at* **Brother Kiyi**'*s hair.*

Norma   Boy, don't shake that ting at me. One sum'ting I don't like, that Rasta ting you have on you head.

Brother Kiyi   And that alien hair you have on your head is better? It don't have nothing to do with no Rasta . . .

Norma   I don't care about you symbol of rebellion stupidness. You should have dropped that jail nonsense years ago. You wash it?

Brother Kiyi   Yes, Norma, is wash me wash me head. You happy now?

Norma   Na man vex me vex. I sit down in front the television nice and comfortable, ready to watch me dog dem run, when the husband come in a start to harangue me soul.

Brother Kiyi   What he want?

Norma   Sex innit! No, hard yard food. He want me to run out the road to buy some cowfoot and pig trotters. I know you doesn't like me to buy from dem people next door, but Dongal and dem is the only place man could find a decent home food. Not one of dem black shop close to me have anything to make old West Indians happy.

Brother Kiyi   That they don't sell that kinda slave food is what makes this West Indian happy.

Norma   My grandfather use to eat cowfoot and there was nothin' slave about him! Except maybe him name.

Brother Kiyi   Which was what?

Norma   George de Third!

Norma *goes round to the desk and carefully pulls out a draughts board. The pieces are still on it.*

Norma   You looking damn thin you know, boy! You use all you corn to pay Mustafar he money innit?

Brother Kiyi *doesn't reply, just smiles slightly.*

Norma   I making a broth tonight, come over na?

Brother Kiyi   Thanks, but I'll pass on the swine!

Norma *plays back* **Brother Kiyi***'s reaction to the money question.*

Norma   You have paid him, haven't you?

Brother Kiyi   Abraham's always use to give me a month or two bligh! Why should I pay as soon as Mustafar ask for it?

Norma   Because Abraham's doesn't own the place any more. Mustafar does.

Brother Kiyi   What's wrong with our people, eh, Norma? The Jewish man come here and buy up the place, then a next immigrant come and buy it off him. Leapfrogging the West Indian. What was wrong wid we, eh?

Norma   A black landlord would ah let you off you rent?

Brother Kiyi   That's not the point.

Norma   You owe the man he rent, pay you rent.

Brother Kiyi   I can't. I spend all me money.

Norma   On woman?

Brother Kiyi (*pointing to bookshelves*)   What need do I have of a woman when I have Morrison, Macmillan and Walker?

Norma   Dem don't bring you cocoa in bed or bury you when you dead. Woman is the only excuse I'll accept. But you've spent it on the books innit? You promised me you wouldn't do that. You promised.

Brother Kiyi   Oh Norma, I couldn't resist it.

Norma   You know what? Talking to you is only going to get my diabetes up. I have time for three moves.

Brother Kiyi (*referring to unpacking books*)   Norma, I'm doing something important!

Norma   That's right, losing. It's time me beat you, Ras – I mean it's time for me to take my victory! I can smell it.

Brother Kiyi   What nonsense you talking . . .

Norma   Don't be hiding behind no books. When is licks time, it's licks time.

Brother Kiyi   Come, three moves and that's it.

Norma   Is my move innit!

Brother Kiyi *pulls a piece of paper from the shelf.*

Brother Kiyi   Whose signature is this?

Norma   Mine.

Brother Kiyi   And what does it say?

Norma   Kiyi has the next move.

Brother Kiyi   Thank you.

He looks over the board slowly.

You see, nothin' like the power of de pen, girl. (*He moves.*)

Norma   How much of dem book you get?

Brother Kiyi   You back on that? Three set a eight.

Norma   Three sets of eight! (*She moves.*)

Brother Kiyi   And another two sets are on order, when I get a little money.

Norma   You don't have money for food, and you ordering two sets ah books?

Brother Kiyi   I'm forced to believe that we can survive whatever we must survive. But the future of the Negro in this country is precisely as bright or as dark as the future of the country. Jimmy Baldwin, 1963. (*He moves.*)

Norma   I bet James wasn't bloody hungry when he wrote that. (*She moves.*) King me, you bitch!

Brother Kiyi   For a woman of the cloth your language is very colourful.

Norma   Don't try dem dirty tactics to put me off. Watch you moves, not my language.

Brother Kiyi   Oh, of that you can be sure. (*He moves.*)

Norma *realises that her king has been blocked in.*

Norma   Ahhhh, man. How you could block in me king so?

Brother Kiyi   By watching the game.

Norma   Rah, last move. (*She moves.*) Scamp. Deal wid dat!

Brother Kiyi   Ummm.

Norma   Haaaa. You see!

She starts to sing a church song.

Victory is mine, victory is mine, victory today is mine. (*She switches back to serious speech.*) I *have* to go.

Brother Kiyi   Eh! Sign the paper.

Norma   Sign it for me na! You know me handwriting not too good.

Brother Kiyi   You too damn lie. Is challenge you want to challenge me when you come back. Sign the ting!

Norma   Alright. (*She writes it down.*) Brother Kiyi has the next move.

Brother Kiyi   Date!

Norma   15th October.

Brother Kiyi   Iiiiech!

She signs. Just before she gets to the door, she takes a tenner out of her purse and gives it to **Brother Kiyi***.*

Brother Kiyi   Na man it's alright. I'm alright. Seriously.

Norma   Shut you mouth and take the ting.

Brother Kiyi   You *could* do me a favour though?

Norma   What?

Brother Kiyi *takes a letter out of the chest of drawers.*

Brother Kiyi   Just got this letter and I don't fully understand it. Could you ask you daughter to look over it for me?

Norma   Thought Beverly does your legal tings?

Brother Kiyi   She's got a lot of work on at the moment. I don't want to burden her.

Norma   You mean you owe her too much? No big ting. I go give Paulette when she come over this evening. I love you yuh na, brother, but (*points to the books*) you too stubborn for your own good.

Brother Kiyi   Where are we without hope?! Say hello to Bernie. And tell him stop eat de master cast-offs!

Norma   I'll tell him that when you cut you nasty locks!

Brother Kiyi *looks through another book. Suddenly he springs up and begins to search for a space to place the books. After much deliberation he decides to take down a row of modern black love stories.*

He takes down the books and, carefully brushing down the bookshelf, places the new ones in their place, in a prominent place in the shop. He stops reading.

Enter **Alice***, thirty-four, mixed race.* **Brother Kiyi** *pulls the book back up as if reading again, but he is not. He is slightly taken by her attractiveness.*

Alice   Hi.

He does not reply. She moves a little closer, tries again.

Alice   Hello?

He looks up from the book and smiles a little smile.

Brother Kiyi   Tende Mwari.

Alice   What does that mean?

Brother Kiyi   Well, in the ancient language of Kwaswahili, it is the greeting that one villager would give to the other.

Alice   Right, that bit I get, but what does it mean?

Brother Kiyi   As you know, translations are always notoriously inaccurate . . .

Alice   . . . but?

Brother Kiyi   Roughly translated it means, 'Hello' . . .

Alice   And I say in return? . . .

Brother Kiyi   It's very difficult, I wouldn't worry yourself about it!

Alice   Right.

He returns to the book. She returns to looking at the bookshelves.

It's Black History month, isn't it?

Brother Kiyi   Indeed it is.

Alice   Must be a good time for business eh? Bet everyone like me comes in looking for something that will broaden their understanding of, well, black history. What do you recommend?

Brother Kiyi   Well, young lady . . .

Alice   I don't know about the young, according to my mother at thirty I should have been married at least once, and had my one-point-six children years ago.

Brother Kiyi   Your mother's from where?

Alice   Oh, um, she's English, from up north.

Brother Kiyi   Oh.

Alice   Why do you ask?

Brother Kiyi   It's a very Caribbean thing to say, that's all. My mother had me when she was twenty-seven and I'm the last of six.

Alice   Wow, what age did you start?

Brother Kiyi   Me? I don't have any children. To the profound disappoint of my mother.

Alice   I'm sorry.

Brother Kiyi   Nothing to be sorry about. I chose to over-share.

But he returns to his book and she to the shelves. He turns the Marcus Garvey tape back on. Marcus is in full-throttle mode. It is passionate oration, and we hear the wild audience response. **Alice** *tries to break the silence.*

Alice   Who is that speaking?

Brother Kiyi (*turning it down a tad*)   The Honourable Marcus Garvey.

Alice   Wow, I'll have one of those please.

Brother Kiyi   The cassette is my own personal property, but if you go to the other aisle on the fifth shelf you'll see many of his books.

She does.

Alice   Are his books any good?

Brother Kiyi   Well, er, I seem to think so!

Alice   Great! Then I'll buy 'em!

Brother Kiyi   There are a few! You might want to buy one to start off with.

Alice   Actually I don't so much as read but have one of those photographic memories. I kind of scan it and it goes in.

She picks up two books and goes to the counter.

I'll have these two. Thank you.

Brother Kiyi   Good.

He methodically puts the books in a brown bag, writes the sales in a little black book and hands the bag to her.

Brother Kiyi   That will be £31.90 please.

She hands him her card.

Sorry, we don't have the facility to process cards. Cash or cheques only. But cash is always best.

Alice   Good thing I bought my cheque book out with me.

She writes it out while he watches. She hands him the cheque and the card.

Brother Kiyi *looks at the signature for a while.*

Brother Kiyi   Do you have any other form of identification on you?

Alice   Why?

Brother Kiyi   The signature on the cheque is, well, it's a little different.

Alice   Let me see. Well, it doesn't look that different to me. Maybe it's a little untidy but I always write fast when I'm nervous.

Brother Kiyi   What do you have to be nervous about?

Alice   I didn't actually mean nervous, I meant excited.

Brother Kiyi *stares at her blankly.*

Alice   *New books!*

Brother Kiyi   I see.

Alice   Here's my driver's licence. Picture's a bit old but, hey, same chick.

He looks at it for a while, then holds the books out so that she can take them from his hand. She doesn't.

Brother Kiyi   Sorry about that, but one has to be careful.

Alice   One?

Brother Kiyi Yes.

Alice Thank you. By the way, I don't know about *Kwa*swalili but in *real* Swahili one responds to 'Hello' with 'Habari Yako'.

Brother Kiyi Is that so? How do you know that?

Alice I had an East African boyfriend. Once.

Brother Kiyi Thank you for telling me that.

Alice It's OK. I wanted to over-share.

He waits for her to open the door.

Brother Kiyi *Safi.* That is also real Swahili.

She turns around, slightly embarrassed, and then leaves.

Brother Kiyi *turns Marcus back up and starts to read his slave narrative again.*

Fade out.

Scene Two

Fix Up bookstore. The following day.

Brother Kiyi *is sitting reading the slave narratives. Enter* **Norma**.

Brother Kiyi Hey girl.

Norma Don't 'hey girl' me, you stubborn old fool!

Brother Kiyi What I do you now?

Norma The letter you asked me daughter Paulette to look at.

Brother Kiyi Yeah?

Norma What don't you understand about if you don't pay your rent within twenty-one days Mustafar is going to send in the bailiffs?

Brother Kiyi I understand it all. What I want to find out is what I can do about it.

Norma   You phone Beverly, get her to inform them you going to pay!

Brother Kiyi   Ah, Beverly's great but she don't have the stamina I require for this battle.

Norma   You mean she has grown tired ah you?

Brother Kiyi   What Paulette say?

Norma   That you need to pay! Like today! You know what the problem is? You think the world is waiting on you, Kiyi! While you're sitting in here being obstinate, Mustafar is moving forwards. Why weren't you at the town hall last night?

Brother Kiyi   I was busy.

Norma   My backside you were busy! All the other leaseholders were there!

Brother Kiyi   I don't go anywhere dem punk rockers will be. If I see them I might just lose me temper and . . . If they'd have stood by me in the first place none of this would have been happening!

Norma   That is history, Kiyi.

Brother Kiyi   No my friend, *his story* are the fables of his winnings. (*Points to slave narrative books.*) This is history. Anyway, it wasn't telling me anything I didn't know already.

Norma   Oh, so you know that he planning to turn the places above you into luxury flats? What do you think is gonna happen next?

Brother Kiyi   They'll pretty up the front, give me a new sign.

Norma   Which parent you think gonna loan dem child money to buy flat on top of an extreme Black bookshop? He has to get you out.

Brother Kiyi   Norma, me know all of that. Me even know he plan to replace my bookstore with shop that sells black hair products.

Norma   How do you know that?

Brother Kiyi   Two people came in here yesterday to measure up!

Norma   To measure up?

Brother Kiyi   Yes. But he's messing with the wrong guy. I'm gonna talk to my MP. I'm gonna start a petition, speak to all the local black celebrities . . .

Norma   I wouldn't count on them if I were you.

Brother Kiyi   You can't replace history with hair gel.

Norma   Kiyi, our MP was there. Smiling. Agreeing. Saying thank you. The only good ting about that meeting is that they asked me to talk. Dem requested that a community woman like myself make comment on dem plans.

Brother Kiyi   What you say?

Norma   I said I was outraged.

Brother Kiyi   And?

Norma   If you were bloody well there you'd have known what I said! We can't mek dem run roughshod over us like that man. Anyway, I went to the doctor this morning and you know what he tell me?

Brother Kiyi   You diabetes getting worse?

Norma   Me diabetes getting worse. This ting go take me to me premature grave.

Brother Kiyi   Hey girl, don't talk stupidness!

Norma   Listen, when me reach de Fadder gate, I want to be able to look he in the eye and say, 'Lord, I did do something down there!' (*Beat*.) So I went to the bank. There was three grand in it. Here's two. Pay the man.

Brother Kiyi   *Don't be stupid!*

Norma *Take it.* I understand where you coming from, man, but you can't fight this from where you are, Kiyi. You need help. We need to keep the shop open. Now take this, pay the man. Pay me back when you can.

Brother Kiyi Norma, you know that's not possible. Listen to me good. If I pay the man his money now, he's gonna expect it on time every quarter. My business doesn't run like that!

Norma And neither does his!

Brother Kiyi I always square up by end of year! What's wrong wid dat?

Norma It's unreasonable, Kiyi.

Brother Kiyi And so is the offer of your savings. I can't take it.

Norma Kiyi, though I don't agree with all you stupidness, you love Black. And all of my life I have been taught to fear it, hate it. That ain't right! Take the money. Please.

She forces the envelope into **Brother Kiyi***'s hand.*

Brother Kiyi Don't think that go stop me whipping you backside at draughts?

Norma Phone him now. Tell them you coming!

Brother Kiyi Now?

Norma Now.

Brother Kiyi *picks up the phone.*

Brother Kiyi (*with smile*) Just cos you give me little money you think you could boss me around? (*Serious switch.*) Hello, put me through to Mr Mustafar please . . . Who's calling? His nemesis . . . No, that's not all one word . . . Thank you . . . Mustafar, Kiyi here. You think you catch me, innit? Well you lie. I coming with you money . . . How about three? I think I can just about make that. Cool.

He slams down the phone. **Norma** *smiles.*

Enter **Kwesi**. **Brother Kiyi** *puts the envelope of money away.*

Brother Kiyi   Tende Mwari, Brother Kwesi.

Kwesi (*not reciprocating* **Brother Kiyi**'s *joyous tone*)   Tende Mwari, Sister Norma.

The slave narratives catch **Kwesi**'s *eye. He stops to look.*

Norma   Kwesi!

She exits to the basement.

Brother Kiyi   So, how's the revolution today?

Kwesi   Fine, my brother.

He is about to walk past **Brother Kiyi** *to the room upstairs when* **Brother Kiyi** *stops him.*

Brother Kiyi   Hey, I just read that Michael Jackson has been a signed-up member of the Nation of Islam for ten years?

Kwesi   How can you have the most prominent manifestation of Black self-hate as a member of a militant Black organisation? Char! Michael should have been shot the moment he bleached his skin.

Brother Kiyi   So what happen? A brother can't look a little forgiveness?

Kwesi   Can you forgive slavery? Can the European repent for that? Only thing this world understands, Kiyi, power. Till we have that, no matter what's up there (*pointing to head*), we're all just joking it.

Brother Kiyi   Good talk, Kwesi, but make sure your words don't take you where they shouldn't. Jail life na nice.

Kwesi   For real.

He makes to go.

Brother Kiyi (*grabbing the opportunity*)   Brother Kwesi, I tried to go into the room upstairs yesterday, but the door was locked.

Kwesi Yeah, that's right. Sorry, I forgot to tell you. But it's OK, I've got the key.

Brother Kiyi There's never been a key for that lock!

Kwesi Oh, at last week's meeting we . . . we changed the locks. The new computers and that. I'm sorry, we should have informed you, but with all this march and all it must have slipped my mind.

Brother Kiyi Right.

Kwesi I'll do a copy and get it right to you?

Brother Kiyi Fine.

Enter **Carl***.*

Carl Brother Kiyi, I ain't got but five minutes so we need to hit it straight away.

Kwesi Hey, Brother Carl, are you coming on the march?

Carl I'm not your brother, and which march is that?

Kwesi The Reparations for Slavery march.

Carl No, I don't think so.

Kwesi You, a recipient of state brutality, can't find one hour out of your day to march for our people's right to be repaid! That's why our race is going nowhere. I'm upstairs, Kiyi.

He exits.

Carl Why is he always so angry?

Brother Kiyi He's a serious young man.

Carl Do you reckon his face is vex like that when he's doing it?

Carl *demonstrates sex doggy-style with a vexed face just as* **Norma** *enters from downstairs.*

Carl Huh! Huh! Huh! Take it, baby! Sorry, Aunty Norma. But it ain't natural, is it?

Norma You want me to come with you at three?

Brother Kiyi   Na, man. I cool.

Norma   Alright, I gone. Later, dutty boy!

She exits.

Enter **Alice***, who crosses with* **Norma** *at the door. She has her headphones on. She smiles and starts to look at a bookshelf.* **Carl** *decides to stay.*

Carl   What you saying, sister?

He walks up to **Alice***.*

Alice   Pardon?

Carl   Are you one of those reparation-marching, hard-faced, straight-talking conscious types?

Alice   I don't think so!

Carl   I knew it. I could see you were different from your hair! I'm Carl.

Alice   Alice.

Carl   Come on, Brother Kiyi, let's get down to it. I haven't got long! (*Showing off.*) Excuse us. Brother teaches me to read. See, I ain't one of those ignorant niggers.

Brother Kiyi (*referring to 'niggers'*)   Carl!

Carl   Sorry – Nubians, that's afraid of edgedumacation.

Alice   I see.

Alice *moves to the back of the shop. Puts her headphones back on as politely as possible.*

Brother Kiyi *pulls out a book from beneath his counter.*

Brother Kiyi   Alright, where were we? Tell you what, try this today. You may struggle a little, but well!

He goes to the shelf and pulls out a book of Selected Poems. *He finds a poem and hands the book to* **Carl***.*

Carl   What is it?

Brother Kiyi Just read.

Carl 'If We Must Die.'

'If we must die, let it not be like hogs,
Hunted and penned in an ingl . . . '

Brother Kiyi Inglor . . .

Carl

'. . . rious spot,
While round us bark the mad and hungry dogs – '

(*Stops reading.*) What does that 'inglorious' mean?

Brother Kiyi I'll explain after. Carry on.

Carl
'Making their mock at our ac-curs-èd lot.' (*He exhales.*)

Brother Kiyi Well done.

Carl
'If we must die, O let us nobly die,
So that our precious – '

(*Pleased with himself for recognising.*) That's that word from *Lord of the Rings* innit? (*Does impression.*) 'My precious.' (*To* **Alice**.) You know there's an actor from *The Bill* who lives right up the road dere, Brian something or other, he knows the guy that played Golom, you know?

Brother Kiyi I see. Carry on with the poem, Carl.

Carl Where was I? Oh yeah. (*He looks at* **Alice**.)

'O, kinsmen! We must meet the common foe!
Though far outnumbered, let us show us brave,
And for their thousand blows deal one death blow!
What though before us lies the open grave?
Like men we'll face the murderous cowardly pack,
Pressed to the wall, dying but fighting back.'

Enter **Kwesi** *from upstairs, who has heard the last few lines. He gently giggles aloud at* **Carl***'s reading. He clocks* **Alice** *and likes what he sees but does not show it, much.*

Brother Kiyi *cuts his eye at* **Kwesi**.

Alice   Who was that?

Brother Kiyi   Claude MacKay.

Carl*'s mobile rings – the theme tune to* Batman. **Carl** *looks at the number and recognises it.*

Carl   Oh my gosh, Brother Kiyi, I gotta run, Mister Dongal done waiting for me. I liked that poem dough. Explain it to me tomorrow?

Brother Kiyi   Tomorrow!

As he walks past **Alice** *he smiles.*

Carl (*about* **Alice** *as he exits, malapropism of course*)   Inglorious!

Brother Kiyi *returns the books to the correct shelves.*

Alice   That's very good.

Brother Kiyi   What?

Alice   What you do. Reading and that.

Brother Kiyi   Care of the community! That is what they meant, wasn't it?

Alice   *In* the commu . . . Speaking of care, I came in today because I wanted to challenge the way you treated me yesterday. Like a common criminal.

Brother Kiyi   Criminal?

Alice   At least that's how I felt, and I wanted to let you know that in fact I am a teacher of much repute. I am a woman that should be respected.

Brother Kiyi   I have no doubts that you are. I apologised yesterday, and I will do so again if you wish.

Alice   You didn't actually.

Brother Kiyi   Didn't what?

Alice   You didn't apologise.

Brother Kiyi   I distinctly remember saying, 'I'm sorry, but one cannot be too careful.'

Alice   Not to split hairs, but that was apologising for having to do it. It wasn't an apology to me.

Brother Kiyi   What today is? Break-me-balls day?

Alice   Sorry?

Brother Kiyi   What is it you want, young lady? I'm very busy.

Alice   For a start, don't you think if you are introducing him to poetry, which I do think is great, maybe you should choose a less sexist poet?

Brother Kiyi   Less what?

Alice   A poet that doesn't exclude women from participating in 'the struggle'.

Brother Kiyi   It is Claude, 'the father of the Harlem Renaissance, the poet quoted by Winston Churchill to the British soldiers before the Battle of Britain', MacKay we are taking about here, isn't it?

Alice   Is it because I'm a woman you use that condescending tone with me?

Brother Kiyi   I'm not using a condescending tone with you.

Alice   Yes, you are! You're talking to me like I'm some 'stupid girl' that doesn't know what she's talking about.

Brother Kiyi   Well, I don't think you do actually . . .

Alice   Well, I beg to differ.

Brother Kiyi   Young lady, you are unknown to me. Why are you raising your voice?

She pauses for a second and gathers herself.

Alice   I tend to get passionate about what goes into the minds of those we are responsible for. I'm sorry.

Brother Kiyi   OK, please explain why Claude MacKay is sexist?

Alice   I don't actually know very much about Claude MacKay. I meant the poem sounded sexist.

Brother Kiyi   Lord have mercy!

Alice   The phrase 'If we must die', that's a call to participation.

Brother Kiyi   Right . . .

Alice   The phrase 'O kinsmen!' makes that call specific: the poem's would-be warriors are men. What about women? He only talks about the race by imagining the aspirations of men.

Brother Kiyi   Rasclaat!

Alice   No, not rasclaat or however you pronounce it – the contest for humanity in the poem is fought exclusively by men.

Kwesi *enters.*

Kwesi   Yes, it is.

Alice *turns and looks at* **Kwesi***.*

Alice   Exactly.

Kwesi   And what's wrong with that?

Alice   Sorry?

Kwesi   What's wrong with that assertion? Battles are fought by men. Not women, not girls, but men.

Alice   I think you'll find that if you look at the number of active service people in the Gulf wars, Kosovo, Afghanistan, you'll see that the number of women . . .

Kwesi   . . . is vastly below the number of men. You guys can't have it both ways, you know?

Alice   What *guys* are we talking about here?

Kwesi   Women! One minute you're the saviour of mankind due to the size of your humanity and now you're the sword-bearers that defend the nation? Which way do you want it?

Alice (*taken aback*)   Wow. I don't know you, sir, but I would say that's a rather archaic viewpoint for such a – (*chooses her words carefully*) modern-looking man.

Kwesi   Books and covers.

Alice   Evidently!

Kwesi *exits upstairs. There's a moment's silence.* **Alice** *switches.*

Alice   What a great place. How many bookstores can you go into and have heated debates like that?

Brother Kiyi   That *was* my dream.

Alice   Who is that guy?

Brother Kiyi   Kwesi, my militant-in-residence. Head of the All-Black African Party. They meet in the room upstairs. (*Suddenly becoming suspicious.*) Why?

Alice   No reason. (*With passion.*) What a hateful man. That's why people don't go out with black men. (*She stops herself.*) I finished *The Philosophies of Marcus Garvey* last night.

Brother Kiyi   You did?

Alice   Yes.

Brother Kiyi   What about the other one?

Alice   No, I haven't started reading that.

Brother Kiyi   Why?

Alice   I kind of wanted to discuss the *Philosophies* book with someone first.

Brother Kiyi   I see.

Alice   But I don't really know anyone that is familiar with the works of Marcus Garvey.

Brother Kiyi   Right.

Alice   I mean, don't you think he's a little racist?

Brother Kiyi   Here we go again!

Alice   No, I mean he comes over to me as a, yeah, a black racist.

Brother Kiyi   You're a teacher, you say?

Alice   Yes, I am.

Brother Kiyi   What do you teach?

Alice   English and – and History.

Brother Kiyi   Just over there you'll find a dictionary – could you pass it to me, please.

She does.

Racist, what does it say here in this *Oxford Dictionary*. 'Racism – a feeling of superiority from one race to another.' Now I would argue, not today, because I'm tired, that we are certainly not economically superior, and I would say, due to the collective lack of knowledge of ourselves and our constant desire to imitate, impersonate and duplicate everything Caucasian, nor are we in a psychological position of superiority. Hence by that definition, we cannot be racist.

Alice   Why are you tired?

Brother Kiyi   I'm fine.

Alice   Cos I'm brown, everybody expects me to somehow know everything black. And I'm like, 'Hey, how am I suppose to know what . . . raaasclaat means, I'm from Somerset.'

Brother Kiyi   OK!

Alice   People down here are so fortunate to have a resource like this.

Brother Kiyi   You don't miss the water till the well runs dry . . .

The phone rings.

Tende Mwari . . . Yes, Brother Peter . . . I see. Have you spoken to our beloved local MP? . . . OK, his surgery days are . . . Yes . . . Monday, Town Hall, Martin Luther King Room. Saturday morning at the Steve Biko Library . . . No, you just turn up. If you'd like I have a book here somewhere on the working of . . . Yes, it will inform you of your rights! . . . Send your son to pick it up. Four o'clock? . . . Yes I'll be here. Tende Mwari.

Brother Kiyi *puts down the phone and gets up to search for the book. He has to squeeze past* **Alice** *to get there.*

Brother Kiyi   Excuse me.

Alice *is quite taken by the smell of his locks.*

Alice   What do you put in your hair?

Brother Kiyi   Um, Oil of Ulay.

Beat.

Alice   Do you do that for everyone?

Brother Kiyi   What?

Alice   Advise them and then bam, sell 'em a book?

Brother Kiyi   I don't sell the books. I loan them.

Alice   Loan them? Do you get them back? . . .

Brother Kiyi   Most times . . .

Alice   In sellable condition? . . .

Brother Kiyi   Sometimes . . .

Alice   How many books do you sell a week?

Brother Kiyi   Why do you ask?

Alice   Curious? How many books did you loan last week?

Brother Kiyi   About twelve.

Alice   Any come back?

Brother Kiyi   They will.

Alice   You have a record of the books you loaned out, right?

Brother Kiyi   What is the problem here? I loan books. If I didn't they wouldn't be read.

Alice   What do you mean by that?

Brother Kiyi   I mean . . . (*Decides to share.*) Do you know what my best-seller has been for the last year? Apart from my Afrocentric cards, that is – you know, black mum kissing black dad. West Indian grandmother in big hat playing with a cat – um, the best-seller was *Shotter's Revenge*, and, oh, *Black Love*.

Alice   What's wrong with that? Who couldn't do with a bit of black love right now?

Brother Kiyi   What is wrong with that? I have on these shelves Van Sertima's *Africa, Cradle of Civilisation*! Chancellor Williams's *Destruction of Black Civilisation*, Peterson's *The Middle Passage*, Williams's *Capitalism and Slavery*. I've books on the Dogons, the Ashantis, the, the pyramids of ancient Zimbabwe, and what do they buy? Nonsensical nonsense about men with nine-packs doing in the sauna with black female executives. What is that, I ask you?

Alice   Six-packs!

Brother Kiyi   What?

Alice   No one has a nine-pack.

Brother Kiyi   I don't care what pack them have! That is nonsense reading when we face the things we face today. You know, you were the first person in an age to buy, well, to buy a book of substance. In fact . . . (*He checks the sales book.*) Yes, here it is! December of last year. One copy of *The Isis Papers* by Dr Cress Welsing. And that customer wasn't even black!

Alice   She was white?

Brother Kiyi   No, she was mixed.

Alice   I believe the term is now 'person of dual heritage'.

Brother Kiyi   I'm sure it is.

Alice   Shouldn't you be up-to-date on that sort of stuff?
Being a leader of your community an' all!

Brother Kiyi   I suppose I should, if in fact I were a leader.

Alice   Why aren't you?

Brother Kiyi   A leader or up-to-date?

Alice   Both?

Brother Kiyi   You ask a lot of questions.

Alice   I need a lot of answers. Always have.

Brother Kiyi   Answers to what? You a policewoman?

Alice   No, I am not . . . Denied histories are fascinating to
me.

Brother Kiyi   I wish that more of my community thought
like that.

Alice   Maybe they do and just haven't told you.

He suddenly remembers and stands.

Brother Kiyi   Sugar, what time is it now?

Alice   Have I kept you?

Brother Kiyi   Kwesi! Kwesi!

Kwesi   Yo!

Brother Kiyi   Come and hold the store for me, please. Got
to run out the road.

Kwesi   I'll be down in a second.

Brother Kiyi   I've got to go *now*!

Kwesi   OK, go, I'll be down in a minute.

Brother Kiyi *grabs his coat, checks that the envelope is secure and
heads to the door.*

Brother Kiyi   You don't have to leave, you can, you know, look around still? There's a chair there.

She runs up to him and hugs him passionately. Almost girl-like, but she's a woman. **Brother Kiyi** *doesn't quite know how to deal with that much affection.*

Brother Kiyi *shouts up the stairs.*

Brother Kiyi   Kwesi! Kwesi!

Kwesi   I'm coming, I'm coming.

Brother Kiyi *strokes his hair. Then exits.*

Alice *walks around the shop looking at things more freely now that she is by herself.*

She sees the slave narratives.

She goes to the desk and looks around. She looks though the contents and then under the counter. She stays there for a little while. Then takes a slave narrative. She decides to read.

The lights reduce to a spotlight on her. We are in her head. She takes on the voice of the story-teller.

Alice   'Mary Gould, Grand Anse Estate, Grenada. One day Masser Reynolds come back from Barbados wid one high yellow gal he just buy. They say she was real pretty but I can hardly remember. But he never put she to live wid the other niggers, no, he buil' she a special little house away from the quarters down by the river which run at the back ah de plantation. Every negroes know Masser take a black woman quick as he did a white and took any on his place that he wanted and he took them often. But most his pickney dem born on the place looked like niggers. But not all. Once, two of his yella children went up to the big house where Dr Reynolds full-breed child was playing in their dolls' house and told them that they want to play in the dolls' house too. The story go that one of the Doctor full breed-child say, "Sorry, this is for white children only." The reply I'm told went, "We ain't no niggers, cos we got the same daddy you has, and he comes to see us every day with gifts and wonderful clothes and such." Well, Mrs Reynolds was at the window heard the white niggers saying, "He is our daddy cos we call him daddy when he comes to see our mammy." That evening that yella gal get whipped for almost three hours. And within one year all her children had been sold away. No sir, it don't pay to be pretty and yella.'

The lights snap on as **Kwesi** *rests his hands on* **Alice**'s *shoulders. She jumps.*

Alice   Ohhhh.

Kwesi   Did I scare you?

Alice   Yes, you did, actually. What are you doing over my shoulder?

Kwesi   You were breathing heavily.

Alice   I was reading!

Kwesi   Do you always breathe like that when you read?

Alice   I mouth the words as well!

Kwesi   You into that stuff?

Alice   Families?

Kwesi   Slavery! Old Kiyi here is addicted to that shit.

Alice   Aren't all you political types?

Kwesi   Hell, no. I only look forward, sister.

Alice   Sounds rather disrespectful to Brother Kiyi!

Kwesi   No it's not. He's cool. Big expert on all things slavery. Which is good for me cos I don't have to go to no Yanks when I wanna know something. I hate going to those Yanks. Been in the belly of the beast too long.

Alice   What does that mean?

Kwesi   It affects you, you know? Being around too much white folk. I seen the bluest of blackest men get too much exposure, bam, they lose their rhythm. Put on a James Brown tune and they start doing the Charleston to ras!

Alice   Isn't there an ointment you can get to mitigate that?

Kwesi   What?

Alice   Over-exposure to white folk?!

Kwesi   Ohhhh, somebody's getting touchy!

Alice   I'm not getting touchy.

Kwesi   Yes, you are. I say the word 'white folk' and you get all arms!

Alice   Two words, actually. Arms?

Kwesi   Vex! Wanna fight?

Alice   I don't want to fight you!

Kwesi   Why not? It's half your people, innit, that I'm cussing!

Alice   Half my p . . . ? You're trying to provoke me. Why?

Kwesi   You look like the type that likes to be provoked?

Alice   Well, Mr Kwesa . . .

Kwesi   Kwesi, Kwes-i, not -ah.

Alice   Sorry. It doesn't exactly roll off my half-tongue.

Kwesi   Very good. If you were 'fuller', I could quite like you.

Alice   Is that of body or of race?

Kwesi   Both.

Alice   If you're gonna come on to me at least engage on a higher level than that.

Kwesi *is slightly taken aback.*

Kwesi   I wasn't trying to come on to you.

Alice   Is that so?

Kwesi   I don't do your type!

Alice   My . . . And what is my type exactly?

Kwesi   West Indians. You guys are weak.

Alice   Yanks, West Indians, mixed. And there was I thinking it was because I'm from Somerset.

Kwesi   You're funny. I like you.

Alice   All of me or half?

Kwesi   Depends what side of you you're showing me. Let me tell you something. I don't trust you type of people. I see you coming in here trying to be down, so when the white man thinks he's choosing one of us you're there shouting, 'Hey, I'm black.' But you ain't.

Alice   Well, you're nothing if not clear, Kwesi.

Kwesi   Nothing, if not clear.

He exits up the stairs.

Lights down.

Scene Three

Fix Up bookstore. Day.

Brother Kiyi *is in joyous mood. He runs over to the cassette recorder and throws in another tape. It gives out a very percussive rhythm made up of hand-claps and foot-stomps He starts to sing an old slave work-chant. It's a call and response.* **Brother Kiyi** *is calling, the recording responding. The lead line sounds like a blues refrain. He begins to dance with it. The dance is as if he is picking cotton from the ground and then cutting cane with two cutlasses.*

Enter **Norma**. **Brother Kiyi** *stops dancing for a moment, then continues.*

Norma   Boy, what you so happy about?

Brother Kiyi   You like the rhythm, girl?

Norma   I would, if it wasn't so blasted loud!

Brother Kiyi   What you say?

Norma　Turn that blasted ting down. You give Mustafar he money?

Brother Kiyi　When I hand it him he shit! All he could do was open he mouth so. (*Imitates jaw dropping.*) You know who was in the office? The same boys he selling it to. Oh God, it was sweet. Thank you, gal.

Norma　Good.

She gets the draughts. They sit down to play. **Brother Kiyi** *suddenly catches sight of her hair. She is wearing a very long and glamorous wig. It stops just beneath her shoulders.*

Brother Kiyi　Hey, gal! A next-animal ting you have on you head. It still alive? . . .

Norma　Don't be feisty. It's hundred-per-cent human!

Brother Kiyi　Human? . . .

Norma　Yes . . .

Brother Kiyi　As oppose to what? . . .

Norma　Horse!

Brother Kiyi　So you will spend your hard-earned money on hair dem chop from a horse?

Norma　I told you it's not no horse hair, it's hundred-per-cent Chinese . . .

Brother Kiyi　Chinese? . . .

Norma　Kiyi! Make we concentrate on the game.

Brother Kiyi *moves.*

Norma　Kiyi, you does need any special qualification to go into politics? (*She moves.*)

Brother Kiyi　Apart from a great capacity for wickedness. No. (*He moves.*) Why?

Norma　I feel community-connected. At the meeting the other night, and when me stand up, you know how they introduce me? 'Madam Norma, a woman who knows this community like no other.' You know how great that mek me feel? The head of the council calling me madam! The only time I get call madam previous to dat in me life is when they come to arrest me husband. (*She moves.*)

Brother Kiyi   What that have to do wid your Chinese wig, Norma?

Norma   If you gonna stand for election you have to look glamorous, don't it?

Brother Kiyi   Election of what? (*He moves.*)

Norma   I don't know. I had this dream last night that I was on me window ledge and all below me was darkness and me feel like me was going to fall off but me say no, and before me know it me just start to fly fly fly.

Brother Kiyi   What you think that mean?

Norma   I don't know. (*She moves.*) But I wake up and the first ting that jump in me mind is 'Norma stand for election'.

Brother Kiyi   You need an agent? Let me find you one na!

Norma   I told you I was just thinking.

Brother Kiyi   Norma, you don't even like politics.

Norma   I don't understand it, Kiyi! But before me dead, I'd like to understand something, something from the inside. That's why me and you generation fail, boy, we didn't engage.

Brother Kiyi *moves.*

Norma   Oh sugar mugar. How you see that move, dread?

Brother Kiyi   By watching the game.

Norma   How long you going to carry on so? No customers, no life . . .

Brother Kiyi   Norma, it's not going to stay so! Na man, I can smell it in the air. (*Beat.*) You see that young girl that does come in here, right . . .

Norma   The half-caste gal?

Brother Kiyi   Different, you know, dread. Angry, political, albeit about woman tings but still fantastic anger. I does sit down and talk to that girl and I does say to meself wooooy, where does that rage come from in these apathetic times? Then the wind whisper in me ears, 'Ah my time again.' That's why I know it's coming.

Enter **Alice**. *They turn around and look at her.*

Alice   What?

Brother Kiyi   Nothing.

Norma *looks at him. The women look at each other.*

Norma (*to* **Brother Kiyi**, *looking at his crutch*)   You sure it's the wind?

Alice   How are you today?

Brother Kiyi   Good. Very good. You?

Alice   Oh, OK! I . . .

She stops herself, taking a quick glance at **Norma**. **Brother Kiyi** *very subtly follows her eyes.* **Norma** *detects a vibe.*

Norma   Kiyi, I gone!

Brother Kiyi   OK, girl. Hail up Bernie.

Norma   Will do!

She leaves.

Brother Kiyi   What were you saying?

Alice   Oh, I didn't mean to . . .

Brother Kiyi   No no no no, Norma was just leaving.

Alice   I was just going to share that I got a call from my boyfriend this morning! Nothing earth-shattering.

His heart sinks, but he doesn't let it show.

Brother Kiyi Boyfriend?

Alice Well, ex.

Brother Kiyi What did he want?

Alice He wanted me to come back to him.

Brother Kiyi Do you want to?

Alice He's no good for me. It's time I either had wild abandoned sex with whoever I want, whenever I want, or settled down to have a family.

Brother Kiyi Can't you do both with him?

Alice He's married. In fact his daughter and I are roughly the same age. I know what you're thinking . . .

Brother Kiyi . . . I don't think you do!

Alice I mean, guys my age are great for sex and that, but, well . . . I need more. I love him, but, ahhh, I'm confused. I don't know what to think. What do you think?

Brother Kiyi You should do. (*He doesn't quite know how to respond.*)

Alice My father always use to warn me, 'What men say and what they really mean are often two different things.' If I were your child what would you tell me to do?

Brother Kiyi Stick with the older man. Only joking . . .

*Enter **Carl** in a rush.*

Carl Brother Kiyi, Brother Kiyi. What's up wid your phone, man?

Brother Kiyi Calm down. What's the matter, Carl?

Carl Beverly's been trying to get hold of you! She needs you to go to see her. Good ting I was passing with Dongal!

Brother Kiyi See me for what?

Carl   She's gonna tell me that innit? But her face looked deadly! Dongal said it's because Mustafar's about to take back the shop.

Brother Kiyi   That's impossible . . . Alright, alright. Come and sit the shop for me. (*To* **Alice**.) Excuse me a moment, yeah?

Alice   Of course. Are you OK?

Brother Kiyi   Some people feel they playing with a boy! Well, they go see. Yes, it's all fine. Little while, yeah?

Carl   Yeah. Everything's safe wid me!

Brother Kiyi *pauses and looks at* **Carl** *for a beat before leaving.*

Carl *stands a fair distance from* **Alice**. *He's kinda smiling at her.*

Carl   Oh well.

Alice   What?

Carl   Nothing. Just oh well! Here we are. (*Sings.*) 'Just the two of us.'

Alice   Is . . . is Kiyi going to be OK?

Carl   Ah yeah, man, he's use to fighting. You don't see the locks? Lion of Judah! . . . They ain't taking nothing from him, dread. This place is too good for anyone to take away. It's great here, don't you think?

Alice   Yes.

Carl   It's a real tribute to Kiyi. Different people coming and going. I mean, look at you. You've come in an' caught the bug, right, like the rest of us?

Alice   What bug is that?

Carl   Culture. Nothing like knowing your roots!

He starts to reggae DJ.

Me love me roots and culture, murderer,
How black people dem a suffer – murderer!

(*A little embarrassed.*) It's an old Shabba Ranks tune. It must be great, being you.

Alice   Wow, where did that come from?

Carl   Yeah, you like must have the best of two worlds innit? Like you got the black beauty bit and you got the white money bit. Hoorah!

Alice   Hoorah!

Carl   Roots, you know, connection! I use to want to be white till I met Kiyi. Now I'm blue black brother. You couldn't make me white if you tried!

Alice   You think people try?

Carl   People try anything in this day and age you know! (*Pause.*) Is your hair easy to maintain?

Alice   Um, yes, I suppose.

Carl   Though I don't wanna be white, that's what I'd like. The mixed flowy type of hair. Girls like that, don't they? It's so beautiful.

Alice   I think your hair is fine. It's like mine!

Carl   You're just saying that to sweet me. You don't have to do that! Look, I'm gonna go do some reading. So, um, feel free to do what you want. Sure Kiyi won't mind.

Alice   Yeah, he said it was OK.

Carl   Good.

He moves across to the desk and takes out a book. He sings to himself:

'From the very first time I set my eyes on you girl,
My heart said follow though,
But I know that I'm way down on your line.
But the waiting deal is fine.'

Alice   Carl, what kind of man is Kiyi?

Carl   How do you mean?

Alice   What kind of man? Is he kind? Loving?

Carl   Mannn, he's got the biggest heart in the world, dread. Everything I am today I owe to Kiyi.

Alice   Is that so?

Carl   Yeah. I was sleeping on the street, everybody else walked over me, but he bent down, pulled me up, took me to his home and fed me. Not a lot of people would do that! Not in this day and age.

Alice   He took you to his home?

Carl   Yeah!

Alice   What did his wife say?

Carl   Kiyi ain't got no wife.

Alice   His woman, then . . .

Carl   You're not getting me. Kiyi's got his books and that's all he needs, bar probably a likkle bit of Norma!

Alice   Oh, he and Norma are . . . ?

Carl   Naa naaa. I put that over wrong. I'm always doing that! Norma's like a man to Kiyi! They like blokes, buddies and shit, stuff.

Alice   Stuff?

Carl   Yeah, between you and me, Kiyi did little time with Norma's husband and they looked after him when he came out. He never forgets a favour.

Alice   How long ago was that?

Carl (*sensing he's talked too much*)   Dunno. Got to take my hat off to him, though, I don't know how a brother goes that long without some grit . . . some . . . some . . .

Alice   Some what?

Carl   You know . . .

Alice (*playing*)   No.

Carl   Some, ha . . . !

Alice   Sex?

Carl   Exactly, that's the one. I didn't want to be rude.

Alice   Sex isn't a rude word, Carl.

Carl   I know, it's just not the kinda utterance you want to use in front of a lady, is it?

Alice (*laughs*)   You are so cute.

Carl   Thanks. So are you.

Alice   Does he ever talk about the old days – you know, his youth, his mother and stuff?

Carl   Naaaa. Not to me.

Alice   But at his house he must have pictures up and that?

Carl   No. He keeps all that stuff here.

Enter **Kwesi**. *He clocks* **Alice**.

Kwesi   You still here, girl?

Alice *gets up and starts to walk out.* **Carl** *is vexed.* **Kwesi**'s *just broken his vibe.*

Alice   I'll see you later, Carl.

Alice *leaves.*

Carl   She's pretty innit?

Kwesi   She alright. (*Referring to the box he has left.*) No, it's alright.

Carl *walks up to* **Kwesi** *and attempts to take the box from him.*

Carl   Hey, my job is delivery. That's what I do.

He pulls the box.

Kwesi   Carl, I said it's OK.

Carl   Your car's gonna get a ticket. Let me take the box. What's the problem?

Kwesi   I said it's alright.

In a sudden burst of temper **Carl** *rips the box out of* **Kwesi***'s hands. It falls on the floor and bursts open. Lots of hair products spill on to the floor.*

Carl   Keep your fucking boxes then!

Kwesi   Are you out your fucking mind?

Carl   Sorry, sorry. I just like things to be clear, you know what I am saying? Know what I'm doing, know where I am?

He gets down to put the stuff back in the box. He notices the hair products.

Kwesi   Move. Move.

Carl (*picks up a bottle*)   Oh shit, I haven't seen one of these in ages. Gerry Curl Max. (*Fake-sprays it on his hair.*) 'Makes your hair wavyyyy.' (*Advert voice.*)

Kwesi   Give it back! Give it to me!

Carl   What you doing with hair products, Kwesi? You boys don't like that shit? (*Impersonates.*) 'Making your hair like white folk!'

Kwesi   Don't worry about it.

Carl   Just looking forward to seeing you with a perm! It's gonna suit you, trust me!

Kwesi *kisses his teeth and exits.* **Carl** *pulls out a hair leaflet he took from the box. He starts to read it. He looks perturbed.*

Lights down.

Scene Four

Fix Up bookstore. One hour later.

Lights come up slowly. **Kwesi** *is in* **Brother Kiyi**'s *chair with his feet on the desk. He is on his mobile.*

Kwesi   Ha! Na, man, the boy's too stupid to put all that together. You're kidding! . . . How much? . . . Niggers, man! We can't afford that! . . . Tell him he's fixing up, not bloody rebuilding! . . .

Enter **Brother Kiyi**. *He looks upset.*

Kwesi   Look, gotta go. Yeah, yeah. Tendai Mwari.

He gets off the phone and out of **Brother Kiyi**'s *chair.*

Brother Kiyi   Hope you ain't planning on fixing up nothing in here?

Kwesi   Um, what do you mean?

Brother Kiyi   What you fixing up?

Kwesi   Um, some stats and stuff we just got from America. Trying to get a professional on the job. You know, for the new classes. Did you know the global buying power of black America ranks eleventh in the world? That's just below Spain and above India, you know? Some serious money Nubians be spending.

Brother Kiyi   How much they spend on education?

Kwesi   Good question, I don't know . . . But check this out. How much are we spending on cosmetics a year? Thirty-five million in this country alone, dread. I mean, come on, it don't take Pythagoras to work out why other people be getting rich off our backs, does it? That's why I always be telling you, Kiyi, I love this shop but niggers ain't ready!

Brother Kiyi *doesn't answer.*

Kwesi   You OK?

Brother Kiyi   I don't know about no niggers, looks like it was me that weren't ready. It's all over, Kwesi, game's over. I no longer have the shop, him take the money for back rent, I thought the option to extend the lease was with me. It's not.

Kwesi   I see.

Brother Kiyi   I mean, maybe I should have heeded your advice, opened this place up. Sold Jamaican videos and bashment-sound tapes and home food in the corner but . . . (*Loses it for a bit.*) This is a place of learning, Kwesi! Not a come-one come-all supermarket, but a sanctuary, a place away from the madness. Away from the pain.

Kwesi *doesn't know what to say. He feels for him.*

Kwesi   He's a businessman, Kiyi, what else is he gonna do? Me, I blame the people around here that have ignored what this is. That walk past safe in the knowledge that it's here but put nothing in. What you gonna go and put yourself in trouble for? For them? For those that buy one book a year?

Brother Kiyi   The road to freedom is seldom walked by the multitude.

Kwesi   It's not being walked by anyone right now, Kiyi. You got to take emotion out of this. You couldn't afford to run the shop because the people didn't support you. That's it. There's a lesson in that for all of us. A lesson for me.

Brother Kiyi   What is that?

Kwesi   Sometimes you got to do stuff in this world that ain't nice. But if you think it's right, you got to do it. That's what my Somalian brothers been showing me. They ain't wrong.

His mobile rings. He glances at the text.

I need to talk to you, Kiyi, not now cos I got to run, but you gonna be around later?

Brother Kiyi   Where else I go be?

Kwesi   Alright. I'll see you in while.

Kwesi *turns to leave.*

Brother Kiyi   Kwesi.

Kwesi   Yeah . . .

Brother Kiyi   You're a good brother!

Kwesi *turns and leaves.*

Brother Kiyi *begins to sob, silently at first. Slowly and quietly we hear his sobs.*

Gently, barely audibly at first, he begins to hear the voices from the books. Passages, statements, prose and poetry all blend.

After a few beats he snaps out of it, inhales and then forcefully exhales the air to pull himself together. He returns to his desk, gets out the key to the chest of drawers, opens it pulls out an old-looking box. He removes the photo album that is inside.

He stares at the first few pictures before drifting off into a state of great sadness.

Enter **Carl**.

Carl   Hey, Brother Kiyi, you OK?

Brother Kiyi   Yeah, man, course I'm OK.

Carl   How did the Beverly meeting go?

Brother Kiyi   Fine, fine. She just wanted to talk to me about future plans and tings.

Carl   Tings?

Brother Kiyi   You know, expansion.

Carl   Right. So the shop's cool?

Brother Kiyi   Yeah man. Safe as it's ever been.

Carl   Seen. Wanna cup of tea or something?

Brother Kiyi   No.

Carl   Hear what! I wanna do something right.

Brother Kiyi   Alright.

Carl   I wanna bust a move on Alice.

Brother Kiyi   What?

Carl   Not bust a move exactly. I wanna ask her out.

Brother Kiyi   Um?

Carl   Truth is I just need to talk to someone and you like a dad to me. Plus I ain't got no mates but that's wholly secondary.

Brother Kiyi (*stunned*)   Carl . . . have I missed . . . do you know if she feels anything for you?

Carl   Yeah, man. I *know* she feels something for me, Kiyi. I feel it in bloodstream. Shit that powerful don't just happen one way, it just don't . . .

Brother Kiyi   Maybe you've misread.

Carl   I can't misread what's in my heart, Kiyi.

Brother Kiyi   I don't doubt that you feel for her . . .

Carl   I don't feel, I know.

Brother Kiyi   . . . Look before you step to *any* woman – you got to make sure that it is something they would like, that you're compatible, that . . .

Carl   You think that I'm not good enough for her? Am I too dark for her or something?

Brother Kiyi   Oh Carl, come on. That's not what I meant!

Carl   Yes it is! I'm alright for all those other girls round here but Alice, noooo!

Brother Kiyi   Carl, calm down! Count to ten, come on, slowly! One . . .

Carl   I'm not a crack addict any more, Kiyi. I mean, you're treating me like the enemy and you don't understand, you ain't looking. What's happening with the shop, Kiyi?

Brother Kiyi   Nothing's happening with the shop, Carl, everything's going to be fine.

Carl You're lying to me. Why does everybody lie to me all of the time? I'm not a fool, I'm not an idiot.

Brother Kiyi I didn't say you were, Carl. I was saying . . .

Carl You're telling me everything gonna be alright. When I know that everything is fucked!

Brother Kiyi Carl, calm down!

Carl I won't fucking calm down, Kiyi, this is serious. I'm trying to tell you something and you won't hear me. Kwesi's going to take over your shop, Kiyi.

Brother Kiyi Ah, Carl, don't be ridiculous.

Carl I'm not being ridiculous. Look . . . here's the order thingy. Now I could be wrong, you know, maybe I read it wrong, I've done that before, but . . . where the fuck is it?

Brother Kiyi Carl.

Carl I'll find it in a minute, just wait a second. I put it . . .

He looks for the hair product order form.

Brother Kiyi Carl, come on. Kwesi! How you gonna be going there? Are you mad?

Carl What did you call me? You see. You see. Do you have any idea how hard it is for me to tell you anything about Kwesi? About your fucking darling upstairs.

Brother Kiyi Carl, look, I'm sorry if I . . .

Carl I don't give a bombo about you're sorry, you think I'd just make that up? I may have done some bad things but I ain't the killer here.

Brother Kiyi I'm trying to protect you.

Carl That's what they use to say in da madhouse before them inject me, in the court house before them send me down, and in my mum's house before she box me in me mouth! You hurt me, Kiyi, you done fucked up.

Brother Kiyi   Carl!

Carl *walks out of the door just as* **Alice** *comes in. They nearly collide.*

Alice   Hi Carl . . .

Carl   Don't touch me.

He exits.

Alice   What's the matter with Carl?

Brother Kiyi   Nothing. We um, just had a little . . . You know, families do that, right. Alice, I've had a really hard day, I'm about to lock up.

Alice   I've never seen you upset before. I only came to return this. (*She pulls a slave narrative from her bag.*) I borrowed it earlier.

Brother Kiyi   You did?

Alice   Didn't think you'd mind, you lend books all of the time, don't you?

Brother Kiyi   Not those, I don't.

Alice   Why not those?

Brother Kiyi   Because they're really not supposed to leave the store. Why would you do that without asking me?

Alice   I'm sorry if I took your book without permission, but I've never seen, read anything like this before, I couldn't put it down . . . I read a story about this woman whose children wanted to play in the dolls' house of their brother and sister, and the children got sold and the mother got whipped, and she was mixed race like me . . .

Brother Kiyi   I know the one . . .

Alice   . . . and I've found this other story, listen to this!

She reads to **Brother Kiyi**.

Alice   'When me mudder see that Mr Reynolds had come to collect me to sell with the other ten or so pickney, she fell to her knees and begged him to spare me. When she seed that

it weren't no good, she simply stood up and asked Him to ask
whoever it was dat buyed me, to raise me for God. I was too
young to understand what was going on, but now I understand.
I never seed my modder again all my living days.' (*Beat.*) I was
given away and I tried to imagine the pain of this mother,
what this mother felt, this parent felt, but I just simply couldn't.

Brother Kiyi   Given away?

Alice   Adopted. Yeah! Can you imagine the pain of this
parent?

Brother Kiyi   No!

Alice   The pain of that child when she realised she would
never see her mother again? Can you imagine?

Brother Kiyi   Have you met your . . . birth parents?

Alice   My father yes, mother no.

Brother Kiyi   How come?

Alice   He was easier to find.

Brother Kiyi   I see. I'm sorry.

Alice   Oh there's nothing to be sorry about. My real mum
and dad were . . . Actually, you know what? There is a book
over there that I wish was out when I was kid. Caring for
black hair. I didn't know you could wear your hair other than
in two bunches until I was seventeen.

Brother Kiyi   This shop, Alice, will soon be, it will soon be
a centre of excellence for black hair products. Run by two
very nice-looking Turkish guys. They don't have a great
grasp of English at the moment, but I'm sure they've enough
to know the difference between Afro sheen and Dyke 'n'
Dryden. It's not a problem, in fact I feel rather good that in
the first months of trading no doubt more black folk will have
passed through here than I'd have seen in my whole fifteen
years! What is a problem is that I must start anew, afresh.
Again. I can handle that, except, maybe, the last time I did
that I had a lot to leave behind. However, today you have

added power to my depleted strength. You're an angel and I thank you.

Alice *just stares at him. Suddenly she bursts into tears and runs out of the store.*

Brother Kiyi *doesn't know how to react to this.*

Norma, *who had entered near the end of their conversation and overheard 'angel', walks forward as* **Alice** *runs out past her.*

Norma   What you and that gal have, Kiyi?

Brother Kiyi   We don't have nothing.

Norma   So what, she just up and bawl so? Is mad, she mad?

Brother Kiyi   I don't know!

Norma   Woman don't just bust eye water so!

Brother Kiyi   Not all woman is hard like you, you know, Norma!

Norma   Indeed.

Brother Kiyi   That sounded worse than I meant it to.

Norma   No, it's OK.

Beat.

Brother Kiyi *starts to busy himself tidying the books.*

Norma   What you doing?

Brother Kiyi   I was about to call you, actually.

Norma   Really? So what was you going to call me to say?

Brother Kiyi   I . . . I . . .

Norma   Boy, something really must a bite you, dread. Cleaning up? Can't open your mouth. What?!

Brother Kiyi   Norma, Bernie vex you or something?

Norma   No. Bernie don't vex me. Is you making a fool of youself that's vexating me soul.

Brother Kiyi   Me?

Norma   Yes, you! One little mix-up girl breeze in here and is turning you head stupid?

Brother Kiyi   What you talking about?

Norma   You don't know that girl, Kiyi, and you be laughing up like a fool, talking to her as if you and she is companion.

Brother Kiyi   Norma, I converse with the girl, she's bright, what is the problem?

Norma   Oh, she's bright, is she? What else is there about this gal that you know for two minutes?

Brother Kiyi   Norma . . .

Norma   No, don't 'Norma' me. Tell me what else she is that makes you talk *shit* you should be keeping to youself? Or to you people them that has been here, with you, since morning?

Brother Kiyi   I don't know what's going on here, Norma, but it should stop. Right now.

Norma   Why? Why should it stop? It's the first real conversation we've had in a lifetime.

Brother Kiyi   That's not true, we talk all the time.

Norma   About what you want to talk about. When was the last time you told me something new? Something you've never said before. Something about you? About your hinterland?

Brother Kiyi   Norma, what you trying to say here?

Norma   How can that rasclaat girl that just reach be your angel, Kiyi?

He is taken aback for a second.

Brother Kiyi   I didn't mean . . .

Norma   Then what did you mean? Because words are everything and you wanna be careful about what you say because people might hear it and believe it.

Brother Kiyi   All I was trying to say was that . . .

Norma   That what?

Brother Kiyi   That I appreciate her being here.

Norma   And what about me, Kiyi? When was the last time you said you appreciate me, Kiyi?

Brother Kiyi   I say that all the time, what you want me to say that for?

Norma   Because sometimes a woman needs to hear it. But of course I'm hard Norma, I don't need to hear nothing.

Brother Kiyi   I appreciate you, Norma, there. You OK now?

Norma   Don't patronise me.

Brother Kiyi   Well, I don't know what you want, Norma, because I was simply expressing . . . Look, the licks I've been taking, I was simply expressing I'm pleased someone young wants . . . wants to engage. That's what this place was built for, Norma. It's what it is . . .

Norma   Well, maybe we give too much attention to the young . . . That young girl is playing you, Kiyi . . .

Brother Kiyi   What is there to play, Norma? I have nothing . . .

Norma   That's the problem – you don't see what you have. You have us, you have your shop.

Brother Kiyi   I don't have the shop any more, Norma! It's gone. I squander you money, OK?

Norma   I know. The whole of the street know.

Brother Kiyi   I'm sorry. I was waiting for you to come, I was going to call . . . But I plan to go out and . . . I'm going to get you money for you, Norma, it might take a little longer than I thought, but . . .

Norma   So that's it, then?

Brother Kiyi   Look so.

Norma   Not the shop, me and you? If you don't have here when am I going to see you?

Brother Kiyi   Come to my yard, I'll come to yours.

Norma   When was the last time you came by my house, Kiyi?

Brother Kiyi   Um, I came . . .

Norma   You know the last time you come? When the car knock me down and I was lay up in me bed for six weeks . . .

Brother Kiyi   Well, there you go then.

Norma   That was three years ago. That's not coming to see your friend. You only came because you thought I was going to dead. When last you just pick up yourself and say you'll come by me?

Brother Kiyi   I don't like other people's houses . . .

Norma   I is 'other people'?

Brother Kiyi   No, but . . .

Norma   But what . . . ?

Brother Kiyi   Family homes are for families, alright?

Norma   What shit is that?

Brother Kiyi   It's not shit, OK. Now I'm gonna get your money by hook or by crook.

Norma *turns to walk out but stops.*

Norma   Give me little satisfaction, Kiyi. When I come back me and you going to see Mustafar. Together.

Brother Kiyi   It's not going to do no good, Norma.

Norma   Did you hear me? If me have to lose ting never let it be said that I didn't fight. Good.

She leaves.

Lights down.

Scene Five

Fix Up bookstore. The next day, early morning.

There's a knock on the front door of the store. It's **Alice**. *She knocks three or four times before* **Kwesi** *eventually goes to the door.*

Kwesi   Kiyi's out.

Alice   Cool, I'll wait for him.

Kwesi   He didn't tell me to let anyone in.

Alice   Oh come on, Kwesi, open the door, it's cold out here.

Kwesi   Let me get the keys. (*He opens the shop door.*) New hairstyle. Nice.

Alice   Thank you for noticing.

Kwesi   Any problems, I'm upstairs.

Alice   As usual.

Kwesi   As usual!

Alice   Would be nice sometimes to converse!

Kwesi   Yeah, it would, wouldn't it?

Kwesi *goes upstairs.*

Alice *takes the key to the chest of drawers from the desk. She opens the drawer and removes the box.*

The box slips and falls to the ground, making a loud sound. She picks it up after looking to see if **Kwesi** *is coming.*

She takes the box to the desk and opens it. She pulls out the old photo album. **Alice** *is a little surprised. She holds it in her hands, but doesn't open it for a moment. She checks over her shoulder that no one is around, and nervously places it on the table.*

If we could hear her heart beating it would be dangerously fast.

As she sits, the lights dim slightly until she is in a spotlight. She opens the photo album and turns to the first page. She gasps, covers her mouth with her hand as if trying to keep in what wants to come gushing out, and stares at the picture.

She turns to the next page and, without trying, tears begin to fall. She quickly turns to the next page, and the next, and lands on one that instantly makes her clench her teeth, cover both her eyes and silently moan.

Suddenly the lights snap back up. A hand lands on her shoulder. She jumps up.

Alice   Ahhh! What the hell are you doing?

She slams the album shut behind her, almost hiding it.

Kwesi   I heard a bang.

Alice   Haven't I told you before about creeping up on me?

Kwesi   I wasn't creeping up on you.

Alice   Of course you were.

Kwesi   Easy na! Calm down. I wasn't.

Alice   Don't tell me what to do! . . .

Kwesi   I'm not *telling* you anything . . .

Alice   Yes, you are!

He attempts to grab her.

Kwesi   Listen . . .

Alice   Get off.

She starts to hit him in his chest.

Get off me . . .

He holds her tighter to calm her down.

Kwesi   I don't know about mans where you come from, but don't be shouting up at me.

Alice   Why, what you gonna do, hit me? I'm use to that . . .

Kwesi   Don't be stupid, what am I going to hit you for?

Alice   Then what? What? Whatever you're gonna do, do it!

She begins to sob. **Kwesi** *doesn't know what to do.*

Still in his arms, she turns away.

Kwesi *starts to look at the desk. It must be something she was reading. He sees the photo album.*

Alice *kisses him deep. Unsure of what is going on, he half-kisses her back.*

The kissing becomes more intense. **Alice** *starts to undo his shirt. He is a little surprised but allows her to do it, then she begins to undo his trousers.*

Kwesi   What are you? . . .

She puts her finger to his lips.

Alice   Ssshhhhh!

She starts to kiss him. He takes her by the hand as if to lead her upstairs. She pulls him back into the desk.

Alice   No. I want you here.

They kiss.

Kwesi   Upstairs.

He takes her by the hand and leads her upstairs. She follows, still staring back at the photo album. As they reach the stairs she kisses him.

Silence.

After a few beats **Carl** *appears from behind a bookcase.*

The anger rises. He runs over to a bookshelf and throws loads of books off.

As he is throwing the books all over the place a bare-chested **Kwesi** *comes running down the stairs. He sees* **Carl** *wrecking the joint.*

Kwesi   Carl! What the fuck are you doing? What you doing?

Carl   No. What are you doing, Kwesi?

Kwesi   What?

Carl   Who's upstairs with you?

Kwesi   What you talking about?

Carl   I said who's upstairs with you, Kwesi?

Kwesi   No one.

Carl   Is Alice up there?

Kwesi   I don't know what you're talking about, but I figure you're losing your mind.

Carl   But you don't even like her, Kwesi?

Kwesi   Don't worry about what I like, you need to be . . .

Carl *makes to go upstairs.* **Kwesi** *blocks him.*

Kwesi   Where you going?

Carl   Get out my way! I need to talk to her.

Kwesi   You ain't got no business up there . . .

Carl   Yes, I have. This place still belongs to Kiyi, you know.

Kwesi   But right now that's my space.

Carl   Then why couldn't you settle with that? Why you gotta have everything, Kwesi?

Kwesi   Carl, I'm not going to tell you again.

Carl *makes to head upstairs again.*

Kwesi   Carl, didn't you hear me?

He pushes him back.

Carl   I wanna see if she's alright. (*Shouts.*) Alice . . . Alice, it's alright, I'm coming. I'm coming to save you. I'm coming.

He runs towards **Kwesi***.* **Kwesi** *tries to grab him They struggle.*

Kwesi   I . . . told . . . you . . . to . . . calm . . . the . . . fuck down.

Eventually they land on the floor.

Carl   Ahhhh, why you got to take everything? Ahhhh!

Kwesi   Calm down, Carl.

Carl (*screams*)   Touch me again and I'll kill you. You – you stolen from me, you're stealing from Kiyi . . .

Kwesi   I didn't steal nothing from no one.

Carl   Yes, you did. It's not no Turkish boys taking over the store, it's you. You and your Somalians. How could you do that to Kiyi? After all he's done for you!

Kwesi   Kiyi ain't done nothing for me. What Kiyi does he does for himself. Is it my fault he can't run his affairs? I made him default?

Carl   You bastard!

He runs at him again. They struggle.

Enter **Brother Kiyi** *and* **Norma**, *unseen by the boys.*

Brother Kiyi   What the . . . What's happening . . . ?

He runs over to the boys and tries to separate them.

Boys, what the hell is going on? . . . Boys, stop this!

Norma   What the arse!

Carl   I told you it was him, Kiyi – him! I told you!

Brother Kiyi   Carl!

Carl   Tell him who's taking over the shop on Monday, Kwesi. Who's got boxes and boxes of curl juice sitting upstairs? You're a thief!

Brother Kiyi   Carl, calm down.

Carl   Will you listen to me for once! I've seen the boxes of perm juice. Ask him, Kiyi, ask the ginal!

Brother Kiyi   Listen, Kwesi, tell this boy that . . .

Brother Kiyi *looks at* **Kwesi**. *He sees the truth in his eyes.*

Beat.

Kwesi (*makes the decision to go front foot softly*)   People don't – want – books. They wanna party, and look good, have the latest hairstyles, and nails and tattoos. That's where niggers be at, Kiyi. They ain't spending shit in here. Why should the other man take our money? That's why we powerless, cos we ain't where the money at.

Brother Kiyi   It ain't about money!

Kwesi   That's why you're on your knees picking up books people don't wanna buy, innit? Where's the respect in that?

Brother Kiyi   Selling Afro-sheen gonna get you respect?

Kwesi   It's gonna get me into the position that when you want to renew your lease you come to me! Five years from now, Afro-sheen gonna buy us a next store and a next store and a next. Before you know it we got all of this place! If we don't do it, Kiyi, the man next door's gonna. I've been trying to tell you . . .

Alice *enters. She is still slightly dishevelled.* **Brother Kiyi** *looks at the topless* **Kwesi***.*

Brother Kiyi *glances at* **Norma***. She stares at him. He looks away, embarrassed. No one knows what to do or say.*

Alice *stands by the desk.*

Brother Kiyi *sees the photo album. As he picks it up,* **Alice** *places her hand on it.*

Alice   Are these pictures . . . ?

Brother Kiyi   Private.

Alice   Is that so?

Alice *opens the album and points to the picture on the first page. It's of a six-month-old baby girl.*

Alice   What a cute baby! Who is this? (*A little more intense.*) Who is this, right here? The one with the ribbons and the silly dress? Aren't you going to answer me?

Norma   Kiyi, don't take this, don't let the young girl talk to you so!

Brother Kiyi Norma, let we talk later, na?

Norma I'm not leaving you!

Alice *produces a picture and shows* **Brother Kiyi** *the photo album.*

Alice You see this? This is the only picture I have of me as a child. Cheeks are a bit bigger, but hey! They look a lot alike, don't they? So I ask again, I wanna know who this is in the album?

Brother Kiyi You already know, there's no need for me to . . .

Alice Yes, there is a need! I need you to say, Alice, this is you. This is the child I gave away, this is the child I had and then couldn't be bothered or be arsed to look after so I dumped into some children's home to fend for herself, away from anything or anybody that cared, away from anyone that looked or sounded like her, away from all that is kin and natural and safe and you're a fucking fraud, Peter Allan, whatever you call yourself now, fucking Brother Kiyi. You're a fraud just like your fake fucking bookstore.

Brother Kiyi It's not fake!

Alice Look. You're more concerned about your stupid shop than you are about me, standing here before you, begging to be named, recognised.

Brother Kiyi You're not begging to be recognised. You know who you are!

Alice I do, do I?

Brother Kiyi Yes, otherwise you wouldn't have come here to play with me, to test me.

Alice I came to find out why I look the way I do, why I cross my legs when I'm afraid. And what did I find? A sad old man who pretends to love but hates everything around him.

Brother Kiyi I do not hate. Disappointed, maybe. Hurt, possibly, but I don't hate. I love my community. I built this for my community.

Alice You're making me want to throw up! What do you know about love? You leave your child to rot, to be raised by the very people you are educating your community against, and you talk about love? What did you build for me?

Brother Kiyi I'm not educating my people against anybody, I'm teaching them to love themselves.

Alice I AM YOUR CHILD!

Brother Kiyi You know that's exactly what your mother would do to me. Twist me up. Lose her temper and start to scream and I wouldn't know what to do. It's her spirit in you come to haunt me, innit? You come to haunt me, Chantella?

Alice My name is Alice!

Brother Kiyi Your mother named you Chantella.

Alice How did she even lay with a beast like you? You forced her, didn't you?

Brother Kiyi What the fuck are you talking about? What do you know about your mother? You don't know nothin'! You don't know what she took to be with me, what shit I took just walking down the street, just fucking being with her. What do you know? What do you know? What does your blasted generation know? Do you have people spitting at you in the street? Do you have shit smeared on your windows? Do you have the pressure that makes you strike at the ones you love?

Alice I don't know because you won't tell me!

Brother Kiyi What do you want me to say? What do you want me to say?

Alice I want to know why I don't have a mother!

Brother Kiyi Of course you have a mother.

Alice Why I don't have a mother that's here?

Brother Kiyi   I don't know – isn't your mother down there in Somerset or wherever you come from?

Alice   No. I don't have a mother, and I want one!

Brother Kiyi   Well, you can't, because I killed her, alright? Is that what you want me to say? Is that what you want? I – killed – her! I didn't mean to but I did, alright? I'm sorry. There! I've said it.

As if all the energy has been drained from her, she stands and simply stares at **Brother Kiyi**. *All his energy has suddenly gone as well.*

Brother Kiyi *looks between* **Alice** *and* **Norma**. *Although she had just worked it out,* **Norma** *has never heard* **Brother Kiyi** *say that before.*

Norma   Kiyi.

Alice *exits.*

Silence.

Eventually **Kwesi** *attempts to speak.*

Kwesi   I . . .

Brother Kiyi   Shhhhh! Please!

Kwesi   I didn't know she was your daughter.

Brother Kiyi *stares at him. He leaves.*

Lights down.

Scene Six

Fix Up bookstore. Saturday evening.

The shelves of the bookstore are half-empty.

Brother Kiyi *is sitting in the middle of the store. He is both physically and mentally in a world of his own.*

Slowly he starts to chop off his locks. When all are gone, he runs his hands through what remains of his hair. His hands eventually fall on his face. He screams.

Brother Kiyi   Ahhhhhhh!

Norma *re-enters the shop.*

Norma   You OK?

Brother Kiyi   Yes. Fine.

Norma   Well, everything done. Bernie waiting to go. What we can't fit in your garage we'll put in the shed. You coming?

Brother Kiyi   No, I'll walk if that's alright.

Norma *stares at* **Brother Kiyi**.

Brother Kiyi   What?

Norma   What do I do with all that I have learnt from you, Kiyi. If even *you* peddle lies, who can I trust?

Brother Kiyi   I don't know, Sister Norma.

Norma   I go see you.

Brother Kiyi   Yes.

She leaves.

He begins to sing the blues slave chant 'Adam' to himself. Very slowly, void of emotion.

Brother Kiyi   Ohhhhhh Eve, where is Adam. Ohhhhhhh Eve, Adam's in the garden picking up leaves.

Enter **Alice**.

Brother Kiyi (*without looking at her*)   An old slave chant from the Deep South. I would offer you something to read but I don't expect you will be staying here that long?

Alice   No.

Brother Kiyi   I like that. No more questions. Statements are clean, you know where you stand with statements, don't you? You weren't abandoned, you were taken.

Silence.

She doesn't answer. After a few beats he realises that it is pointless trying to explain.

He picks up the photo album and brings it to her.

She opens it and looks at the picture of her mother.

Brother Kiyi *stares at her, confirming the truth that she does look like her mother.*

She puts the photo album to her chest.

Brother Kiyi   I built this to shut out the cries. Of you.

Alice *takes that in.* **Brother Kiyi** *stands up, looks deep into* **Alice**'s *eyes and walks out.*

Alice *is left alone in the store still clutching the photo album.*

The lights go down.

Statement of Regret

The government is considering issuing a statement of regret for the slave trade on the two-hundredth anniversary of its abolition. Commemorations are to be held across the UK on 25 March, two centuries after the passing of an 1807 parliamentary bill outlawing the trade in the British empire.

The deputy prime minister, John Prescott, ruled out a formal apology for Britain's part in slavery earlier this year. But he will chair a meeting next month of the advisory committee overseeing preparations for the commemoration, at which proposals for a statement of regret are expected to be discussed.

Guardian, 22 September 2006

If you are the son of a man who had a wealthy estate and you inherit your father's estate, you have to pay off the debts that your father incurred before he died. The only reason that the present generation of white Americans are in a position of economic strength . . . is because our fathers worked for their fathers for over four hundred years with no pay . . . We were sold from plantation to plantation like you sell a horse, or a cow, or a chicken, or a bushel of wheat . . . All that money . . . is what gives the present generation of American whites the ability to walk around the earth with their chest out . . .

Malcolm X, *Malcolm Speaks*, 1962

We need first of all (for) the Caribbean Blacks to acknowledge we are not the same group as they are – to begin to learn about Africans, to begin to listen to us, to begin to understand that even if they have the African heritage they are not Africans any more.

Lola Ayonrinde,
Former Conservative Mayor of Wandsworth, 2006

Statement of Regret was first presented in the Cottesloe auditorium of the National Theatre, London, on 14 November 2007. The cast was as follows:

Kwaku Mackenzie	Don Warrington
Michael Akinbola	Colin McFarlane
Idrissa Adebayo	Chu Omambala
Issi	Angel Coulby
Lola Mackenzie	Ellen Thomas
Kwaku Mackenzie Junior	Javone Prince
Val	Trevor Laird
Adrian Mackenzie	Clifford Samuel
Soby	Oscar James

Directed by Jeremy Herrin
Designed by Mike Britton
Lighting design by Natasha Chivers
Music by Soweto Kinch
Sound design by Yvonne Gilbert

Characters

Kwaku Mackenzie, *late forties, early fifties. Black British of African Caribbean descent. Founder of the Institute of Black Policy Research (IBPR) think-tank.*

Michael Akinbola, *forty-nine. Black British of Nigerian descent. Deputy Director of IBPR.*

Idrissa Adebayo, *thirty-four. Black British of West African heritage. Research Director of IBPR. Oxbridge educated, gay and very clever.*

Issi Banjoko, *female, twenty-eight. Black British of West African descent. Very bright research fellow at IBPR. Oxbridge educated.*

Lola Mackenzie, *fifty-five, wife of Kwaku. Born in Nigeria but moved to Britain when she was sixteen. Head of Human Resources.*

Kwaku Mackenzie Junior, *twenty-six, son of Kwaku and Lola. Events manager at IBPR. Not as well spoken as the others. Did not go to university.*

Val Thomas, *late forties. Born in Trinidad, came to Britain with parents when he was three. An eccentric, glorified postman. Has been with Kwaku from the beginning.*

Adrian McKay, *twenty-five. Black British. Well-spoken. The office intern.*

Soby, *late sixties. West Indian businessman.*

Ideas and arguments are second nature to all of the characters. Thus related dialogue should almost fall out of their mouths with ease, comfort and pace; there is constant overlapping by the others who have often got the argument before a sentence has been completed.

Act One

Scene One

*We are in the offices of the Institute of Black Policy Research (IBPR) –
a privately run political think-tank. Chairs, eight in total, are being
placed along the edges by* **Kwaku Mackenzie**, *founder and director
of the company, immaculately dressed, authentic West Indian accent
when he wants to, but his straight English accent defies his working-class
roots – something he is very conscious of in this world dominated by
middle-class intellectuals.*

*On the walls are geopolitical maps of the Black world: Africa, the United
States, the Caribbean, Australia, etc. Socio-economic breakdowns of
Britain and America are mixed in with pleasant Afrocentric art – Chris
Offili, etc. – and pictures of* **Kwaku** *shaking hands with every prime
minister since Callaghan.*

There is a plaque on his desk with the words:

> At some future time the civilised races of the world will almost
> certainly exterminate and replace the savage races throughout the
> world – Charles Darwin, Descent of Man

The radio is playing via the internet on a computer in the background.

Lola Mackenzie – **Kwaku**'s *wife, head of Human Resources,
beautiful but sometimes strangely absent, mostly because she doesn't
really 'like' politics – enters the room quickly with a big Jamaican ginger
cake in her hands. She gives it to* **Kwaku**.

Lola   You forgot the cake!

Kwaku   Oh, thank you, wife. What would I do without you?

*She stops and stares him right in the eye. After a beat or so she lets out a
small huff and walks out.*

Kwaku *removes the Jamaican ginger cake from the wrapper and starts
to cut it into pieces. When done, he places it in the centre of the table and
steps back to see if it is indeed centred.*

The song on the radio changes to Johnny Cash's 'There Are More Questions than Answers'. **Kwaku** *slowly stops what he's doing and looks towards the computer. It is as if a dark cloud has suddenly descended. He pauses for a moment, unsure quite how or what to do. He moves quickly to the computer and switches it off. Still unsure what to do, he lets his head slowly fall, till eventually, even though he has tried not to, his eyes begin to swell – not crying, just simply swelling. Embarrassed at his sniffing, he catches himself and wipes his eyes just as* **Michael Akinbola***, his partner, deputy director and best friend, not quite as clothes conscious but well dressed, with a cut-glass English accent, enters.* **Michael** *is Nigerian but never uses his Nigerian accent in the office.*

He knows what has just happened but tries to avoid it for a moment. Giving **Kwaku** *enough time to gather himself,* **Michael** *spots a bottle of 'home' white rum on the table and points to it.*

Michael (*not looking at him until eyes are clear*)   How many bottles of rum did you bring back with you, boy?

Kwaku (*laughs*)   A whole suitcase! That's what happens when your best friend flies you first class. Dem na look in you luggage!

Michael *smiles.*

Michael (*sensitive but straight*)   What else have I got to spend my money on . . . You OK?

Now **Kwaku** *is together,* **Michael** *switches on his computer without mentioning it.*

Kwaku   Yeah yeah, of course . . .

He returns to laying out the drinks. **Michael** *then joins him.*

Kwaku (*changing/avoiding subject*)   So, here's one for you: US elections it's down to Condi or Hillary, who you vote for?

Michael   Condi's not standing!

Kwaku   Don't be a claat, I know that . . .

Michael   . . . Plus I'm not an American!

Kwaku . . . Alright, if you wanna be obtuse, for the purpose of this discussion, you are a Yank, you're at the polling booth –

Michael I'm not trying to be obtuse –

Kwaku No, you're doing what you normally do when you don't want to answer a question, you're being fucking rude – now answer the bloodclaat question!

Michael And you're doing what you normally do when you want to bully an answer out of someone – you start swearing in Jamaican.

Kwaku (*knowing full well*) I don't do that! . . .

Michael You blatantly do.

Kwaku I swear when I'm getting vex . . . frustrated that a very fucking simple question takes you eight bloodclaat hours to answer. Put the cake over there, it looks better.

Michael Holidays are suppose to relax you, you know!

Kwaku It was an extended business trip that you told me to go on.

Michael (*deliberately*) I didn't tell you to go away for three months.

Kwaku Answer the question, Michael!

Michael What was it again?

Kwaku *pauses, stares, knowing he's being wound up.*

Kwaku (*spells it out*) You have the power to make Condoleezza Rice the first black female president of the United States. Do you do it and hand power back to the right, or do you give the power back to white folk?

Michael What do you think I'd do?

Kwaku Hillary.

Michael That's right. You?

Kwaku Mind your own business, voting is private . . . Condi.

Michael (*outraged*)   That's madness, you hate the right . . .

Kwaku   I didn't say it was correct, did I? But it's what ninety-five per cent of the human race would do – vote for their own.

Michael (*empathically*)   Well, they're are wrong!

Kwaku   You said 'three months' as if as if I'd done something wrong.

Michael (*suddenly catching up*)   I don't think it's wrong, it's just, well, when you were away I had to work really hard to keep everyone motivated.

Kwaku   I was at the end of a line.

Michael   That costs the company money. And anyway I don't want to disturb you over little things . . .

Kwaku   Little tings like what?

Michael   Well, like today, for instance. Steve at the bank called, said there wasn't enough money in the account to cover payroll.

Kwaku   I told you to bounce everything back to me, why'd he call you?

Michael   Cos he didn't know if you were back.

Kwaku   Tings that bad?

Michael   For now.

Kwaku   What did you say?

Michael   I'd get back to him once I'd spoken to you.

Kwaku   OK, I'll call him in the morning, get him to bump some over from the surplus saving account . . .

Michael   Are you sure? Now you've said that, I can do it.

Kwaku   That's why we got the savings, ain't it?

Michael   I know *that*, but . . .

Kwaku   Listen, maybe it's you that needs the break, it's simple tings! You're too conservative with money, I tried to tell you . . .

Michael   It's not the money, I just wanted to make sure that you'd remember to do it, that's all.

Beat.

Kwaku   Of course I'll remember. I'm fine, Michael – really. Top of the world.

Michael *stares at him, aware that* **Kwaku** *is playing up for him.*

Michael   Hey, I know, today is your father's day . . . in fact, forget words – come here – come here, come here . . .

Kwaku (*knows what's coming*)   What? Ahhh, stop that stuff . . . No go away, go away . . . What's wrong with you, man? You know I don't do that huggy stuff!

Michael *runs and catches* **Kwaku**.

Michael   When Maria left me, did I tell you that? No, you said, 'I'm your brother and I love you' and that you'd put a hit out on the fool she left me for.

Kwaku *stops and accepts the argument.* **Michael** *gives him a big hug.* **Kwaku** *eventually hugs him back. Then pulls back and smiles.*

Kwaku   Thank you, comrade. But umm, he's here with me! Ever here . . . (*Changing the subject.*) Maybe you should take that holiday – I'll even pay.

Michael   What you, you tight git? I'll think about it.

He hugs him again. Enter **Idrissa**, *research director – casual smart dress, Rolls-Royce brain, very quick, very clever. The kind of person who is biding their time in a think tank till they break into mainstream politics. He sees the men hugging, something he has seen many times.* **Issi**, *research fellow and finance officer, also enters. A do-gooder by nature, should really be at a big charity or NGO.*

Idrissa   Bundddle – group hug.

Kwaku   Heyyy! Stop that stupidness.

The group cheer and do the group-hug thing. **Kwaku** *breaks away and he and* **Michael** *pop the bottles of champagne.*

Issi   Hey, Kwaku, you look great!

Kwaku   That's what a man likes to hear on his first day back. And it's all because of him. (*Pointing to* **Michael**.) I love this man.

Dashing in just as the biggest champagne bottle pops is **Kwaku Mackenzie Jnr**, *better known to all as* **Junior**. *He is very sharply dressed, very verbose in an almost childish way, but very lovable.* **Kwaku** *looks at him without warmth.*

Junior   Immaculate timing as usual, even if I say so myself.

Kwaku (*plenty of side*)   No one ever need talk for you, Junior.

Junior (*ignores him*)   Hey hey, watch this joke I just get.

All   Oh nooo, Junior, no more of your jokes!

Junior   Alright, your loss, this one was a classic.

Enter **Lola**.

Kwaku   Where's Val?

Lola   He'll be here soon.

Kwaku   OK everybody, grab your glasses. And for those that want something a little stronger – I have a bottle of Clarke's Court from home. Two thousand per cent proof. Puts hairs on your chest.

Issi   Not a good look for me, I'm afraid. Hope that wasn't produced using child labour or anything?

Kwaku *smiles at her knowingly, then catches himself. He and* **Michael** *fill the glasses.*

Kwaku   Anyway, Michael said the press launch went well this afternoon . . . ?

Issi   Brilliantly. Well done, Junior.

Junior   Thank you.

Kwaku   Well, on behalf of Michael and me, thank you. An organisation such as ours is judged by one thing and one thing alone – its results. And today, we, you, got a result . . .

All   Hurahhh, damn right we did.

Kwaku   But, well, it's ridiculous me talking, I wasn't here doing the hard work. Michael, finish off na, you speak posher than me anyway.

Michael *reluctantly accepts. But this is always his role.*

Michael   Well, I'd just like to second Kwaku's words – everyone said we were crazy coming up with this whole Minister for Race thing, but the power of your research and the quality of our arguments today have borne fruit. Hayden Johnson, the first ever Minister for Race. And even the *Daily Mail*, actually only the *Daily Mail*, attributed the idea to us. It wasn't very complimentary but a mention is better than a kick up the proverbial. So, (*he lifts his glass*) to you, the best think-tankers in the game, well done, cheers.

All   Cheers.

They all swig their drinks down.

Kwaku   There's some Jamaican ginger cake there. I've already cut it, so help yourselves and, yep, top up, and then pull the chairs up and lets get down to some work.

As the assembled top up, in dashes **Val Henry**, **Kwaku**'s *eccentric oldest employee. His official title is Communications Director – but what that really means is he is a glorified postman who sits in at all meetings on* **Kwaku**'s *say-so. He is* **Kwaku**'s *eyes and ears, almost his talisman. Today he is wearing heavy boots and matching Hawaiian shorts and top.*

Junior (*half showing off to* **Issi**)   Hey, Valerie, hurry up, you gonna miss all the – how he call it? All the devil brew, and you wouldn't want to do that, would you?

Val   I done told you a hundred times, don't call me no fucking Valerie, sorry ladies, my name is Val. My modder call me Val. Val, OK?

Junior (*spooky*)   Oowww, the brew is calling youuu.

Val (*warning*)   Stop provoking me.

Kwaku   Leave the man alone na, Junior. One day he's gonna flip on you arse, and you go see.

Junior   Yeah, yeah.

Kwaku   Val, I've got you some sorrel juice, OK?

Val (*snaps*)   I don't want nothing . . . I'm fasting!

Kwaku   What you fasting for?

Val   You forget, Thelma Burgess child dead last week? Tonight is the nine night. Man has to be clean for when the spirit leaves the earth for the last time.

Kwaku   Right . . . fine. So, Val, you want to kick us off in customary fashion?

Val   Fadder, bless the minds, the thoughts and the deeds that may come from this union. In your blessed name.

They open their eyes. **Kwaku** *looks to* **Lola**, *who indicates that she's ready to take notes.* **Idrissa** *didn't close his eyes in the first place.*

Kwaku   Alright, I just want to say on record it's great to be back at work. Now, we've not been hitting the back of the net much of late so now, while we're hot, this is the time to really press our new and existing idea home. Michael, how's the tax relief on the African remittance project going?

Michael   Meeting at DfID went well this morning, they like the idea in principal and are willing to fund the initial research.

Junior   Does our new Department of Race have a say on it?

Michael   No, no, International Development.

Junior   Pity, I'd say we could double the budget.

They all laugh.

Kwaku Issi?

Issi Having difficulty finding a model for African Remembrance Day that they think Gordon will run with . . .

Kwaku Can we tie it up with our reparations agenda at all?

Idrissa *huffs under his breath.*

Issi We shouldn't, people have had slavery overload. If they're separate ideas, we have to get two separate 'no's.

Kwaku There is not going to be a 'no' – now's our time! . . . Hayden will be up for this I know, but I'm wary of throwing everything at him in his first few weeks.

Junior We are his favourite think-tank!

Kwaku Yes, which is why we have to think strategically. Never your strong point, Junior.

Idrissa (*huffs loudly*) Junior?!

Idrissa *looks towards* **Michael**.

Kwaku What?

Beat as they all look to the ground. **Idrissa** *still looking at* **Michael**.

Kwaku What?

Michael (*carefully*) Well, we kind of had a unit discussion on Friday ahead of this just to get you up to speed, and Idrissa had some thoughts that maybe we should take the opportunity to speak about now?

Kwaku Indeed. Idrissa?

Idrissa I'm used to success, Kwaku, one mention in the *Daily Mail* in six months is not my definition of it. We're not publishing anywhere near enough material for us to be viable any more, and that's because . . .

Kwaku I wouldn't say that's true!

Idrissa   . . . Well, you've not been here. When was the last time we were asked to comment on anything in the press or even had an editorial written about an idea we've put out there?

Kwaku   Today!

Idrissa   That wasn't an editorial and the idea wasn't really ours. You guys know me – I'm sorry, but I speak my mind. We run this place as if the Brixton riots were something anyone actually fucking remembers. Our thinking is in the Ice Age, people, our agenda is old school . . .

Kwaku (*calm*)   I don't think fighting for a Minister for Race is old school. Neither do I think that fighting for reparations for the holocaust of slavery is . . .

Idrissa   Reparations is a dead dog. When those children are killing each other on the streets like animals, think anyone cares about reparations?

Kwaku   Did the Jewish community say that? Did the Japanese say that to the Americans, if I remember de de de facts correctly . . . (*he tries*) in umm, umm, 19 . . .

Then looks to **Michael**.

Michael (*quickly*)   '88.

Kwaku   . . . '88, that's right, they received . . . (*Grapples with his mind for the numbers.*) How much again, Michael? Tell him.

Idrissa (*irritated, he reels off*)   We all know for the internment of Japanese Americans during World War Two the Yanks gave 1.2 billion dollars, payments of 20,000 dollars to each of the 60,000 internees still alive and for the establishment of a 50-million-dollar foundation to promote the cultural and historical concerns of Japanese Americans. That – was – yesterday!

Kwaku (*almost smiling*)   Really? So, at this meeting you had, was this 'we are in a time warp' theory the general consensus?

Idrissa   The consensus was that self-flagellating liberalism is dead. It was never going to last for ever and we are stupid to think that it was. The agenda has changed and we've got to skip to the beat or die. Today my friends, the money is in self-criticism.

Junior   What does that mean when it's at home?

Idrissa   That they want to know that we can look at our problems objectively and not always blame the white man for our every fucking woe.

Kwaku   Oh, self-hate you mean?

Idrissa (*perplexed*)   Why does introspection have to mean self-hate? Isn't that what democracy . . .

They are all shouting.

All   Twenty quid – In the sin bin – haaa! You know that word's not allowed . . .

Idrissa   Oh shit! I wasn't being lazy, sometimes you have to just use that word. Maybe we should look at that rule too.

He takes twenty pounds and places it in the middle of the table. **Junior** *gets up and puts the money in the swear box.*

Michael   Carry on, Idrissa.

Kwaku *clocks the tacit encouragement.*

Idrissa   I've run a couple of things past a few people – advisors, journalists and the like – and they all have responded positively.

Kwaku (*surprised*)   You've spoken to people already?

Idrissa   Friends. Bear with me, OK, these are just headlines, suggestions – things to just get us out there again.

Kwaku   OK.

Idrissa   OK. Ready? Why black men beat black women –

Kwaku/Junior/Lola (*outraged*)   What . . . ?

Idrissa   I know we can get money for that. Listen, listen, we do an authoritative report on the social causes of domestic violence seen through the prism of race. It serves women in our community that are victims of domestic abuse but it also serves the wider community – violence amongst the underclasses. Debate will run from Derry to Glasgow to Harlesden bloody High Street. Right at the heart of it – your social agenda. Invest in people, or it costs more in the long run.

Kwaku   How does that serve us, Idrissa?

Idrissa (*riffs*)   Alright, another angle, on the equality platform or even health – have white men caught up in the genitalia department? The myth of black male genitalia. How has that contributed to notions of modern inferiority, or even current social dysfunction? I mean, I can't speak for anyone else, but I'm experiencing very little difference . . .

Val (*exclaims*)   Stop that batty-man business! I rebuke you in the name of Jesus.

Idrissa   I mean, there's another one – rampant homophobia in the black community – causes of and cures for.

Kwaku   We can't put out that kind of stuff . . . what does it say?

Idrissa *stands.*

Idrissa   It says debate, people – debate. Debate, ideas are everything.

Junior   But . . .

Idrissa   But nothing . . . for Christ's sake let's stop lying to ourselves. We've always been in the business of giving white people what they want. Now they want something else. And if we don't give it to them, someone else will. The revolution will not be subsidised, my straight brothers.

Kwaku   Anyone else see it like Idrissa does?

All are wary of comment.

Michael   I think there's an element of truth in it, yes.

Issi   There's an argument that post-7/7 we're in a different world. Yes, I suppose I am in agreement.

Kwaku   Lola?

Lola   Oh, I leave the thinking to you guys –

Kwaku (*slightly irritated*)   Lola?

Lola   From my point of view – it's hard enough finding good-quality black folk that *want* to work for us. If we're being perceived as behind the curve – it's a discussion we should be having.

Junior   I don't like the sound of it.

Kwaku *looks at* **Val**.

Kwaku   Val?

Val   I don't know, what would Jesus say at a time like this?

Junior *bursts out laughing. They all want to laugh but stare at* **Junior** *till he stops.*

Val   I suggest we all read Psalm 111 and pray on it.

Kwaku   Right. OK. Well, I think we've gone just about as far as we can with this debate. I'm due to meet Hayden tomorrow, let's see what he thinks about where we stand in the marketplace . . . Final point on the agenda, the shortlist for our new intern.

Issi   It's not my decision, but it comes down to two for me and I have my favourite . . .

Junior   I don't give a toss, intern is an intern . . .

Val (*to* **Junior** *with side*)   . . . So long as they pretty, right?

Junior *ignores this.* **Kwaku** *looks at* **Junior**, *then continues.*

Kwaku   What I was going to say is that I met this wonderful young man a few nights ago, Oxford and, um, some university in the States . . .

Lola *looks up and stares almost violently at* **Kwaku**.

Kwaku   And, um, as you said an intern is an intern but I think this guy is perfect for us. So – if you all don't mind? – I have his CV here for you all to browse at your leisure.

He looks in his case, but it is not there.

Oh sugar, must have left it at home. I'll email you all tonight. In principle, everybody cool wid dat?

They all shrug shoulders, nod in gentle agreement.

Issi   We did say, Kwaku, we were going to try an' balance out the testosterone in this office.

Junior   How many women do you want? We already got three – you, Valerie and Idrissa.

Val   . . . I told you already.

Kwaku   Junior, stop being an arse. So, if everyone's in agreement, meeting adjourned. Val?

Val   Father, thank you for the wisdom, thank you for the guidance. And thank you for not letting me put a sharp pickaxe in Junior's brain. Amen.

Kwaku   See you all in the morning.

Val   Sunshine, come back – when you was gone them forgot you start this cos of me, you na! (*Whispers.*) Is like them wanted to push me out.

Kwaku   Well, I haven't forgotten – as long as I'm here you're OK.

Michael   I gotta dash to a meeting at church, K, I'll call you in an hour.

Michael *leaves with the others.* **Lola** *turns to* **Kwaku** *and speaks so that the others cannot hear.*

Lola   I know where you're going with this intern business. Don't do it, Kwaku. I'm warning you, I tolerate many things, but I won't tolerate that. You hear me?

Kwaku   Is that all you have to say to me – today – on this day?

She walks away without answering.

Issi   Kwaku, can I see you for a moment?

Kwaku   Of course.

Lola *is the last one out of the door. She looks back at* **Kwaku** *and* **Issi** *over her shoulder.*

Issi   Sorry about all of that Idrissa stuff.

Kwaku (*angered*)   Why didn't you tell me last night?

Issi   That's outside my job description, Kwaku . . .

Kwaku (*with doubt*)   You really think we have to go down that road, Issi?

Issi   Maybe for a little while.

Kwaku   Twenty-five years fighting every negative thing they've thrown at us, black organisations can't survive without ripping themselves off or apart, there's no constituency for black thought, etc., etc., only to put out ideas more racist than the men I came into this to fight? Maybe I'm getting too old?

Issi   You're the sharpest man I know.

Kwaku   Used to be, maybe. (*Sensitive.*) You think I should wrap this ting up, Issi?

Issi *kisses him very gently on the lips. We can see that they have been intimate before.* **Kwaku** *quickly looks over her shoulder at the door. Still in the kiss, she bites his lip and draws a little blood.*

Kwaku   Owi!

They have done this before as well. **Kwaku** *wipes the blood away, without expression. But* **Issi** *smiles a little.*

Issi   Whatever you decide, it will be the right decision. I know that.

She moves away. **Kwaku** *looks hard and long at her. That was not the right answer. When she gets to the door she smiles and leaves.*

Lights. Over Max Romeo's roots rock reggae classic 'One Step Forward'.

Scene Two

Issi *is working at her computer.* **Val***, dressed today in a Native American outfit – headgear but not the full feathered business – is handing out mail, but covertly attempts to listen in on* **Idrissa** *and* **Michael***'s conversation.* **Idrissa** *is sitting on* **Michael***'s desk and they are speaking quietly.* **Michael** *keeps glancing to see if* **Val** *is listening.*

Idrissa   . . . And they've called me three times to see if we've spoken yet. That's how much they want you, Michael.

Michael   Really?

Idrissa   Now this is not for me to say . . .

Michael   . . . But you going to say it anyway.

Idrissa   Baby, you don't have to turn twice and you'll be fifty, let this opportunity pass and I don't know how many more offers like that you're going to get. You gonna play second fiddle to that drunkard for ever?

Michael (*firm*)   Don't speak about him like that, OK?

Issi (*shouts*)   . . . What's the name of the female President of Liberia again?

Michael   Umm, umm, Ellen Johnson-Sirleaf.

Idrissa *gets off the table and walks back to his desk with his manuscript.*

Idrissa   Johnson-Sirleaf! That's not a very African name, is it?

Michael   Her great-grandfather was a freed slave who repatriated – or was he European?

Idrissa (*innocently*)   Oh yeah, they're like the West Indies up there. Full up of whitey.

Michael   Idrissa!

Val   That's not a very nice thing to say, is it?

Idrissa   What, that Liberians have a lot of European in them? It's not like I called them slave babies or something.

Val *kisses his teeth loudly. The others shake their heads.*

Idrissa   What? What? You gonna deny it now? It's all up on the TV in that genealogical show – West Indians have like sixteen or twenty per cent white blood in them. Are they being horrible when they say that?

Junior *walks into the office, having heard the end of the conversation.*

Junior   Idrissa, what nonsense you going on about now?

Idrissa   I was simply explaining the genealogical history of the African Caribbeans. You guys – well not you, cos your mother's African, you're more like three-quarters . . .

Junior   Sometimes you sound like pre-emancipated Germany, boy. Anyway, fuck all this, hear da joke I just got on my phone. You gonna love this one, Idrissa . . . Wait, wait, it wasn't you that sent it me, was it?

Idrissa   I doubt it. What gag is it?

Junior   'Bush in hell . . . '

Issi   Where he goes down on Clinton?

Junior   Oh shit, you've heard it?

Idrissa   Why did you think I'd like that?

Junior   Cos he sucking dick innit! Haaaa!

Idrissa   OK, OK, that's how we playing it today huh? If racism didn't make it two -isms, you homophobes would lose my black arse in a heartbeat. Backward black people!

Adrian   . . . Where?

*They all turn and see **Adrian McKay** – attractive, very bright and smartly dressed, except for the mud on his shoes – standing at the* *entrance to the office. He is scanning every detail of the room from where he stands.*

Michael   Hello, can I help you?

Adrian   This is the IBPR, right?

Michael   Yes.

Adrian   Then I doubt if I'll find any in here.

Michael   Any what?

Adrian   Backward black people . . .

They all look at him. The gag didn't work.

I'm Adrian McKay.

Michael   Adrian?

Adrian   The new intern?

Beat as we see that something is wrong for **Michael***.*

Michael   Are you sure?

Adrian   My letter says quite clearly the IBPR . . .

Michael (*catching himself being watched*)   Of course, I just didn't think you were starting today.

Adrian (*humble*)   You must be Michael . . . I've read much of your work, sir. Your early essays on culture, media and race have influenced me greatly.

Michael (*wary*)   Thank you. Actually, could we speak outside?

He stands, still working out what is the best thing to do.

Issi   Introductions, then. I'm Issimama, our brilliant research fellow. I also do payroll on the side. Good person to know.

Adrian   Pleased to meet you.

Issi   Pleased to meet you too. This is Kwaku Mackenzie Junior – our Operations/Events manager . . .

Junior   Junior! Good to meet you.

Adrian So you're Junior?

Junior That's what the lady just said.

Adrian You look different to the picture on the website.

Idrissa He was having a bad hair day.

Adrian Gosh, must be weird having your father's name and working in the same place?

Junior Which is why people call me Junior.

Junior And this is Val, our longstanding postman . . .

Val Spiritual officer . . .

Issi Of course.

Val Greetings!

Junior Val. Why are we dressed as a Native American today?

Val (*isn't it obvious*) Black Indian power, innit. Chávez, the role of people of colour is rising. (*He points violently to* **Idrissa**.) And you, shut your mouth. I don't want to know what he is or isn't to you, OK? (*Back to* **Adrian**.) We got to let the people them know. Communication isn't just about TV. Gotta make them see it on the streets, on the Tube.

Adrian You, you travel on the Tube like . . .

Val (*smiles*) Yeah man, every day.

Adrian Respect, I dig Chávez big time.

Val Love-ins.

Issi And last but not least . . .

Idrissa Idrissa Adebayo. Head of Policy.

Adrian Good to meet you, sir.

Idrissa Not quite, sir, yet, but it's coming! How you doing?

Adrian Good, thank you.

Idrissa   Welcome to the IBPR.

Junior (*jumps in*)   Don't think I'm rude, I'm just checking, but being an intern and all, you're not adverse to doing the morning coffee run, are you?

Adrian   Not at all . . .

Junior   Here's a tenner, mine's a latte, chai latte, his is a double capp, hot chocolate for Val, and what you having, Idrissa?

Idrissa   I'm fine actually.

Junior   Oh yeah, and an *Evening Standard*.

Adrian *stares at him for a beat.*

Enter **Kwaku** *who has a suit-carrier in his hands. He is not drunk but all can smell the drink on his breath. He walks past* **Idrissa**. *He's in a steely-eyed, down-to-business mood.*

Kwaku   What you fine about, Idrissa? You're never fine. Adrian, you're here already?

Adrian   You did say eleven.

Kwaku   Did I? Never mind, it's good to be early.

Once **Kwaku** *has walked past* **Idrissa**, **Idrissa** *doubles, sniffs, and recognises the smell. Alcohol. He looks up at* **Michael**, *a look* **Michael** *reads and understands. Sadness falls over his face.*

Adrian   I tend not to do BPT.

Kwaku   Black people time can sometimes be an advantage.

Idrissa   When?

Kwaku   I can't quite tell you off the top of my head, but got to defend your people, right?

Adrian   Yes, sir.

Michael   What's the suit for, K?

Kwaku   Race in the Media Award ceremony tonight innit!

Michael   It was last Tuesday.

Beat.

Kwaku   Oh shit, I must have put it on the wrong day . . .
my bloody hand-held keeps messing up. (*Quickly turns to*
Adrian.)

Michael (*jumping in*)   Kwaku, can I talk to you a moment?

Kwaku   Not just yet. Adrian, sit down everybody, gather
round right away. As the ragga DJ Cutty Ranks was fond of
saying, 'Wait dere man – uno think me did done.' Roughly
translated for our non-ghetto employees . . . hold up a minute,
you thought I was all washed up. Junior, take the minutes. I've
been thinking . . . Let's have an hoorah for that!

All   Hoorah!

Kwaku   Though money has never been a motivating factor,
as we've established, we need to bring some in. I accept maybe
our output has not been reflective enough of what we all think.
I want to throw some ideas at ya and see if you agree with the
direction of travel. I think this will revitalise our stock, and
that's what you've been speaking about, right?

Idrissa   In essence.

Kwaku   So, point one: if we wish to influence public policy,
we need more profile . . .

Idrissa *looks at* **Michael** – *is he OK?*

Kwaku   Issi, I think one of your discussion papers last year
looked at the disproportionate number of black homeless kids?

Issi   The Centrepoint Report.

Kwaku   So, I got on to the phone last night, called Michael
at the *Black Nation*, pulled in the Blair apology exclusive favour,
and he's going to run a big spread about us in next week's
edition. 'Why Black People Need to Think!', something like
that.

Idrissa   The *Black Nation*?

Kwaku   Yes – problem?

Idrissa   No, I love the paper but –

Kwaku (*speeds*)   Right. Also called Maddy at the *Guardian* – she's willing to do the same, but one proviso, it's got to be around something new. So, Issi, I want you to get in contact with a handful of the most deserving kids you interviewed – and I'm going to call a couple of the famous 'ballers, get them to stump up some money. Oprah style. We buy three small little terraces – redo them and a few of the childs dem are rehoused – a black housing system inspired by one of our ideas. (*Points at* **Idrissa**.) With our own black money. Use that template all over the country.

Michael   Footballers don't put up money.

Adrian   Rio Ferdinand did.

Kwaku (*ignores*)   And then there's education – well, that wide open for us now – and it's one of Hayden's and Gordon's pet subjects.

Michael   What would be our angle on education? We've already done –

Kwaku   That was five years ago! We find the new research that will support a big recruitment drive for young black teachers helping to tackle institutionalised racist exclusions of black boys, and let's call them racist – always causes a stir.

Idrissa (*laughs almost*)   Not that old chestnut?!

Kwaku   You know, Idrissa, sometimes you can be really aggressively negative.

Idrissa   If these white teachers are so racist, why are African boys doing well?

Kwaku   What do you mean?

Idrissa   Just what I said – African Caribbean are the ones fucking up, not Africans.

Kwaku   Umm, well . . .

Idrissa   Well what? See, you can't answer that, can you? Dragging out old chestnuts like racist white teachers and institutionalised . . . Aaghhhh.

Kwaku   What, what are you trying to say, it's the kids dem fault?

Idrissa   Yes I am! There's research in the States that shows African Americans are scoring beneath their white peers from primary school to law school. Yet new African immigrants with English as a second language are outstripping the Afro Americans every time. Why? Those are the questions we should be asking if we want to be relevant. Jesus, did you say new ideas?

Adrian   Maybe it's because the African boys did not have to go through the trauma of slavery.

Kwaku   That's it, boy, in at the deep end.

Idrissa   Now that's depressing. (*Almost disbelief.*) Where were you educated again?

Kwaku   Careful now, 'Drissa fights nasty.

Adrian   Oxford and Portland State.

Idrissa (*ignoring the other*)   Oxford, and you allow yourself to think like that?

Adrian   Like what?

Idrissa   Like a . . .

Michael   Leave the boy alone, Dris.

Idrissa   No, he's part of the team, gotta treat him like an equal. Thinking like a dinosaur. Please name me one person alive in Tottenham, say, that you know was a slave? Or even knew someone that was a slave, apart from to crack. I mean, I'm as right-on as the next guy, but . . .

Adrian   . . . Was that to the right of the next guy?

Idrissa   *Touché*, but you're too young to be looking backwards. Issi, tell them your idea. It's fantastic. I've already identified a sponsor for this report.

Issi   Oh, um, OK. It's a discussion around 'Black Women and the Crisis Facing Black Men', how this informs their experiences of rape and sexual assault.

Kwaku   WHAT?

Val   Rape?

Issi   Its central point being that not only are black women dealing with racism and sexism from white mainstream society, but we're also dealing with sexism from within our community, and who are we going to tell?

Kwaku   'We'? Who is this 'we'?

Adrian   What about the women that like rape?

Kwaku   OK, maybe that's jumping in too deep . . .

Adrian   Not strangers-jumping-you-down-an-alley kind of stuff, but for kicks.

Issi   That is so objectionable . . .

Adrian (*looks at* **Idrissa**)   Yes it is, isn't it? As objectionable to me as hearing 'those who are not from the continent are somehow inferior wherever they are in the world'.

Val   Murderrr! Gwan, new boy. Idrissa, you meet you match!

Idrissa (*eyes snapping right back*)   That's not what I was saying.

Adrian   It's what it sounded like to me.

He looks down, sensing he's now gone too far.

Kwaku   Who did you say wants to fund this report on black male rapists?

Issi (*slightly offended*)   That's not what it is, Kwaku.

Idrissa (*slightly reluctant*)   I was speaking to Hayden's new policy advisor.

Kwaku   And he said Hayden would want to go with something like this?

Idrissa   In fact he said as soon as we get the proposal to him he'd be in a position to green-light it.

Kwaku   Seen. Well then, I suppose you should do that then, shouldn't you?

Idrissa   Thank you.

Michael, *who has been glancing at the newspaper, picks it up and passes it to* **Kwaku**, *pointing to the headline.* **Kwaku** *scans it quickly.*

Kwaku (*almost embarrassed*)   Good. Any other ideas you guys want to run past me that you've spoken to others about already?

Everybody looks at the floor.

And my ideas? Do they tickle anyone, or are they deeply bedded in the misguided philosophy that we are here to *help* black people?

Silence.

Right then, meeting adjourned.

Val   Heavenly Fadder we thank . . .

Kwaku   Junior, my office.

He steams out to his office.

Issi *looks with concern after* **Kwaku**. *They all slowly return to work.*

Issi   I think you need to chill a little, Idrissa, you make your point and then you go a little too far.

Kwaku's *office.*

Junior   How did the meeting with Hayden go?

Kwaku   He cancelled.

Junior   Again?

Kwaku   When was the last time you went to your grandfadder grave?

Junior   I haven't . . . been in ages. I've been really busy . . . When I'm not here, I've been at home doing my internet business stuff . . .

Kwaku   You may or may not know that the bank refused to cover the payroll this week.

Junior   I had no idea things were that bad. Have you fixed it? (*Trying to be funny.*) Cos I got me some bills to pay. You know what I'm saying?

Kwaku (*ignoring*)   I tired telling you. Don't bring that street talk in here . . . I tried to bounce some money over from our surplus savings account, should be about a hundred grand in there, but when we looked you know how much was there? Three thousand, two hundred pounds and twelve pence, to be exact.

Junior (*suddenly realises*)   Why are you telling me this? . . . I hope you're not implying what I think you're . . . ?

Kwaku   What am I implying, Junior?

Junior   Naaaa . . .

Kwaku   Once a thief, always . . .? I'm asking myself how can cheques be cashed with my signature on them?

Junior   Maybe you signed them and forgot, you know what your memory's like these days?

Kwaku (*outraged*)   My memory? I wasn't in the country – how could I sign the fucking cheques if I wasn't here? You think I would forget signing away a hundred thousand pound?

Junior   Once – I took money from your account once, and it was back in five days. You're gonna hold that over me for the rest of my goddam life?

Kwaku   Who you talking to like that, boy?

Junior   Why are you always accusing me? What do I need that kind of money for?

Kwaku   That's what I wanna know.

Junior   Well, before you go accusing people maybe you should work that the hell out.

He storms out of the office on to the floor and exits. After a beat **Michael** *walks in.*

Kwaku (*vexed*)   My memory, you know! You see what I'm talking about? That claating boy and his mother, not one of them, you know, not one of them had the decency to go to my father's grave yesterday. After all he did for them, not one of them could say, 'Hey Dad, husband, I know today's a heavy day for you, come let we . . . ' And he wants to talk about my memory!

Michael   Kwaku . . .

Kwaku   You know what I did last night? I just sat here, on my jones, on my jones. Good ting man has a little relief (*he subtly indicates* **Issi**) or I'd have gone the whole night just me and me white rum, not one of them, not nobody, you know . . .

Michael (*calm but ignoring* **Kwaku***'s outburst*)   Kwaku, what is that child doing here?

Kwaku (*still wrapped up in his son*)   What child?

Michael (*firm but whispered*)   You know exactly what I'm talking about! . . . Even though your time away was supposed to put an end to it, when you walk into work with your breath stinking of alcohol I don't say anything. When you sleep with members of our staff in the same office as your wife, I don't like it, but I –

Kwaku   Don't like it? Is not you that does sit down licking your lips when I tell you the details?

Michael   Licking my lips? I listen to the stories maybe, but –

Kwaku   There you go – so I do it for the both of us.

Michael   *Kwaku! Stop!* Stop that right now. I don't know what is going on in your house, but send that boy home before Lola comes in. What you're doing is wrong.

Kwaku   Wrong? I tell you what was wrong – you having secret meetings with our employees behind back! You set me up to look like a fool yesterday.

Michael   I didn't set you up – I didn't have time to tell you cos you were too busy screwing our research fellow to take my calls.

Kwaku   Fuck you, Michael. That's no excuse. What's happening to you?

Michael   Me?

Kwaku *takes a bottle of rum out of his desk and pours himself a quick shot.*

Michael   Don't you think you've had enough of that for the day already?

Kwaku   What are you, my fucking modder now?

Michael (*takes the calm approach*)   Without your advice in my life, Kwaku, I would have crashed. I value it as I feel you value mine. Please send that boy home . . . please.

Kwaku *finishes the drink.*

Kwaku   I'm not sending anyone home. I run this company, not you, not my wife, or fucking Idrissa, alright?

Michael   No, it's not alright . . .

Kwaku   Well, it's going to have to be.

He leaves his office. They all look at him.

Adrian *enters with coffees.*

Val   Me hot chocolate reach.

Adrian   Shall I leave Junior's coffee and paper on his desk?

Michael   Sure.

Adrian   Please forgive me if I spoke inappropriately just then.

Idrissa (*waves it off*)   Not at all . . .

Adrian   Hardly the correct behaviour for an intern first day, contradicting his boss, but you see it's my pet subject.

Idrissa   Like they said, that's how we do things here. Pet subject, huh?

Adrian   Yes, though I studied History and Philosophy at Oxford . . .

Idrissa   What did you get?

Adrian   First.

Idrissa (*approving*)   . . . Carry on.

Adrian   It was at Portland that I . . .

Idrissa   Portland?

Adrian   It was the only place I could find the right supervisor. Dr Joy Leary, I don't know if you've heard of her?

Idrissa   Ah, makes sense now. Isn't she the woman who . . . Post-slave, ah . . .

Adrian   Post-traumatic slave syndrome yes. My PhD placed it within the African Caribbean context.

Idrissa   I see. And how did we meet Kwaku?

Adrian   Umm, he was at a party I was working at. I approached him and – *voilà*.

Idrissa   Right. OK, young Adrian . . .

He makes to go.

Adrian   Forgive me, but may I ask you a personal question?

Idrissa   My, you're forward. Go ahead.

Adrian   Why do you work here?

Idrissa   Why do you ask?

Adrian   You seem . . . not really on the same page as . . .
I suppose if I were to find a word it would be 'restless'. Do you
find your sexuality makes you . . .

Idrissa *stares right at him.*

Idrissa   You're working class, aren't you?

Adrian   I beg your pardon?

Idrissa (*working it out*)   Your sentences. Sometimes too
formal, other times, little grammatical slips . . . yeah – ghetto
kid done well but out to prove that he's not going to 'sell out',
so studies post-traumatic slave syndrome or some other hocus
pocus to explain away why so many of his peers just damn
right fail. But it doesn't really give him comfort, does it?
Doesn't really help, does it, Adrian, because it can't explain
away why you have succeeded and the others have simply
become prison fodder? Yes, the guilt of actually feeling more
comfortable around the thinking white classes than those you
grew up with haunts you, doesn't it, young Adrian? Are you
afraid that a little white man lurks beneath that deep chocolate
skin? Yes, that's your story, isn't it? You're really a little
coconut parading as radical black intellectual.

Adrian   I think it was the American writer Elbert Hubbard
that said, 'If you can't answer a man's arguments, all is not
lost – you can still call him vile names.'

Idrissa   I didn't call you anything.

Adrian   Nor did you answer my question.

Idrissa   I think you'll find I did, young man. Your assumptions
are presumptuous. And apart from being dangerous,
assumptions are always, always insulting. Never insult me
again, do you hear?

Enter **Lola**. *She has two bags in her hands.*

Idrissa   Hey, Lola, have you met our new upstart, I mean
intern, Adrian McKay?

They look at each other for a beat before **Adrian**, *almost reluctantly, stretches out his hand.*

Adrian   Pleased to meet you.

Still staring at him, **Lola** *leaves him hanging for a moment too long. Eventually she refers to her hands being full so not being able to return the handshake.*

Lola   Indeed. (*To* **Idrissa**.) Is he in there?

Idrissa   No, he stormed out in a sulk, I think.

She can't take her eyes off **Adrian**.

Lola   Fine. Fine.

She shuffles for a moment and then heads out of the office. **Idrissa** *is puzzled for a beat, then shrugs his shoulders.*

Idrissa   She doesn't take to you, does she? Oh well, that makes two of us!

Adrian *does not respond at all.*

Lights. We hear the vocal 'woooo-oooops' before the kicking, driving rhythm of Aswad's 'African Children'.

Scene Three

Later that night. **Kwaku** *walks into the office. He looks around and sees several packed boxes.* **Lola** *is packing up.*

Kwaku   Don't be silly, Lola.

She doesn't answer. He moves towards her.

Lola, stop it . . . We need to talk.

Lola   Don't touch me.

Kwaku   Look, I'm not at my best right now, but I need you to speak to your father.

Knowing what that means, **Lola** *stops what she's doing and looks at* **Kwaku** *incredulously.*

Lola (*exclaims in Nigerian*)   Ah ah! You have to be kidding me.

Kwaku   I'm in trouble, Lola, we're in trouble. Is our child I'm trying to protect, you know . . . I so shame, I can't even tell Michael . . .

Lola (*deep roaring anger*)   Don't you dare! Think I don't know what you're doing? I see straight through you . . . You bring your bastard child into our work space and then blame our child for stealing money . . .

Kwaku   My signature was faked. How else could the money go out? Who else could do that?

Lola   Half of Kingsland bloody High Street.

Kwaku   Half of Kingsland does not have access to Michael's or Issi's counter-signature.

Lola   Oh what, so Michael's in on it as well now?

Kwaku   I don't know! You can't trust anybody these days. And Junior could easily have got Michael to sign them by presenting some fake invoices or something.

Lola *stares at him and carries on packing.*

Kwaku   All I need is enough to cover the wages for three months. I'd have pulled it back by then, I know I would have. I'm adapting, Lola, that's what you always tell me I need to do . . . I'm listening to them . . . Back in the day I would have knocked that fucking Idrissa in he face . . . I can't afford to go down now, not in the year of the abolition – if we let them off the hook now, reparations will be dead.

Lola   Didn't you read today's paper? Are you dreaming? Hayden's said such discussions do not contribute to the integration agenda.

Kwaku   When he tells me to my face I'll believe it, OK? This is politricks, baby.

Lola   I'm not asking my father for anything, Kwaku. You want money, ask him yourself . . .

Kwaku   You know he hates my guts. Never got over you marrying a bloody West Indian . . .

Lola   He hates your guts because he saw you for the opportunist bastard that you are . . .

Kwaku (*trying to be soft*)   Ask him for me, na?

Lola   I warned you not to bring your bastard child in here.

Kwaku (*momentary flip*)   The boy has a name, OK . . .

Lola   Call one of your many friends.

Kwaku   I have . . . They're not calling back . . .

Lola   There's a surprise. After trying to have an affair with Eric's wife behind his back . . . and smashing up Thomas's party and half his house in a drunken display . . . You need help, Kwaku . . .

Kwaku   Exactly . . .

Lola   No, therapy kind of . . .

Kwaku (*flares*)   There you go again! I don't need them stupidness dere. Therapy is for idle white people. What I need is money!

Lola   I warned you, K, bring that boy into our sanctum and my heart will turn to ice . . .

Kwaku   He is my son, he needed a job, I gave him one, OK? . . . I know you don't want to hear this but (*filled with pride*) he's brilliant, Lola, so bright, I can't tell you . . .

Lola   You haven't told Junior about him, have you?

Kwaku   . . . No.

Lola (*points straight at him*)   You make our son feel less than he is, and I will ram a knife through the centre of your heart and slowly drag it to the edges. Do you hear me? . . .

Kwaku   Fine. I've got a few other people to contact anyway. I mean, I'm having a meeting tonight with –

Lola   Good luck. Anything to do with work, get Michael to call me on my mobile. I was going to move out, but, as you know, it's my house.

Kwaku   As you never fail to remind me.

Lola   So I'm just going to go away, and when I'm back, Kwaku, make sure you have a good solicitor.

She picks up her box and exits. **Kwaku** *throws himself into one of the chairs. After a few beats he gets up, looks to the heavens, thinking. He picks up the phone and dials.*

Kwaku (*friendly at first*)   . . . Hayden? At last! Kwaku . . . What's wrong wid you, man? You're treating me like a coot, you know . . . What, you's a big man now, you can't call me back? . . . Look, all that integration thing you talking is bullshit, right? You know that, and I . . . Come onnn . . . This is our only chance to honour the ances . . . Don't make me look like a fool, Hayden . . . Remember who you came to to put the idea out – to put the idea of you out there? . . . I'm not raising my voice . . . I have to read in the fucking *Evening Standard* that my reparation report funding might be cut? . . . I have to hear from one of my staff what you're considering and what you're not? Why, I got to hear from . . .

Hayden has put down the phone.

Kwaku   Hayden, Hayden . . .

He calls again. Goes through to answerphone. He slams down the phone and puts his head on the desk.

Soby – *sixty-eight, a fast-talking man in plain dark suit, white shirt and tie* – *knocks on the door and walks in.* **Kwaku** *jumps up.*

Soby (*referring to his telephone call*)   I hate them too . . .

Kwaku   What, answerphones or politicians?

Soby Oh, I could never hate the answerphone. Not in my business – got to be able to reach me at all times. Anyway. How are you?

Kwaku Fine. Thank you for coming to see me, sir . . .

Soby I think you is big and ugly enough to call me by me name.

Kwaku Thank you, Soby.

He indicates **Soby** *to sit.* **Kwaku** *holds up the rum bottle.* **Soby** *waves it off.*

Soby You go ahead.

Kwaku *does.*

Soby Now first things first. I went to the graveyard today on business, and you mean you father's grave still don't have no stone.

Kwaku We're waiting for the ground to . . .

Soby The ground ready and waiting. You shaming youself and your fadder – most time a gravestone is the only monument, only proof that you pass through this place – fix it up, you hear me?

Kwaku I will.

He swigs down the drink.

Soby So, you broke?

Kwaku Well, I wouldn't say that exactly. May I talk straight? You know me, I'm a man for the community, of the community. I didn't take my education and run go work in the city, I didn't run stand for political office – I stayed here and served us. Well, it's time for the next phase. I'm looking for a group of men to help me. To help the community, in fact.

Soby You've said community three times, you're making me nervous.

Kwaku Soby. The white man have me by me balls.

Soby What's new?

Kwaku . . . No, not me balls, he have me by me cerebral cortex. You know what that is? (*Speeds through.*) The largest part of the brain, the part responsible for thinking, memory, problem-solving. I started this think-tank, Soby, because I wanted to . . . take the baton and move forward, show them . . . that dem just can't run roughshod over we, tell we how to think . . . what to say, and cos dem is we paymaster. We have to just do it.

Soby . . . Piper and all that, uh huh?

Kwaku I want the tune to be different, Soby. The road I'm having to travel, I can't take it – our community can't take it – so I'm asking mans that have made their fortunes, to help me.

Soby Ahhh! So you do want me money?

Kwaku I want your support. Now what we do here is . . .

Soby (*leans back*) I understand what you do here, but the truth of the matter is – well, I have a problem.

Beat.

Kwaku Carry on.

Soby This name-changing thing you did, I know is a long time ago, but I didn't like it – it still today don't sit right with me, you know.

Kwaku I see. Well, I thank you for your honesty.

Soby It embarrasses me – in fact, it embarrasses all of us when you West Indians go and change your name to some African something. You're not African – they use to tell us that much when we first came to this country. We're the slave children. The ones dem throw away. And what do our children do? Throw demsselfs at them.

Kwaku That may have been the case back then, but now –

Soby (*cutting in*) What are you saying? We must forget history? Let me talk straight – I want to support something . . .

worthwhile, but how do I know that I, that my grandchildren, would be served by you and your 'thinking ting'?

Kwaku   That's easy. Right now our big thing is to press hard for reparation for –

Soby   My point exactly. For who, Kwaku – or can I call you Derek?

Beat. **Kwaku** *takes the bottle to pour himself another drink.*

Kwaku   May I?

Soby *nods.*

Soby   Who is there for us?

Kwaku   And when you say 'us', you mean . . . ?

Soby   We West Indians. You know how many times I would go downstairs into the room we keep the bodies and I would just bawl, 'Oh God, what we did do?' You know how many young West Indian children I did look at? Have to bury before they taste the sweetness of life! Hey, I shouldn't complain, death is me business, but lord, who is dere for we? . . . We stupid you know. The Indian man come – when he start to catch hell him start to call himself black, prime position for when the grant money was flowing, and we was like 'cool'. I even remember a time even de Irish and Greek man use to call demself 'political black'. What de hell dat mean, eh? And we was like 'cool'! Now dem all gone and leave we, all of dem, left us wid black. Me na want dat now, I's a West Indian. We love other people too much, Derek. We love everybody but us. I want someone who can put out ideas that can change that, that can sow our seeds, who's carrying our baton forward – ploughing our seeds, Derek? Show me someone who's willing to do dat and I would support it with all I have.

Kwaku (*unsure, nervous*)   Well, that's what we're here for. Turning intellectual seeds into influence . . . I should just say at this point, this company historically –

Soby   History has not always served us well. Speaking of the company, your partner – what is his name, Michael, that's right – has he decided whether he's going to accept?

Kwaku   Accept what?

Soby (*leans back in seat*)   See what I'm saying? No matter how long you know them –

Kwaku (*don't mess*)   Michael is my best friend.

Soby   But he didn't tell you that he was interviewed to be candidate for that safe seat in Enfield.

Kwaku   Of course he di . . . For who?

Soby   The Tories, of course.

Kwaku   Yes, yes, yes, sorry, I forgot he did mention it . . .

Soby   Of course he did. You mean Val mentioned it?

Kwaku   Mind if I have another?

Soby   Boy, you really can hold dat thing like an old West Indian. That's the third I've seen you put away and you standing strong.

Kwaku   I'm me father's child, you know. Ever the West Indian.

Soby   Word on the street is since he gone, you're no longer the man you were . . .

Kwaku   Nonsense. Idle street gossip.

Soby   I hope so. So look, I have a little idea I'd like to run past you? See if it's something you could, I don't know . . . give legs, as they say . . .

Kwaku   Of course, throw your idea at me.

Soby   Something I'd be willing to back all the way.

Lights. The drums kick into Aswad's 'Natural Progression'.

Scene Four

Everyone is in the office except for **Kwaku**, **Idrissa** *and of course* **Lola**. *All are working away at their desks silently.* **Junior**'s *mobile rings. He jumps up.*

Junior   Hello? . . . Yeah, yeah, Roger, good to hear from you . . . Could you give me a sec . . . Just getting out of a taxi . . . Keep the change, mate.

He fakes the car-closing noise. The others look up as he leaves the office.

Adrian   What's that about?

Issi   Never know with Junior, if it isn't one guaranteed-to-make-you-a-million-in-a-week scheme, it's another. Hustler number one.

Michael   What product is he on to now?

Issi   Last week it was property, some internet business thing, I think. Who knows?

Val, *today dressed in a white gown and his boots, enters from the toilet.*

Val   Oooh something don't smell holy in that toilet, you know?

Michael   Probably what you just dropped! Any man who doesn't eat cooked food but can drink hot chocolate all day, that's a belly that's always going to be dicky.

Val   Don't watch my belly, I'm going to live till I'm a hundred and twenty like the man dem in Tibet and you're going to die very soon – like he man dem in England.

Michael   We're all in England.

Val   Only in the mind, Michael, only in the mind.

Issi *turns to* **Adrian**.

Issi   So you studied under Dr Joy Leary? How was it?

Adrian   Apart from missing my mum, I loved it.

Issi   Ahh a mummy's boy? You single, mummy's boy?

Adrian   Umm . . .

Issi   Must mean no. Don't worry, you're a bit young for me, but you are bound to know other bright men, hopefully older than yourself?

Michael   . . . She's about to ask you to set her up with a blind date. Just say no.

Issi   Michael! OK, now I want you to think of three men who are solvent, intelligent – but when I say intelligent I don't just mean have qualifications, I mean those who think outside of the box – and then choose the one you think I'd be most attracted to, and set us up on a blind date. Simple . . .

Val *kisses his teeth.*

Issi   Oh yes, he's got to be currently unattached and pref – though I know it's hard post-thirty for any race – without children.

Adrian (*playing along*)   Black – white?

Issi   Preferably of African descent, but I wouldn't say no if it were the Crown Prince of Denmark, say.

Val (*exclaims*)   Gal, you too loose.

Issi   . . . Be quiet, you.

Enter **Idrissa** *on his mobile.*

Issi   Now if Idrissa didn't work here, wasn't gay, and didn't love his mother so much, he'd be perfect.

Idrissa   What you say about my mother?

Issi   Which is why we're doing the next best thing – moving in together.

Idrissa (*into phone*)   Hello, yes, account number – 32167.

Issi   So now you know the brief, I'll expect the names by, say, four o clock today?

Michael (*surprised*)   You and Idrissa are going to move in together?

Issi (*deliberately provocative*)   Yeah. Love the idea of watching gay men have sex. You are going to let me watch, aren't you, Idrissa?

Val (*kissing teeth*)   Backside!

Idrissa   Have your own threesomes, you dirty girl . . . (*Into the phone.*) No no, not you, madam . . . Idrissa Adebayo – yes, I was just told I have insufficient funds in my account – that's a damn right lie. I get paid on the third of the month, today is the seventh . . .

Enter **Kwaku** *with a bounce in his step.*

Idrissa   If there was a problem with my pay I would . . .

Kwaku   Oh, Idrissa . . . Idrissa . . .

Idrissa   One moment, I'm just cursing out my bank . . .

Kwaku   I know you are. Put down the phone . . . Put down the phone, I can help.

Idrissa   Madam, I'll call you back.

Kwaku   Guys, I just wanna say, we're bankrupt . . . only kidding! There was a little mistake but it's been dealt with. (*Points to* **Michael**.) While I'm on that point I just want to say, ladies and gentlemen, there is a man that I trust implicitly. He has saved my life more times than I care mention and I love you, Michael. Just wanted to say that.

Michael *looks nervous. Where's this heading?* **Idrissa** *raises his eyes to the heavens – and cuts the call.*

Kwaku   This is the first day of a new day. (*To himself.*) Does that makes sense?

Enter **Junior**.

Kwaku   Ah, Junior. Great timing as usual. Idrissa, I want you to get me those stats you spoke about – African and

African Caribbean boys at school. You're damn right, why are African Caribbean boys at the bottom? Michael, can I have the stats on, I can't remember how you phrased it – percentage level of self-employed in the various ethnic minorities. Issi, prison population juxtaposed against university entrances for African Caribbean . . .

Michael   Fine. Why?

Kwaku   People, it was the second anniversary of my father's death day this week.

Junior's *eyes hit the ground.*

Junior (*under breath*)   Fuck.

Kwaku   And you know what he said to me before he died? Apart from, 'You should have caught me, you bastard.' He said, 'Son, remember who you are, where you come from.' Last words. I intend to do just that. Idrissa, you were right – reparations is dead.

Idrissa   Thank God.

Kwaku   Gotta go through all that Africans-sold-themselves crap – who was complicit, who wasn't. Michael, you're right again – our focus is too broad. We're going to drop the relief for Africa crap, in fact we're going to drop everything to do with the motherland. It's a crowded market. Fuck it. We're going to focus on where it's needed. Those born here – this country. Which is why we're going to argue the case, indeed sell the case, that reparations should only go to the direct descendants of those who were enslaved. Yes, to the African Caribbeans exclusively. Use the money to set up a foundation for *us*.

Idrissa   Us?

Kwaku   Yes, those that need it, those that languish at the bottom, those maligned by everyone, those poor little Jamos, Idrissa.

Adrian *whoop-punches the air.*

Adrian   Wow!

Idrissa   He's drunk, isn't he?

Kwaku   No, Idrissa, I'm not drunk – well, maybe I am, but only on joy, baby!

Issi   Why would we do that, Kwaku?

Kwaku   Cos it makes sense in the marketplace! Who else is suggesting it? When the African Americans are talking, it's reparations for African Americans. I'm talking about it for West Indians. Fuck serving everybody else – before I know it Somalian Muslims will be pulling on our cheque . . .

Michael   But there isn't a cheque, Kwaku . . .

Idrissa   . . . And it's a divisive debate to be having in public.

Kwaku   Well, it's a debate we're going to have. What, so it's only in private that you can say to Val that he's only eighty per cent black? That Liberians are like West Indians? Full up of whitey, I think the expression was.

Beat as **Val** *looks down.*

Kwaku   Now if this is too thick for anybody's blood, fine. No offence will be taken if you wish to hand in your resignation this very second. But this is what we're going to do. Jump now or for ever hold your tongue.

Silence

Excellent. Let's get our figures sorted, get the stats together, get this out to the press and get this party started. It's reparations time. It's time to save my people.

He walks off. The others are all staring at each other. Only **Adrian** *is smiling. The opening horns of 'Warrior Charge' play, and then echo out.*

Act Two

Scene One

Institute of Black Policy Research.

We are in the office. The phones are going off the hook. It sounds like a telephone exchange/call centre, everyone talking at once. As he pounds the floor we only just hear **Michael**'s *conversation above the others at first. He's on the back foot, and we can hear the suppressed tension in his voice.* **Kwaku**, *however, is not on the phone but watching* **Michael** *from his office as he speaks. There is a darkness in his eyes.*

All   Yes, I'll try and put you through . . . No, if you look at the stats . . . We'll need three cameras . . . Security will be . . . (*Etc., etc.*)

Michael   No, no, no, we are simply setting the parameters for a useful and, can I say, essential debate.

Everyone in the room stops momentarily and points at him. He throws his eyes to the heavens and as he continues the conversation takes the twenty pounds out of his wallet.

. . . If it's not about looking out for the rights of minorities, what is democracy? . . . And the African Caribbeans are fast becoming the smallest group in the ethnic minority family . . . It soon will be . . . No, there isn't anything outrageous being said here . . .

Issi (*shouts over*)   Michael – Gola from *Africa Today* on line six . . .

Michael   Yes, yes, I know.

Issi   Says he's been waiting twenty minutes . . .

Michael *looks at* **Junior**, *who picks up his phone.*

Michael (*carrying on*)   . . . I understand that, I can see how it can be perceived that way, yes, I do . . .

Junior (*over*)   Hi Sophie, so sorry to cut in, I know we came to you late but we've overrun and Michael's next interview has been waiting for . . . Thank you. Thank you. Excellent.

Michael   Thank you, Sophie, hope you got all that you needed.

He puts the phone down momentarily.

Junior   When did you say this is going to print? . . . Excellent.

Michael *sits in his chair. He exhales from deep within. He looks exhausted. He glances up at* **Junior**, *who patches through the next call. Before starting to speak he gives a quick glance at* **Kwaku**. *Their eyes make four for a mere second.*

Michael   Junior, what is this thing she's talking about on the website?

Junior *shakes his head in ignorance.*

Issi   Michael.

Michael   Hi, Gola, sorry to have kept you, you know what you journalists are like . . . Right . . . No, I'm ready for you.

Adrian (*over*)   Junior, conference centre on line seven . . .

Junior   Tell them one minute . . .

Adrian   I'll put you on hold.

Michael (*over*)   No, no, no . . . All we're saying is the previously held orthodoxy that 'we all' need to descend on the white man as one homogenous mass demanding reparation for the injustice perpetrated against us is in realpolitik terms – naive . . . No, we're not being anti-African . . . Tunde, sorry, Gola, you know me, we have spoken for many years. Do I strike you as someone that is anti-African? I am African.

Adrian (*overlaps*)   . . . Junior, he says he needs to speak with you now or they're going to cancel. Something about threats to the . . .

Junior   Shit, send it through.

Adrian   . . . I don't know, speak to him.

He does. **Junior** *takes centre stage now.*

Junior   Gerald, how are you today? Good . . . Really? . . . Your director's concerned about the possibility of . . . ? This isn't a hip-hop concert, Gerald . . . Believe me, good middle-class black people debating the way forward.

Idrissa   Where's the goddam coffee, Adrian? You said you were going thirty minutes ago.

Adrian   In a moment, I promise, I'm just trying to finish . . .

Idrissa   How could Lola go to Nigeria at a time like this? We need more people in this bloody office, Michael.

Michael (*getting irate*)   . . . What does that mean, Gola, I'm a sell-out? . . . (*Raises his voice.*) Self-hating African? Before you start calling people names, those that actually do something on the front line for our people, as opposed to those who just talk about it and do nothing . . . No, no, check the mirror, which one of us is the parasite, Gola? Which one?!

He slams down the phone. Everybody looks over and then away.

Fuck! Fuck fuck this shit!

Idrissa   Anyone know anything about a radio car outside?

Junior   Excuse me, Gerry – yeah it's *Five Live*. Michael, when you're . . . ready, they're . . . It's Jenny – she's . . . nice. It's only a two-minuter.

Michael   Call Gola back and apologise for me, I shouldn't have lost my temper.

He gets up and walks out.

Junior   Sorry, Gerry . . .

Issi   Junior, someone from Channel 4 News on line two. They want to know what you mean by –

Junior   Tell them to hold.

Issi (*screams*)   How the hell am I supposed to get any work done?

Junior   OK, OK. Gerry, can I call you back? . . . Two minutes . . . Thank you, sir . . . Where's the bloody press release?

He starts to look around his desk. Then around the office.

Anyone seen the box with press releases?

Adrian   Yes. I put them in the recycling bin.

Junior   Why the fuck did you do that?

Adrian   Um, Kwaku told me to. Said something about them not being correct or something.

Junior   Is he losing his goddam mind? No one answer that! Issi, tell them I'll call them back in a min.

Issi (*shouts*)   I'm not your bloody secretary, Junior.

He steams over to **Kwaku**'s *office.* **Kwaku** *is on the phone. He signals one minute and then looks up.*

Kwaku   Junior?

Junior (*suppressing outrage*)   Dad, why did you tell Adrian to throw away my press releases?

Kwaku   I've been thinking, I don't think they're right.

Junior   . . . But you passed them!

Kwaku   I know, I know. Maybe, I don't know, it just wasn't saying enough.

Junior   Saying enough? What did you want it to say?

Kwaku   Well, I'm glad you asked that.

Pops his head out.

Adrian, bring in the revised press release you wrote up for me, please.

Adrian *nods.*

Junior   You asked . . . Why would you ask an intern to . . . That's my . . . Press is my job.

Kwaku   He may be an intern, Junior, but he's no fool.

Junior   Meaning? (*Snatches it*.) Let me see this.

Adrian (*humble*)   It's very much like yours, but I just added a little . . .

Kwaku (*smiles*)   Yeah, but it's the seasoning that makes the meat taste nice.

Junior (*reads quickly*)   'The trauma of the deculturalisation process as it pertains specifically to the African Caribbean community has been a territory political correctness has forbade us enter. Now is the time to release ourselves from the shackles of monocultural perceptions and – '

Kwaku   Exactly.

Junior   What? Monoc . . . This is bullshit. What are you talking about? What is this deculturalisation when it's at home?

Adrian   The seasoning process when we arrived in the Caribbean and they took away our gods, our names, our identity in order to, to have us become mules for labour.

Junior   Well, that's very nice, but this is bullshit – long-winded bullshit at that – certainly not something we should be putting out to the press, it's not professional . . .

Adrian   With respect, my PhD is in this area of trauma. It's a subject I know very well.

Junior   I may not have a PhD but writing press releases is a subject I know very well. Dad, are you going to let this bullshit go out there . . . ?

Kwaku   I like it, Junior. In fact I told him to post it on our website this morning.

Junior   What?

Kwaku   I think this helps service the debate.

Adrian   With respect, I don't think that this is bullshit. Right at the heart of this claim is that your *mother*, say, as oppossed to mine, could probably trace her ancestry. The African Caribbeans were made into another tribe and are treated as inferior not only by Europeans but by other members of the African family.

Kwaku   Now that's the stuff we want out there.

Junior *looks at them both.*

Junior   I'm speechless. I . . . again, this – is – bullshit.

He leaves the office and returns to the floor.

Michael, wanna know why you're being called an African-hater? Adrian here has posted the most reactionary drivel I've read in a lifetime on our website. Pull it up, see . . .

Michael (*to* **Adrian**)   Why would you do that? That's not your area of responsibi . . .

Kwaku   I told him to. I told him to rewrite our press release and post it. The other one was crap.

Junior (*clearly devastated*)   Thank you, Father . . . At least you know this before you hit the news this evening, Michael . . . They'd be crucifying you and you wouldn't know why.

Michael   God, do I have to do another interview?

Kwaku   Actually, I'd like Adrian and me to do that interview, Junior.

Silence. No one quite knows how to respond to this. Eventually:

Michael   Umm, I was only joking . . . when I said . . .

Kwaku   No really. I was going to say that anyway. I'd want Adrian and me to do it. That can be done, right?

The phone rings.

Michael (*snaps*)   Put the phones on answer . . .

Issi *does.*

Michael   You hate dealing with the press, Kwaku, that's why I always do the . . .

Kwaku   Yes, you do, don't you? They didn't ask for Michael specifically did they, Junior?

Junior (*struggles*)   They asked for a representa –

Kwaku   Exactly. And the truth is, Michael, I don't know if you're the right man to continue doing all the 'representing'.

Michael   Can we speak in the . . . office about this?

Kwaku   No. I'm fine speaking right here.

Michael (*calm*)   I really think we should . . .

Kwaku (*barging over*)   Of course I can see why you'd want to be on television all the time . . .

Michael   Why would that be?

Kwaku   Isn't it obvious? . . .

Michael   Kwaku, let's go into the office . . .

Kwaku   It's my office and I said no, OK? Truth is, I hear the way you've been tiptoeing around the subject matter and I don't like it . . .

Michael   Stop it, Kwaku . . . The enemy's out there, not in here.

Kwaku   Enemy? Now that's an interesting word. Who exactly is the enemy right now, Toks? That is his real name, everybody, Toks. Just at uni Toks decided that Michael would allow him to fit in better – wasn't that right, Toks? . . .

Michael   Why are you doing this, K?

Kwaku   What do your new Tory boys think? Toks opens up the new African demographic, or maybe they're happy with Michael? Just any black will do!

Michael *glances to* **Idrissa**.

Kwaku   Oh, what, think I wouldn't find out about your little interview? (*Raises his voice.*) I thought they were the enemy, Michael? Those who stood for the status quo, those that saw us as inferior trespassers on their glorious land . . . or have you too bought into the hype?

Michael (*glances at* **Val**)   I spoke with them, K, what's the big deal?

Kwaku   They offer you a safe seat? No doubt a speedy ascent to – what, Shadow Secretary for Race? I don't understand why you haven't screamed it from the rooftops, why you haven't told everyone. (*Darkness descends.*) Why you haven't told me, Michael?

Michael   I didn't take their offer, there was nothing to tell. What? I have to tell you every time I get offered a job?

Kwaku   No, just the ones (*screams*) THAT CONTRADICT EVERYTHING YOU'VE EVER STOOD FOR!

Michael   And you think this doesn't? You think exacerbating . . . shouting that West Indians should be given money that we haven't even got, and Africans shouldn't, doesn't do exactly that? Doesn't split us right down the fucking centre? God, must you always be the fucking martyr? You know what? Do what you want. Do the fucking interview – word of advice to you though, Adrian, I'd make sure there's no alcohol in the studio or you might be holding up more than just an argument.

He steams out. Silence.

Kwaku   Right, well, that's settled then. Back to work everyone. Answer those phones.

Val *looks at* **Kwaku** *and indicates he's going after* **Michael.** **Kwaku** *walks away.*

Lights. Max Romero's 'War Inna Bablyon' kicks in.

Scene Two

The next morning. Very early.

Issi, *iPod on, dressed in tracksuit, runs into the office. She takes off her computer rucksack, then trackie jacket, and starts to warm down. She takes off her iPod and connects it to the speaker system next to her computer. It's playing a 'bashment' tune, 'Me Gal Pon de Side', by Frisco Kid. She sings along with it as she warms down. The rhythm starts to move her. She lifts her left leg in the air, holds it aloft and starts to rock back and forth, bashment dancehall-style. She changes from the lyrics to the chorus. Since she is dancing she doesn't see* **Junior** *walk in. He stares at her.*

Issi (*touching her arse and breasts*)
   'He love me bumper an me chess . . .'

Eventually **Junior** *coughs. She jumps, startled, and switches off.*

Issi   I, I was, cha, what you doing in this early?

Junior   'My girl on the side sexes the best?' You wanna be a little more careful than that. Gives it right away.

Issi   Gives what away?

Junior   That you're an old reggae bashment queen. Respectable intellectual like you should be ashamed of yourself . . .

Issi   Shouldn't I just.

Junior   Song gives away your age, though. Who uses 'Chini brush' now Viagra's here? (*Quickly.*) Not that I have used either.

Issi   Uh-ha.

Junior   You ever had sex with a man who's taken Viagra?

Issi   Umm, a few times.

Junior   Thought so.

Issi   Excused. You don't usually get in this hour.

Junior   No I, know. I just . . . well!

She looks at his clothes. Same as yesterday.

Issi   Did you actually go home last night, Junior?

Junior (*smiles*)   I meant to, but I was going through everyone's computers and . . . I got carried away . . .

Issi   You went through everyone's computer?

Junior   I do it all the time. Little scans, just, just, you know, see what everybody's doing. But last night I couldn't seem to stop. I just kept looking and looking to see if, if, well other things that I written or done had been, I don't know, stupid, I would have known . . .

Issi   Had been what?

Junior   Corrected, rewritten or something . . . I know, stupid . . . just everyone here is Oxbridge or whatever and I . . . I just got a bee in my . . .

Issi   Junior, you do great work here – honestly. Your events are always well organised, well planned . . .

Junior   Then why do you think he asked Adrian to –

Issi   I don't know . . . and I think you should forget it.

Junior   Did you watch last night?

Issi   No . . .

Junior   Me neither . . . Well, I did, a little . . . The smashed monitor . . .

Issi   That bad, was it?

Junior (*back to press release*)   I mean, he'd have to know I'd feel humiliated? The boy's an intern.

Issi   Maybe he didn't, Junior. He's not himself right now.

Beat.

Junior   Look, we're both adults here, so forgive me for what I'm about to say, OK?

Issi (*wary*)   OK.

Junior   I know you fucking my dad . . . my mother knows – which makes it even harder to say what I wanna say . . .

Issi   There's more?

Junior (*friendly*)   Don't act all surprised, Issi, I knew you were in touch with your 'inner freak', but I was a little surprised when I saw your most frequently viewed website . . .

Issi   You checked my web viewing? You bastard!

Junior   Bloody hilarious! Does my father know?

Issi   It's where I met him, actually.

Junior   You met my father on illicitaffairs.com?

Issi   Yes. I was rather specific, you know how exacting I am, 'Black, solvent, thinks outside the box lives inside, interested in politics,' etc. – and only two came up.

Junior   Why married?

Issi   'One should jettison themselves away from love as far as possible till the right one appears . . . ' Can't remember who said that, but I read it at college and it makes sense, right? You said you had something else to say?

Junior   . . . My father actually respects you, Issi. I know he does. Speak to him for me, please . . . Do you think you could do that?

Issi (*confused*)   About what?

Junior   There is an issue about some money going . . .

Issi   Oh, I don't want to get into money stuff, Junior.

Junior   Please, it's really important. He listens to you . . .

Issi   At best, right now your father is a functioning alcoholic, Junior. I don't think he listens to anyone . . .

Junior . . . He listens to Adrian.

Issi Then that's who you should be speaking to.

Beat.

Junior He has told you who Adrian is, right?

Issi *shrugs her shoulders, not understanding the question.*

Junior At first I couldn't work it out – the face – then it hit me . . . Every so often, as a child, I would see this car drive by my house and there was a kid there sat in the passenger seat, staring into the home. It wasn't regular, but I began to feel – to know when it was going to happen – when he was going to drive by . . . and stare at my life. I'd ask my dad about it, but he'd push me away, 'Stop talking stupidness' – then one day, thirteen, and it stopped. Adrian is . . . my father's son. He had him a year or so after I was born, at least that's what I think and . . .

*Enter **Adrian**, taking off his iPod. **Issi** spots him.*

Issi Morning, Adrian!

Adrian *(taken aback by the enthusiastic welcome)* Hi. Good morning, Junior.

Junior Adrian.

*He doesn't realise that **Adrian** hasn't overheard anything.*

Adrian *(to **Issi**)* We're informal today, Issi.

Issi I ran in. I do that sometimes.

They all just stare at each other, no one knowing what to say, but the air is thick.

Issi Look, I'm going to get in the shower upstairs. See you guys in a minute. We'll catch up later, Junior.

She picks up her bag and leaves.

Adrian *walks to his desk, switches on his computer. The boys sit in silence.* **Adrian** *is waiting for some kind of communication. Eventually he bows.*

Adrian   So, what did you think of last night?

Junior   Sorry, I missed it.

Adrian   Oh.

Back to silence.

Junior   Where did you say you grew up again, Adrian?

Adrian   I don't think we've had that conversation. Any conversation actually.

Junior (*friendly*)   So I'm asking now. Where did you grow up?

Adrian   All over, really.

Junior   Where is all over?

Adrian   Exactly that. We moved so many times.

Junior (*restrained anger*)   Can you remember just one of the places then?

Adrian   Well . . . Um, between three and seven, we – my mother and I – lived in Norbury – then we moved north for a while, Highbury, before it went upmarket, my mother liked the whole 'bury' thing – then we moved to Tilbury after a while. Then finally where we are now –

Junior   Where's that?

Adrian   Stamford Hill.

Junior   Big Jewish area.

Adrian   Yeah, I kinda grew up with um, um, a big dose of Jewish envy.

Junior   Jewish envy?

Adrian Yeah, well, they were discriminated against, right? But through what they achieved intellectually, educationally, they became strong. I'm not talking about world conspiracy stuff – just that no one fucks with them now. Or if they do . . . they're wary, even scared. Unlike us, of course, who they don't care if they insult because we're nothing. Powerless.

Junior And you think that's right? You think people should be scared of you?

Adrian As I said, I grew up with it. A black US college cured me of that.

Junior Must have been hell moving so much?

Adrian No, my mum always had a nice big car. And where did you grow up?

Junior (*not looking at him*) I know who you are, Adrian . . . I don't want to talk about it. Just don't take the piss and try to pretend . . .

Adrian I . . .

Junior (*raises his voice a little*) I said, I don't want to talk about it . . . Not now. I just want you to know. (*From the heart.*) I . . . know . . . you. And whatever your plan is here, I will quash it like a bug under the heel of my shoe.

Adrian Fine. I'm glad you know.

Enter **Idrissa** *and* **Michael** *Idrissa sees the two boys together. He feels the tension. He decides to break it.*

Idrissa Another bright and wonderful day at the office. Hey, Junior, you haven't put on the phones yet have you?

Junior No.

Idrissa Good. Don't . . . Listen, I didn't get time to stop off for brekky. Adrian, you wouldn't mind doing the honours, would you?

Adrian (*a little reluctantly, as in 'I thought I was past that stage'*) Oh, not at all. Would anybody else like anything?

Idrissa   Just do the rounds – croissants and coffee galore.
Here.

Hands him a tenner.

Adrian *shuffles for a moment, then leaves the office.* **Issi** *re-enters.*

Issi   Hey, boys.

Michael   Junior, is your father here?

Junior *shakes his head as* **Idrissa** *checks that* **Adrian** *has completely cleared the building.*

Idrissa (*referring to the TV programme*)   Did you see that fiasco
last night?

All shake their heads.

Idrissa   How the hell did you miss that?

Michael   I couldn't face it.

Idrissa   You'll be facing a lot more than that today, I tell
you. It'll be on their website. He has got to go, Michael.

Michael (*snaps a little*)   And I told you about saying things
like that, Idrissa.

Idrissa *taps into the website.*

Idrissa   Junior, you been snooping on my computer again?
You're such a wanker! How'd I get this thing on to all your
computers again?

Junior   Hit 'streaming' – under 'connections' – and it should
do it . . .

Idrissa   This shit is gonna be on YouTube before the day is
out, trust me . . . Here, found it.

They all swing round and watch the wall-mounted TV.

We see **Kwaku** *and* **Adrian** *sitting on one side of the interviewer's
desk and the interviewer laid back in his chair on the other. The picture
is streaming quality. They are speaking, but we can't hear the sound.*

Idrissa   What's wrong with the sound?

Junior   Rebuffer it! . . .

Idrissa *presses something on the computer. It pauses, then continues, this time with sound.*

Interviewer   . . . The former Prime Minister and Deputy Prime Minister gave an apology –

Kwaku   The former claat, you mean. Statement of what? Dem don't regret nothin. And it should have come from de bloody Queen.

Interviewer   The Queen?

Kwaku   Yes. That is you head of the state, innit?

Interviewer   Well, ceremonial –

Kwaku   And den she should ah tell she government to pay we – we reparations.

Interviewer   OK, moving on. There is the point being made that as abhorrent as slavery was, it was legal at the time . . .

Adrian   The kidnap, rape, murder and forced servitude of humans was always an illegal act. 'It was "illegal" to aid and comfort a Jew in Hitler's Germany. Even so, I am sure that, had I lived in Germany at the time, I would have aided and comforted my Jewish brothers.' Martin Luther King, April '63.

Kwaku (*to* **Adrian**)   Me na inna dis Jewish ting yeah? Come off dat.

Interviewer   Pardon?

Adrian (*jumping in*)   What my fa – Kwaku is is is saying is –

All pick up 'What my fa –' in the office.

Interviewer (*not really understanding*)   What was that you said about Jews?

Kwaku   I didn't say anything about Jews, but I tell you what I do say: black people need to be racist, not just against Jews but against everybody. And it's not until we do that, that we do unto you as you as you did unto us, that the fire will come down . . .

Michael (*shouts*) Switch it off, for Christ's sake switch it off, Idrissa.

Idrissa *does. Silence descends.*

Michael We're fucked . . . On every front we're . . . Oh my God, it's all my fault . . .

Issi You can't blame yourself.

Michael Yes I can, I shouldn't have let him bully me out of doing –

Idrissa It's what I've been telling you for the last eighteen months. The man is mentally unstable, trust me . . . What I want to know is, what we going to do now? . . . The man is out of control and it's dangerous, Michael. I don't think I can stay here. I don't think any of us can . . .

Michael I'll talk to him . . .

Idrissa Talk? It's too late for talk, Michael. Something drastic needs to be done or he will bring us all down . . . We'll never be able to work in this game again, in politics – forget it. We'll be the ones – the black racist guys – who –

Michael Idrissa, will you shut the fuck up and let me think!

Issi What do you mean by drastic, Idris?

Idrissa I don't know. But if something isn't done today, I'm outta here. And if you guys have a self-respecting African bone in your body so would you be. If not, then ma wah for youoo.

Just as he finishes **Adrian** *re-enters.*

Adrian So sorry I forgot. Did you say croissants or bagels?

Lights.

Scene Three

Later that day.

Idrissa, **Issi** *and* **Junior** *are at their desks, not really working.*
Adrian *is at his desk, typing away. A deadly silence hangs over the*
office. **Kwaku** *is in his enclosure reading newspapers and on the phone.*

Michael *enters with a small carrier bag in hand. He can hardly look*
at any one. Eventually:

Michael   Anyone seen or spoken to Val yet?

All   No.

They shake their heads, no one really looking up at him either. **Michael**
understands.

Junior   The Equality Commission called.

Michael (*knows bad news*)   Oh yeah?

Idrissa   Ref big headline in this afternoon's London paper.
'Black racist thinkers slam Jewish community' . . .

Michael   OK.

Silence. **Michael** *makes to head towards the office.* **Junior** *jumps up.*

Junior   Can I speak to you a . . .

He indicates the far corner. They head there.

I know this is probably going to sound a bit odd, and I'm not
saying all, but I think that this is partly my fault . . .

Michael   Kwaku Junior, come on, we've established that . . .
no one is to . . .

Junior   No, seriously, Michael.

Michael   I won't, I won't let you do this, Junior . . . There
are things that have happened I should never have allowed . . .
and I'm not going to allow you to do this to yourself. Do you
hear me?

Beat.

Junior   Has he told you about the money? . . . The hundred grand missing from the savings account? If I didn't tell Mum that he blamed me, she wouldn't have left . . . Without her, Michael, he can't function properly, never has . . .

Kwaku *enters, singing quite loudly the Maze song 'Happy Feelings'.*

Kwaku (*sings*)
'Happy feeling in the air, touching people everywhere!'

Everyone looks up before casting their eyes to the ground again.

Kwaku (*to* **Michael**)   Remember dem tune dere? Old-time classics! Na, na, na, na, you gonna know this one . . . (*Sings.*)

'You make me happy, this you can bet,
You stood right besides me and I won't forget –
Before I let go.' (*Sings bass line.*)
Bom bom bom, bom bom bom.

No one responds.

Ah, you guys are dry, man.

He heads off to his office singing the bass line.

Everyone then looks up at **Michael***. He heads to the office. He knocks.*

Michael   K, can I . . .

Kwaku   Since when you start knocking?

Michael (*innocent*)   K, remember when we had the payroll problem the other day – how did you sort it?

Kwaku *turns to him for an extended moment. His eyes look as if they've swollen or reddened in a matter of seconds.*

Kwaku   Have you read these papers?

Michael   Yes . . .

Kwaku   Fucking white people, make me laugh, they been practising they shit for years, we say one likkle ting, identify their secret weapon and I'm Idi fucking Amin . . . I mean, what de fuck? You know even the freeholder called this morning, wanted to talk about our tenancy. I told him to fuck off.

Michael   You told Glen to fuck off?

Kwaku   Yes. His secretary, yes! Is the truth, it's the truth you know that's frightening them. When they start hitting you like this, you got to know you on to something.

Michael   What's the truth?

Kwaku   . . . Then the conference centre pulls out, but ha, I got us another one. Just like that . . . Is a bwoy dey think they playing wid? I mean, you saw the interview, right?

Michael   Yes, I did.

Kwaku *waits for his opinion.*

Kwaku   The boy was good, wasn't he? You should have seen his mother when I dropped him home.

Michael (*surprised*)   You spoke to Gloria?

Kwaku   Yes. I should never have left that woman, you know.

Michael *stares at him.*

Kwaku   Where you been all morning anyway? I've had to handle all this shit by myself.

Beat.

Michael (*changes subject*)   I was walking past Waterstone's when you were away and in the window there was this book –

Kwaku   Oh yeah?

Michael   *Grief and the Mind.* Jumped out at me, so I bought it.

Kwaku   What you got to grieve about?

Michael   Started reading it and I just couldn't put it down. All the things it says grief can make us . . . what drives us humans to do certain . . . things. I can't explain it properly, you'd have to read it.

He tries to place it on the desk but is rebuffed.

Kwaku   I ain't got time to read stupidness right now.

Michael   But there was this chapter, right, on the effect of grief. I reread it last night, and it suddenly began to make sense. Showed me how . . . it can sometimes contribute to making us, almost tribal . . . all this hatred can come out. But it's not really hate, it's grief . . .

Kwaku   Sounds like a load of rubbish to me.

He places the open book on the table.

Michael   Grief, it says, has three stages. Denial, then suffering and disorganisation – which she calls the heart of the grief, where you begin to feel the truth, that this loss is for ever, and there's tremendous psychic, spiritual, emotional and physical pain.

Kwaku   Is that so?

Michael (*spells it out*)   Yes. And its symptoms can include lethargy, memory loss and great, great anger . . .

Kwaku   And what does the book say about nosey bloody parkers that should keep their stinking psycho, new-age bullshit to themselves?

Michael (*staring right at him*)   Personally, I'm at number, number two. Because I feel that I have lost a friend, a companion and one of the finest cultural warriors I have ever known, and I think you are not well, K. I think this whole adventure is misconceived and it is killing us. And what's worse, I know you don't believe it . . . Is this what you think your dad would have wanted? Everything we've worked towards over these years – to be dashed away?

Kwaku (*shouts*)   Don't fucking tell me about my dad! What do you know about my dad? – You hardly met my dad, you was nothing but a fucking little African booboo boy that spoke posh.

Michael (*ignoring*)   Kwaku, if we continue down this line
I don't know how we can get out of it in one piece . . .

*The others outside who have deliberately not been looking in now do so,
and* **Kwaku** *sees them. He also sees that* **Val** *is in the office now.*

Kwaku   I tell you how we get out of it, we can get out of it
by you bloody supporting me, getting behind me . . .

Michael   But it's misguided, Kwaku. It's working on the
assumption that reparations is even on the agenda.

Kwaku   Misguided?

He steams over to the door, opens it and stands in the doorway shouting.

I tell you what's misguided. You think that I haven't noticed
over the years how you and Lola only employ people that are
fucking African?

Michael   K, stop it.

Kwaku   You think I'm stupid? You think I haven't seen?

Michael   I have, we have employed the best people for the
job . . .

Kwaku   What are you saying? There are no West Indians
that can do our job? There was a time when this office was
filled with West Indians and we were doing better than we are
now! None of them were writing in right-wing rags that black
kids are more interested in mugging than mathematics.
Michael, Michael, can't you see what's happening?

He walks on to the floor.

Issi, who employed you?

She doesn't answer.

Idrissa, who employed you?

He doesn't answer.

You see, they won't answer me cos you're one little motherland
clique, aren't you? Good to see you, Val.

Idrissa   I told you, the man's gone mad . . .

Kwaku (*flips*)   Don't you call me mad, you little fag!

Idrissa *tries desperately hard not to lose his rag but points right back at him.*

Idrissa   Don't you call me names – I don't have to take dat.

Kwaku   Den fuck off then.

Michael   Kwaku!

Kwaku   Think I don't know what you all been saying about me? Think I don't know? . . .

They look at **Adrian***.*

But you're wrong. Look, see, we've not been as hot as this for years. Do you know how many people are asking about us today? . . . *Newsweek*, Radio 4, bloody Australian TV to ras . . .

Michael   Of course they're calling, K, hoping to be the one that strings you up!

Kwaku   Rubbish. People are talking about it, people are arguing about it. Debate, people – debate is everything!

Issi   My cousin called me this morning. Her kids are fighting in the playground with West Indian kids.

Idrissa   They use to do that shit back in the seventies!

Kwaku   That's right, and you lot use to get a bloody good kicking then too . . .

Idrissa   What are you talking about?

Michael (*loses it a bit*)   Do you think that's something to be proud of? That you, not the white kids, were the ones calling us jungle bunnies, that you, not them, were the ones shouting from across the street, 'African booboo, take the bone out of your nose,' making our lives hell . . . Do you think that is something to be proud of?

Kwaku (*shouts*)   What's that in comparison to selling us, Michael?

Michael (*shouts back*)   I didn't sell you!

Kwaku   But you benefited from it?

Michael   How? How? Letting them into our country so they could take over and plunder it? We were a great civilisation that stretched from –

Kwaku (*screams from the heart*)   If you were so great why didn't you come and get us? Why didn't you come and reclaim us when we were dying in the fields, raped in the huts, being brutalised and made half fucking human . . .

Idrissa   Ohhh! My God . . .

Michael   There were Africans that resisted, you know . . .

Kwaku   Not hard enough! We beat you and called you jungle bunny because it was the first time in four hundred years that we could tell you: you – hurt – me. The first time that we could show you our pain. And I'll be damned if right here and now, when our old folk are dying and half our fucking men are with bloody white women, and the other half are in jail, and you guys are multiplying and multiplying that I'm gonna have anyone, anyone stand in the way of me defending my people. Defending those that need me . . . you lot don't need me . . . they do . . .

Idrissa   Rubbish, you attacked us because you were jealous, cos we have families, cos we came here to work and educate ourselves, not laze about the streets, smoking ganja, depending on the state to . . .

Val (*hands on ears screams at the top of his voice*)   Ahhhhhhhhhhh!

Kwaku   Val, Val, Val, stop it. Stop it . . .

Val   Ahhhhhhhhhhh! (*Chants.*) We were not slaves, we were not slaves, we were enslaved . . . people, human beings . . .

Michael   Val, Val, Val, stop, stop.

Kwaku Get off him . . . Val.

Kwaku *slaps him hard across the face.* **Val** *cools a little.*

Val I can't take this! (*Chants.*) I am not a slave, I'm a human
. . . I can't take it, K. I can't take it. You know, I couldn't get
out de bed this morning the weight, the weight of my head.
I couldn't get it off the pillow. All I could hear in my mind
was de shouting and the noise . . . How wicked we are, how
bad, how low, how poor and how sick and . . . I can't take
no more bad talk, K . . . How am I suppose to raise my
head? How we children suppose to . . .

Kwaku Valdon, we fighting *to* raise your head. If we fight
this thing right, we will *never* have to fight it again. We children
won't have to fight it. Now calm down, Val . . . I need you on
side, I need you to be a West Indian right now, OK?

He pulls **Val** *next to* **Adrian**, *leaving* **Michael**, **Issi** *on one side
and* **Junior** *in the middle. He stares at them.*

Michael (*incredulously*) You gonna divide this office now into
African versus West Indians?

Kwaku It was the join that was artificial.

Adrian That's right!

Idrissa I've had enough. He'll be rounding us up next. I'm
outta this madhouse.

Michael *grabs him.*

Michael Idrissa!

Junior *looks at his father.*

Junior Dad. You didn't take my hand, Dad. Where am
I suppose to go?

Kwaku You were always your mother's child!

Junior *just stares at him.*

Michael *looks at the pain in* **Junior**'s *face.*

Michael   That's it. That's . . . You've gone too far, K . . .
I want this to stop now. It either stops this second or I will . . .

Kwaku   You'll what?

Michael   I have only ever wanted to serve your vision,
Kwaku, but if that vision means I have to push you aside,
I will do that.

Kwaku   Push me aside?

Michael   It doesn't have to be that way. Please, K, let's not
travel this road, please . . .

Kwaku (*contained*)   Fuck you, Michael. You're not man
enough.

Michael   I made you go on holiday, K, because I thought
maybe the time away would be good for you. Bring you back,
mind refreshed . . . But you can't remember key things, who
you've spoken to, what you've signed, what month or even
year we did this or other . . . We are in dire financial difficulty
and as of now I'm sure I can say you no longer have the
confidence of your staff. But most of all, you are losing your
mind. I know that now and I can't allow us all to go down
with you. That will be my report to the board, to the Charity
Commission, but most importantly, to my conscience.

Kwaku (*laughs*)   Is me crown you after, Michael? Is war you
really want? I long know it is me pussy you want – well, watch
her there na – (*Points to* **Issi**.) Tek it! But you don't have the
guts to take my company from me? Remember burying
people is in me genes. You sure you want to war with me?

Michael   Like I said, it doesn't have to be that way, Kwaku.

Kwaku   It already is. I'll accept, no expect, everyone's
resignation by first thing in the morning. And your desks
cleared by the end of the week.

Issi *picks up her bags and walks out.*

Issi   You can have mine right now.

Kwaku   You know what, fuck the end of the week . . .

He moves to the desk and starts throwing the papers and computer screens on to the floor.

Fuck it. I want you out now . . . get out now, all of you – nowwww, fuck off out me place.

Adrian *and* **Val** *run to calm him before he smashes up the whole office.*

Kwaku   Fuck dem, I want them outtttt! Get them outta me place!

Lights. The echo chamber hits the horns of Aswad's deep dark dub, 'Rockers' Medley'.

Scene Four

Three days later.

Michael *and* **Junior** *are sitting in the office in silence. It's a little tidier but still ransacked – well, their desks are anyway.*

Eventually **Lola** *runs in. She has one of those suitcases that can be used as hand luggage on an aircraft and is wearing a big coat.*

Lola   So where is the fool? Jesus, he did this?

Michael *gently nods.*

Michael   Two days ago. All of us refused to resign except for Issi – so every night he ransacks our desks . . . Leaves big scrawling notes. 'When you coming out me place?' He'll be in soon, so we should get to it.

Junior   When I went round he put his arse out the window and tried to fart at me. 'That's all you are!' he said.

Lola   Did the neighbours see? Don't answer that.

They all sit.

Michael   We normally clean up straight away, but I just needed you to see what we've been going through.

Lola   What have the board said?

Michael   I haven't told them. Yet.

Lola   Ohhh, Michael, Michael.

Michael   I know, I know. I wanted to wait for you . . .

Idrissa *comes rushing in.*

Idrissa   Sorry, my Oyster card had run out. The bloody Jamo conductor decided that this was the day he wanted to embarrass someone. Starts shouting at me . . . I'm 'taking the piss'. 'Who do I think I am?' Blah blah blah. I wanted to say 'I know who I am, you cultureless West Indian, do you?' (*Calms.*) Sorry . . . Good to see you, Lola . . . How was Nijah?

Lola   Fine, Idrissa, fine.

Michael   I asked Idrissa along because he has had direct experience of . . . what I want to talk about.

Lola   Which is?

Michael   I was wondering if there is an argument for Kwaku being . . . made to seek help.

Lola   Made?

Michael   When people find themselves in his situation, where they can't, or maybe refuse to see their condition for what it really is, it's up to the family and friends to sometimes be pro-active. I do consider myself family . . .

Lola (*surprised*)   You're not suggesting that we . . . section him? Is that what you've called me back to do?

The men look at each other.

Junior (*outraged*)   You didn't tell me about that, Michael.

Michael   I don't know what else to suggest! He's sticking his arse out of windows, he's shouting for black racism on the television, he's telling his own son that –

Junior   I know what he's doing, but that doesn't mean we have to put him in a madhouse!

Michael   One more outburst like that on telly, on the street even, he'll be arrested – and then what?

Junior   You know what? I'm thinking maybe he is right, maybe you *are* trying to take his crown . . .

Lola (*cuts him off*)   Junior? Calm down.

Junior (*screams*)   I won't calm down, I've been calm too long, do you hear what this traitor is saying?

Lola *approaches to calm him down with an embrace.* **Junior** *doesn't know what to do with his level of frustration. He's almost crying.*

Junior (*still there*)   You sure, you sure it's not you that's going mad, Michael? It's not you that's engineering all this so that you can . . . 'bout putting him in a madhouse.

Michael   Me? It's you guys I'm trying to pro – Look!

He grabs some papers from briefcase.

The company's bank statements for the last six months. That's the business account, savings *one*, savings *two*, umm, look at the figure at the bottom of savings two – tell me what it says!

Lola   One hundred and one thousand three hundred and . . . (*Surprised.*) He got the money. Who gave him that?

Michael   Look again, Lola, and look carefully, there's not been a withdrawal from that account – in over a year.

Lola   What are you saying?

Michael   There never was any money missing. Our payroll was covered last month by Steve putting us into unofficial overdraft . . .

Lola   No, the money had to be missing . . . He asked me to ask my father for some – couldn't the bank have just made a mistake?

Michael   It's everything they say happens when you begin to suffer from dementia. The mind is not working the way it used to. He didn't read the statements properly, Lola.

Junior   How'd you know that?

Michael   If it's not that, then he engineered the whole thing to push you out and let Adrian in – choose whatever version you want . . .

Beat.

Idrissa   When my aunt was . . . OK, what you need are two doctors, one of whom knows him well, and a social worker or a close relative to agree this is the right thing to do.

Junior   Who fucking asked you?

Michael (*a little heated*)   Trust me, if his mind deteriorates further he could be a risk to himself, Lola. No offence. There's no one at home.

Lola (*not convinced*)   Go to the board, sack his arse – nothing like a good fall to get Kwaku's juices flowing. He's not mad, he's a crazy fool, but he's not, he's just, just . . .

Michael (*firm*)   Just what, Lola? The man cannot put his father's death into context, he blames himself for not being there, for not saving him from the fall, for changing his name, for marrying an African, for . . . His father is ever-present, it's textbook stuff.

Lola   And I don't want to put my husband in a madhouse.

Michael   You think I do?!

Lola   You know what they do to black people in those places?

Michael (*shouts*)   You don't want to section him, find a way to walk him in!

Lola   Think he listens me, Michael? Do you think we'd be standing here if he listened to anyone?

Junior   Exactly!

Michael (*loses it for a second*)   If you were half the man your father was then you would find a way to make him listen.

Enter **Adrian**. *They don't know how much he's heard.*

Junior *clocks him and just stares at* **Adrian**. *We're not sure what is going through* **Junior**'s *mind at this moment.*

After a beat or so **Adrian** *walks over to his desk, one that is tidy, and starts to go through different papers.*

After a few beats **Michael** *speaks.*

Michael   Umm, I don't know about you guys, but I'm bursting for a coffee. Idrissa? Did I tell you about that new deli on the corner, Lola?

Silence. **Adrian** *of course does not respond.*

They get up and move out of the office.

Adrian   Guys, if you're getting yourselves a takeaway, mine's a latte! Thanks.

Michael *and* **Idrissa** *look at each other and exit.* **Adrian** *smiles.*

Lola *rises very slowly, staring at* **Adrian**. *She walks towards him.*

Lola   You look like her.

Adrian *doesn't know what to say for a beat.*

Adrian (*pointed*)   Mum always thought I looked more like my father, actually, but when she stared at us both together the other night she agreed I look like myself.

Lola   Please be sure to tell your mother, I'm back.

She exits. **Junior** *indicates that he will catch them up. He's not sure what he's going to say, but he's going to say something.* **Adrian** *is still staring at* **Lola**. *After a few beats:*

Adrian (*unnerved*)   Why would she do that? Why would she take the piss out of my mother?

Junior   I don't think that's what –

Adrian   Why did she do that? I mean, doesn't she think you guys have given my mum enough pain as it is?

Junior   I don't –

Adrian   Do you think laughing at us is funny?

Junior   We're not laughing at . . . Why would we do that?

Adrian   Oh, come on, Junior.

Junior (*undercutting*)   No, you come on, Adrian, I need to speak to you about something more important than –

Adrian   What? You want me to run out and get you a coffee, or some croissants, maybe?

Junior (*sincere*)   Give me a break here, Adrian. I'm trying to –

Adrian   Well, try harder! You never did quite learn to do that, did you?

Junior   Do what?

Adrian   Try hard enough. He used to bring your school reports home, you know – cussing. 'Big private school and look?' Do you know we had a whole wall full of you. Junior in school uniform, Junior at a football tournament, Junior in Grenada on holiday . . .

Junior   Why did she put them up?

Adrian   Don't be stupid . . . isn't it obvious? It was so embarrassing when my friends came round, they'd say who's that? I'd have to say – it's my cousin.

Junior   I'm sorry, I didn't know . . .

Adrian   How would you know? You were there in the big house – one big happy African family. While we, the lowly West Indians, were moving from pillar to post. So you'll

understand when I say you want something from me, you
need to try harder.

Junior   Alright, you wanna bring this down? Come we go.
I may not know what it's like to be the 'outsider'. I do know
though what it's like to not be the child your father wants you
to be – that was you, obviously. When he would rage at my
lack of academic success I now know who he was comparing
me to. Yep, I may have had the big house but you're the
one he's proud of – you, Adrian, Oxford, Portland, PhD, etc.
He listens to you. Go tell him he needs help . . . walk him into
somewhere, please . . . somewhere where someone . . .
professional can help . . . help him heal. Don't let them have
to force him. That man has done too much for his community
to end up . . . There's so much guilt floating around him . . .
so much pain – it's killing him, Adrian . . . and only you can
help . . . because he'll listen . . . to you.

Adrian   What? Because he's finally realised that what we
need is an African Caribbean think-tank, he's crazy?

Junior (*firm*)   The man needs therapy.

Adrian   The streets are filled with the walking wounded.

Junior   He needs it now before he cracks up. All this
shouting from the rooftops –

Adrian (*exclaims*)   – Is his therapy. Believe me, I know.

Junior   What do you know, Adrian? That he screamed like
an animal being skinned alive when he found his father had
been laying dead for three days at the bottom of his stairs?
That his father left everything he had to his thirty-year-old
girlfriend of two years and the rest of us nothing? That he
didn't say a word to us but went to the grave every day for
eighteen months crying, asking for forgiveness? What do you
know? Tell me what you know, O favoured one? I tell you
what I know – that if we don't help him he will fall and die.
And any legacy that the man's had will lay at the bottom of
the gutter that they pick him up from. Gloved and masked . . .

You think we're wounded now? Wait till we have to visit him in Rampton.

Beat. The boys stare at each other.

I may not be as bright as you, know all this slave history stuff, but I do know that this is how they got us to sell each other in the first place . . . told one tribe they were better than the other − while arming and saying the same to the neighbouring tribe. I want to kill you right now. If we get caught up in our own shit − no one wins. I paraphrase but I'm sure I quote a great work.

Adrian   You flatter me.

Junior   It was there to be read. I also read your conclusion. One needs to say sorry. Even when you are unsure of the harm you have caused . . . unsure of how one has personally benefited. So . . . sorry, Adrian . . .

Adrian   Stop it . . .

Junior   For all you've had to go through . . .

Adrian (*screams*)   Stop it . . .

Junior   I am sorry . . .

Adrian (*loses it*)   Just . . . stop. I neither want or need your cheap-arse apologies, alright? You can't give me the years back, can you? Can you? So it is worthless to me.

But we can see that he has been affected.

Leave me alone.

He steams out of the office.

Lights. The dub rhythm of Aswad's 'Tuffist' echoes around the room.

Scene Five

Night time. **Kwaku** *is in the office. The bottle of rum is next to him. He's opening letters and reading them.*

Soby   How's it going, boy?

Kwaku (*as if he's always been there, almost laughing*)   Really fucking badly. What have you got me into, Soby? I'm this high in shit . . . You know who I just received a letter from? The BNP. Before that, UKIP. Both asking me to be keynote speakers at their next . . .

Soby   That's good, people from all side want to hear your view?

Kwaku   They don't want to hear my view . . . they want a black face to confirm their anti-integration, anti-immigration anti-fucking . . .

Soby (*anger*)   And they right. Integration is what has failed we West Indians, boy . . . When we came here instead ah keeping we self to we self and telling we children about the horrors of de white people . . . all we wanted to do was follow dem to the pub. Come here wid all we dream and mek dem take dem from we? And we doh do nottin. We *deserve* to die. Anyone who comes to a land and doesn't know how to fight properly will *have* to die.

Kwaku   That's what you always used to say.

Soby   Because it's right. But you're not going to be like that, nooo . . . You are the first generation of university-trained Caribbeans born in dis land – dem shouldn't be able to run roughshod over you like they did us . . . You know the rules, the rules of their game . . . You have to strategise.

Kwaku   Yes, I'm sure you're right, but . . . are you sure this split thing is the right . . .

Soby   You've got to be bold, son, like I was. You going to always let me down? We is bottom of the pan-African tree? Everywhere you go, people ask you where you're from, who your people of letters are? Which thinkers had ideas that changed the course of history?

Kwaku   I'd simply say . . . Toussaint l'Ouverture – I'd say T. A. Marryshow, the father of the West Indian Federation . . . I'd say C. L. R. James, I'd say Marcus Garvey, I'd say Eric Williams . . .

The lights change as **Adrian** *walks into the room.*

Adrian   Who are you speaking to, Dad?

Kwaku *looks around. He can't see* **Soby***.*

Kwaku (*slightly confused*)   I was, I was just telling Soby . . .

Adrian   Soby? Who's Soby? Wasn't that Grandad's home name?

Kwaku *doesn't answer.*

Kwaku   What are you doing here this hour, boy?

Adrian   I came to look for you.

Kwaku (*relaxes a bit*)   Huh! (*Laughs.*) That's why me love you, you know, boy. You think about your father . . . If there's one regret I have . . . I should have followed him into the funeral business, I should have looked after 'we' first . . .

Adrian   Dad . . .

Kwaku   He's was right, you know, I lived to be exactly what he said I would be – dependant on the white man's handouts for everything . . . and it's sending me maddd, son! But I'm a warrior!

Adrian   Dad, do you think there's a possibility that you . . .

Kwaku   That I what?

Adrian (*struggles*)   I was thinking you're under a lot of pressure right now. Maybe it might be worth us checking in with someone that can help.

Kwaku *springs up.*

Kwaku   Help? What de arse you talking about? What I need help wid, Adrian? . . . I've never been better. I love this – forget Michael and dem people dem . . . War is what I'm here for . . . Look, look . . .

He picks up a piece of paper from his desk.

Check this paper I just write. We're not going to stop until the Africans say sorry too – Good heading, huh?

Adrian   But they have!

Kwaku (*stops in his tracks*)   W-w-when was that?

Adrian   December '99: President of Benin, the Ghanaian President, and forty African kings apologised for their nations' involvement in the enslavement of their fellow African people.

Kwaku   And so they should. But what's the point in doing it African to African. The ones they sold are in –

Adrian   Dad, Dad, Dad! In 2003, they toured America apologising to African people in the diaspora.

Kwaku (*angered*)   Well, they haven't said niche to we West Indians, to those of us born here, so . . .

Adrian   Dad, they all think you're going crazy . . .

Kwaku (*spells it out almost*)   Do you know how bored I am after thirty years in the race business of speaking-about-race? Of hearing my father's generation and then mine and then yours say the same things, measuring and celebrating each minute incremental step forward as if Jesus Christ had landed? I'm not crazy, son, I'm bored, and this is new, or old, or at least just something not said. Can you understand? Do you think it's crazy to want to say something that has not been said before?

Adrian   No, but it might send you crazy trying to find it! Let's prove them wrong. Let's go see someone.

Kwaku   Adrian, Adrian, what are you saying? Father in heaven! . . .

Adrian   That's where he probably is, but you were . . .
speaking to him . . .

Kwaku   Of course I was speaking to him. That's cos he's
here, that's why. Who do you think helped me out of the
situation I'm in now? Who do you think . . . He's here . . .
Who do you think I have to turn to? No one but him.

Adrian   Dad, I believe you, but put that on top of losing
your memory sometimes . . .

Kwaku   Fuck you . . .

Adrian   Not being able to concentrate . . .

Kwaku   Everybody has that . . .

Adrian   Becoming irritable, saying or doing inappropriate
things . . . Losing one's ability to keep track of finances . . .

Kwaku   Get lost, leave me the hell alone . . .

Adrian   You recognise any of those things, Dad? I want to
fight this fight too, but . . .

Kwaku   No you don't, you just want to run, like everybody
else. 'I am owed, OK', I am owed. Just as I begin to get close
to him he's . . . In fact, you know what . . . I don't want to talk
to you anymore. Go, go, just like the others.

Adrian   No one can reparate you for your father. Let's both
be strong, let's both be . . . healed, Father. That is why you
brought me here, wasn't it?

He steps to hold him . . .

Kwaku   Get out! Out! Should have left you in that stinking
hovel when you was a child. Make sure you tell your mother
what you have done to me today. Make sure. Come out! Out!

Adrian *eventually leaves.*

Kwaku   You hear them? You hear them? They saying I
crazy. Crazy, you know . . . because I can feel you . . . Crazy
cos I refuse to drop the baton but runnnn, Fadder, like you

did, run bring we to where we should be . . . These poor children, they need me, they need me to talk the truth, to tell it the way it is . . . and when they hear it, they'll know that someone cares, they'll start to hold their heads up high . . . I'm right, aren't I? Talk to me na! Do I need a healing, Daddy? You think so? Where do I find that? Am I not the one who built this place to do just that? I am right, aren't I? Tell me I was right.

Lights.

Alternative Ending

The radio version of Statement of Regret *continued with the optional alternative ending that follows.*

Kwaku   Talk to me na? I am so lonely, Dad . . . So lonely . . . I mean, if you don't speak to me, who will?

But **Soby** *has gone.*

Kwaku   You think I gone crazy too? You think so, Daddy? Just tell me I've done right. Tell me I do what you say I should. I'm so tired. Tired. Just so . . .

He lies down heavily. We hear his deep breathing, almost asleep.

After a short while **Lola** *enters. She kneels on the floor and pulls* **Kwaku** *up in her arms.*

Lola   (*firmly as if almost invoking*) Get up, Kwaku . . . Get up.

He doesn't move.

Lola   I said, get up, Kwaku . . .

After a few beats he slowly rises.

Kwaku   What you doing here Lola? Thought you were in Nigeria. (*Trying to gather himself.*) Excuse my appearance right now, I'm just . . .

She stares at him, stopping him in his tracks.

Lola   I'm taking you . . . We going to find someone to heal you, let us find someone . . . someone that can rest their hands on your head . . .

Kwaku   He tell me I need to heal! Where do I find that healing, Lola? Am I not the one that built this place to do just that?

He doesn't know what to do.

Lola   Come.

Eventually he walks towards **Lola**. *When he is close they stand looking at each other. Eventually he hugs her, for the first time in years.* **Lola** *hugs him back, in fact holds him up.*

Kwaku (*whispers*)   I'm sorry.

Lola   I know. And so am I, Kwaku. The battle has changed, Kwaku. Maybe it's time we rest. Maybe it's time we let the young ones make their mistakes.

Kwaku   Maybe. Take me home, Lola.

They walk out of the office.

Let There Be Love

Let There Be Love was first presented at the Tricycle Theatre, London, on 17 January 2008. The cast was as follows:

Gemma	Sharon Duncan-Brewster
Maria	Lydia Leonard
Alfred	Joseph Marcell

Directed by Kwame Kwei-Armah
Designed by Helen Goddard
Lighting design by Rachael McCutcheon

Characters

Alfred, *sixty-six. West Indian male. Quintessential grumpy old man, a cross almost between Alf Garnett and Victor Meldrew.*

Maria, *mid- to late twenties. Young Polish woman. Bright, sprightly and confident.*

Gemma, *thirty. Alfred's daughter. Classic last child of the pioneer generation. Struggles to know where she fits. Very attractive.*

Act One

Scene One

Front room of **Alfred Morris**'s *house. It is decorated like a classic West Indian home circa 1980. The radiogram holds pride of place in the corner, the 'globe' on a trolley that opens up revealing itself to be a bar, is somewhere close. The flowery wallpaper is almost back in vogue. The place is not dirty but is in need of serious sorting out. Only the sofa and chairs look somewhat new.* **Alfred**'s *electric wheelchair is somewhere in the room. In a another part of the room is a suitcase.*

We hear the toilet flush. Enter **Alfred**, *sixty-six. His right leg is in a light bandage, but he walks well. Waiting in the room is his daughter* **Gemma**, *thirty: a pretty girl with short cropped hair, baggy jeans but nicely fitted top. Her look is that of a trendy lesbian woman – not explicitly, but those who know can see. Although she doesn't have to,* **Gemma** *speaks most of the time in a deliberate old-school Eastern Caribbean accent. It's not an impression, just her choice. When it flips, it's back to London black.*

The atmosphere between them is frosty.

Alfred (*almost cold*) All right, well, you've seen me back home, you could go now.

Gemma *ignores him, heads for the globe bar and fixes herself another drink. The top half of the globe, however, is very wobbly.*

Gemma (*kisses her teeth*) Why you does keep dis ole ting I'll never know. And dis. (*Referring to the radiogram.*) There are music players created this side of the millennium, you know. What you running me for anyway?

Alfred I was perfectly fine to come home by meself, you know. What the damn hospital have to call you for I'll never know.

Gemma If they didn't think you needed someone to take you home they wouldn't have asked. What was you in there for anyway? Your bandages don't come off for another month.

Alfred (*ignores the questions*)   It's only because I didn't want to disturb them why I didn't call Stix's from across the road's children. *They* know when to leave.

Gemma   Stay with you for an hour is what they said, and that's what I'm going to do. (*Carefully.*) Anyway, there's something else I need to talk to you about – what you want to drink?

Alfred (*glares at her*)   At least you sister tells me straight she wish I was dead, but you is always the sneaky one, innit?

Gemma   What?

Alfred   The bungle-load ah pill you know I'm on for me pressure, me urine and me heart, and yet is drink you want to offer me?

Gemma   She didn't wish death upon you, she said she wished you weren't deaf! If you'd wear your hearing aid you'd have heard . . .

Alfred (*getting vexed*)   Hearing aid? What, hearing aid could cover the hate in she eye?

Gemma   Can you blame her, you start calling she husband a . . . (*Decides against it.*) You know what? I'm going to fix you your shake. What you want, strawberry, vanilla or chocolate?

Alfred   I don't want any.

Gemma   Well, you've got to. You've got to eat something, the doctor said . . .

Alfred (*suddenly concerned*)   Which doctor? One in the hospital?

Gemma   No, your GP.

Alfred (*relieved, kisses his teeth*)   You think I does listen to dem Indian doctor?

Gemma   He's South African, Dad.

Alfred   . . . And no matter where they come from, they is always an Indian – they will tell you dat themselves . . . you think dem like we? More West Indian dead in this town from bad advice from Indian than cock does crow.

Gemma (*tries to change subject*)   Dad, look . . .

Alfred   Look what? In me own house I can't finish a sentence? Every time I try to talk you have to stop me, Gemma?

Gemma (*taking deep breath*)   I'm not trying to stop you finishing your sentences, but, truth be told, I've heard it all before . . .

Alfred   What have you heard before?

Gemma   Your quite frankly offensive statement about Asian doctors.

Alfred   How can you be offended by the truth? You know how I have to beat up that man to give me me painkillers for me to sleep when I twist me foot?

Gemma   Dad . . .

Alfred   No, don't 'Dad' me, tell me why would you find the truth offensive?

Gemma   Maybe because it's not.

Alfred   Not what?

Gemma   Da truth. You know this isn't worth –

Alfred   – arguing about? Why, cos you can't defeat my thesis, that's why . . .

Gemma (*almost mumbles*)   That's right, Dad. I'll never be able to defeat your super-superior intelligence . . .

Alfred   That's right, bloody leave school with nothing in you head, how you go beat my intelligence?

Gemma *doesn't answer. Her mobile rings. She moves well away from her father.*

Gemma (*almost whispering*)   Saved by the . . . What you playing at? You suppose to be here. Like now . . . No, talk, he can't hear . . . For Christ's sake . . . Tell them to get someone else . . . Today! . . . Char.

She puts down the phone.

Alfred   Who was that? Your coolie *boyfriend?*

He pushes 'boyfriend' as if to provoke her. She ignores the provocation and just stares at him.

Gemma   So, do you want the shake or not?

Alfred   What don't you understand about the letters N-O, when they are in close proximity to each other?

Gemma   You *need* to eat something.

Alfred   When you're *gone*, I'll call Stix – he'll send one of his children when they get in to get me some proper food – though I have to say I doesn't like the way them new Jamaican does cook . . . Food does smell frowsy . . .

Gemma (*straight*)   Do you like anyone, Dad?

Alfred   Yes, me.

Silence.

Gemma   Dad . . . when the hospital called yesterday, Janet and I . . .

Alfred   Don't mention that girl name to me, you hear?

Gemma   My sister and I have been thinking – the whole idea why we had you move in with her, in the first place was to –

Alfred   – humiliate me! . . .

Gemma   – to have someone there that could look over you . . . Wandering around this big old house, I mean it's a potential minefield, as we done know.

Alfred That coulda happen to anybody. I'm perfectly fine looking after meself thank you.

Gemma No, you're not . . . the reason you in the hospital backside every five minutes is –

Alfred I am not in hospital every five minutes – this was a routine test, booked months ago. And the reason I'm not eating is because you try swallowing after you've had a camera on a wire shoved down your throat . . .

Gemma Why were they doing that?

Alfred (*avoiding*) Ohhh, what do you care anyway? Leave me alone. Pussyhole!

Gemma What you call me?

Alfred You heard. I said you are a pussyhole . . .

Gemma *takes a deep breath, like she's counting to ten to control herself.*

Gemma I tried tell you, you know, Dad – don't talk to me like that.

Beat. He slightly retreats, but he has succeeded in getting her off the subject.

Alfred (*kisses his teeth*) You hear you Uncle Trevor dead last week?

Gemma (*short*) Yeah, yeah.

Alfred West Indian dying like fly boy. Heart just give way, bam! Lucky bitch.

Gemma Lucky?

Alfred Better it sneak up on you than tell you in advance. Is the funeral next week, Tuesday. I can't go – cos ah me leg – but I tell he son that you would go for me, represent the family and ting, so mek sure you dress nice . . . like a *woman*, OK.

Gemma You said I'd do what?

Alfred   Represent the family. You is the eldest –

Gemma   No I'm not – Janet is.

Alfred   What you shame to represent me now? You shame ah me?

Gemma   Dad, I ain't seen Uncle Trevor or his kids since I was about six.

Alfred (*getting irate*)   And?! You see, you see, that is why you black children killing yourself on the street . . .

Gemma   What?

Alfred   Dat is we tradition, the eldest represent de fadder if he can't be there – but . . .

Gemma   I've told you, Janet is the eldest.

Alfred   Don't make me have to tell you about that again, gal.

Gemma (*finding her way in*)   Dad! I think you're absolutely right. Your leg *doesn't* allow you to do the things you want to. Rather than let me bring your suitcase up you'd rather fall down the stairs –

Alfred   I don't need your help. What help I need?

Gemma   – which actually brings me neatly to what I wanted to talk to you about. Your *daughter* and I have decided to arrange some 'assistance'.

Alfred   For who?

Gemma   A private home-help person to come here.

Alfred   Come where?

Gemma   Three times a week, just for a couple of hours . . . To check up on you.

Alfred   I don't need no one to check up on me.

Gemma   See that you're eating . . . You won't let Janet near you, and –

Alfred   She kick me out she house in the middle of the night!

Gemma   – and I'm not the look-after-Dad-at-home kinda gal, so . . .

Alfred   I don't want you to look after me.

Gemma   Good, cos it's already sorted.

Beat.

Alfred   And who paying for this?

Gemma   Janet and me . . .

Alfred   Oh, really. You, with your broke self?

Gemma   Yes, me. I'm going to pay her back, alright.

Alfred   Let me tell you something. I don't want anything from any of all you, you understand me? Now get you arse out me house. Get. Get. And the next time you come to my house ever talk stupidness to me like that again and I'll throw hot water in you face.

Gemma   You're ignorant, Dad, proper ignorant. Your prescription of painkillers from the hospital . . . Make sure you eat, Dad.

Alfred   And don't you just love me for it?

She takes a packet and a prescription from her pocket and puts them on the radiogram.

Alfred   Pussyhole.

Gemma *slowly walks out. After she's gone* **Alfred** *picks up the packet, opens it, looks at the painkillers.*

Lights.

Scene Two

The next day.

Alfred, *in his house clothes, is sitting on his sofa. He is holding the top part of his chest. We can see that he is in pain.*

He stands, walks to the drawer and pulls out the painkillers. He just stares at them and then throws them back in.

He pulls a joint out of his pocket and lights up. After two or three pulls he's settled again. Suddenly he hears a key go into the front door lock. We hear a slight struggle with the door. After a few beats we hear it open.

Alfred *heads to the sitting-room door, raising his walking stick high in the air. As* **Maria** *– twenty-five, dyed red hair covered with baseball cap, and very pale – walks into the front room,* **Alfred** *brings the cane down with force, only missing her head by inches.* **Maria** *jumps back in fright.*

Maria   Jesus!

Alfred (*snaps out*)   Who are you? What you doing in my house?

Maria   I Maria, you help . . .

Alfred   I'll bust this stick in you arse . . . how'd you get keys to my house?

Maria   Look . . . look . . . you helper.

She takes paper out of her bag and shoves it in his direction.

From agent-cie. They tell me to come – 21 Johnstone Avenue. Go see . . . see – you Mr . . . Mooorishh.

Without putting down the cane, he takes the paperwork from her and reads. After a few beats he slowly puts down the cane and looks at her.

Alfred (*sharp*)   Where are you from?

Maria   Eh, um, Good Home Services – they have all reference . . .

Alfred   No, no, no, I say where you from, which country you born?

Maria   Oh, um, Poland.

Alfred *laughs.* **Maria** *is unsure why he is laughing.*

Maria   Why you laugh?

Alfred   Well, look at me crosses – my children really don't know me. Dem don't send me a non-English-speaking immigrant to look after my needs. Listen, Polish – and I'll speak slowly so that you understand – what did they tell you to do at 21 Johnstone Avenue?

Maria   They say look after sick man.

Alfred   Could a sick man nearly knock your head off with a cane?

Maria   Depends where sick. If in the head – then, yes . . .

Alfred *(slightly wrong-footed)*   Well, there is nothing wrong with my head or any other part of me. I don't need no home help . . . I definitely don't want no Polish thieving the Englishman job neither.

Maria   They warn me you would be – how they say – upset.

Alfred   Who is they?

Maria   The agent-cie.

Alfred *(correcting her)*   Cy, cy, the agen-cy.

Maria   Agency.

Alfred   You know – when we come to dis country dem wouldn't let we *into* they house and we could *only* speak the Queen's – you lot just reach and look? Everyone breaking down they house so they could bring all you in to fix it up. Not me a rass! This blasted country makes me sick.

Maria   So you do sick.

Alfred   No, it's an English figure of speech, Polish.

Maria   No!

Alfred   No what?

Maria   No Polish. You say is English figure of speech and Polish.

Alfred   No, I was calling you Polish.

Maria   My name is Maria . . .

Alfred   What you say, Polish?

Maria   Not Polish, my name's Maria. Your name?

Alfred   Doesn't it say on the letter?

Maria   Mr . . . A. Moorishhh – sorry, Morrris. What is first name?

Alfred   Who are you, social se-bloody-curity?

Maria   I tell you mine, is only fair you tell me yours.

Alfred   Fair? You think is fair that they let so many of you into the country thieving work from we young people?

Maria   I don't . . .

Alfred   Give a monkey's. Get de fuck out me house.

Maria *looks at him.*

Maria   This word 'fook' – is bad word in English, no?

Alfred   Yes, it is.

Maria   Then why you use?

Alfred   It brings a wonderful focus and clarity to my sentences. Now, tell your agency that it is not your fault, just those that employed their services were incorrect in their assessment of my needs.

Maria   May I sit for moment before I . . . ? My heart still fast beating from attack.

Alfred   I didn't attack you.

Maria   No you, on street before here. Two young boys.

She shows him bruise on her arm.

Want phone – I give – when they see old make, they push me, give back and run. Old trick I use in Poland – always carry shit – people no like shit . . . This is big house. How many rooms you have?

She sits.

Alfred   Five. Why?

Maria   Plenty cleaning.

Alfred   No one lives in the rooms, what they need to get clean for?

Maria   My, how you say, unc-lel . . . Unclel is right word?

Alfred   I struggle to understand your sentences, you think I can work out singular words?

Maria   My brother . . . my mother brother – unc-lel . . .

Alfred   Ohh, uncle.

Maria   Yes, is word. He too has big house – not so big, but look like this. You used to have money, yes . . .

Alfred   I beg your pardon?

Maria   Well, house now looking little . . . well, how we say in Polish . . .

Alfred   Listen, young lady, I'm not interested in how you describe my house in Polish, Yiddish or Azerbaijanish. How I choose to display my wealth is my own private affair. Now before you so impertinently put my key in my door, I was on my way to a calling that people of my age ignore at their peril. When your heart has settled you can see yourself out. Leave my keys on the table. Goodbye Ms Polish – Maria.

Maria   You want help toilet?

Alfred   No! I do not . . . my leg is bandaged, I have not lost it. I'm going to keep the door open. Any nonsense and I'll be out swinging . . . as it were. Goodbye.

He leaves, quickly. **Maria** *takes a bottle of water out of her bag. Then she unwraps her sandwiches from the foil, takes a single bite and wraps them back again.* **Maria** *looks around and spots the gramophone and globe. She thinks for a second, then gets out her cleaning liquids and starts to polish the globe.*

Maria   *Tom to jest.* [*There you are.*]

And then she continues. When she finishes the globe she looks at the gramophone and marvels at it.

She lifts the head of the gram and sees the turntable inside.

Mr . . . A. Morriss, what is this – ?

She looks at the name of the machine.

Bluespot . . .

Alfred (*shouts from off*)   What are you doing near my gramophone? Get away from my gram.

We hear the toilet flush and **Alfred** *moves as fast as he can back to the front room.*

Who told you to touch up me tings? Step away from the gram.

Maria (*ignoring his stress*)   How beautiful is this machine . . . I no see before . . . I take back, you man of taste . . .

Alfred   Take back?

Maria   Oh when I came in I thought you like most English, rich but no understanding of history.

Alfred   History?

Maria   Is wrong word but I know what I mean. How many years you have this?

Alfred   Umm, if you must know, July 12th 1963. First thing I ever bought in England.

Maria   Wow. Many years older than me. You must be old Mr . . . Morrisss.

Alfred (*ignoring*)   Thank you. Is the only way I does remember my children birthday actually. Janet was born four years after I bought Lillie – that's she name – and then the mistake – Gemma – eight years after that . . .

Maria   Mistake? What is that mean?

Alfred (*softer, but correcting her*)   What *does* that mean.

Maria (*trying it*)   What does that mean?

Alfred   Exactly.

Maria   So?

Alfred   Oh! It means, how can I say this politely? I thought we were covered against such mishaps – but nothing in life is one-hundred-per-cent safe.

Maria   I think I know what you speak of. Yes, life can throw – how Americans say – curve ball.

Alfred *looks blank.*

Maria   My boyfriend love baseball. Lillie is nice antique.

Alfred   Antique? This is a hi-tech, hi-spec, fully functioning gramophone. This baby doesn't only still play, it polishes the record before she plays them . . .

Maria   Nooo, she still can work?

Alfred   What you mean?

He dashes over to 'Lillie' with joy.

OK, you ready for this?

He slides open the bottom drawer and takes out three LPs.

Which shall it be, Lillie? Who will show you off the best to our Polish friend here that thinks we don't have class or pedigree?

Eyes closed, he places each LP on 'Lillie' as if waiting for her to reply. After placing all three, he goes back to the second one: The World of Nat King Cole.

He places the disc on the turntable and it starts to play the jazzy introduction to 'Let There Be Love'.

Alfred *smiles all over his face as Nat's dulcet tones glide their way through the words. He starts to sway almost with the rhythm.*

Alfred (*shouts over music*)   You have them rhythm dere in Poland, girl? Heyyy! Who needs people, eh, when you have Nat? I tell you something – forget CD, DVD, greenray or stingray, you have a problem in this world, Nat and Lillie guaranteed to have the answer. Doesn't she sound glorious?

Maria   She does. But must you play so loud?

Alfred   Oh!

He bends over to turn down the volume, but has a shooting pain in his chest.

Ah!

Maria   Are you alright?

Moves to help him. He pushes her arm off quite violently.

Alfred   I'm fine . . .

Maria   Here, have chair . . .

Alfred   I said I'm fine. I'm not an invalid, you know.

He slowly makes his way back to his chair. Once seated he begins to breath in and out, in and out, quite deeply while gently massaging his chest. He takes a packet of Polo mints out of his pocket and places one in his mouth.

Eventually he returns to breathing normally.

Maria   It say nothing on medical record of heart.

Alfred   That's because there is nothing wrong with my heart. Let me see that?

He takes a sheet from her and stares at it, checking out what it says about him.

Where did they get this information?

Maria   I don't know. Why you rub?

Alfred   Because, Ms Noseache Maria, I very occasionally have problems breathing.

Maria   Do your doctor know?

Alfred (*kisses his teeth*)   Don't get me started on my doctor – huh! Char, I have my own remedy. Is not everything you must wait on the state to do for you. Your people know all about that, don't they, Polish?

Maria   Know what?

Alfred   Horrors of the state doing everything for you . . .

She looks blank.

Alfred   Lech Walesa? Solidarity?

Maria   I know very little of politics, Mr Morrisss.

She moves next to the gram. Opens her arms as if about to twirl.

(*Changing subject.*) But I know lovely music. It reminds me of America . . . I learn all my English from American film. You ever been to America, Mr Morrisss?

Alfred   Once or twice.

Maria   Is it wonderful there – like in movie? 'Make my day, punk.' 'I be back.'

Alfred   Of all the glorious black-and-white romantic movies, that's what you know?

Maria   Is what I want to say to those boys today.

Alfred   You wanted to shoot them?

Maria *just smiles as if entertaining the thought.*

Alfred   You been in the country two minutes and you want to start shooting black children already? You have no idea what those children are going through, no idea what their parents and grandparents have been through, so don't you come here and start to judge them . . . Do you hear me, Ms White Polish?

Maria   Who say they black?

Beat. **Alfred** *coughs.*

Alfred   Like I was saying, I've been to America a few times. Nothing like the movies at all.

Maria   What is like then?

She sits, almost eager to hear. He takes a second to take in that **Maria** *actualy wants to hear him speak.*

Alfred (*surprised she wants to hear*)   You really want to (*know*). . . (*Smiles.*) Big. Everything is double the size you think it should be. Including the women.

Maria   I don't think is very funny, Mr Morisss.

She shows him the badge on her jacket: 'Route 66'.

Have you been here? Route 66? Tomas, my boyfriend, say he see it. But I don't believe him. He lie very much.

Alfred *smiles, indicates for her to wait a minute. He places the needle on a track. The jazzy opening of Nat King Cole's 'Get Your Kicks on Route 66'.*

At Nat's words, **Maria** *laughs, and she asks:*

Maria   Is really two thousand kilometre?

Alfred (*jumping to music*)   No, miles, that's about what? Three thousand kilometre? Isn't this baby jumping?

Maria *starts to dance to the music.*

After another verse, **Alfred** *switches it off.*

Maria   I am beginning to believe you – this Nat . . . ?

Alfred   King Cole.

Maria   He do – (*correcting herself*) *does* have answer to questions.

Alfred *smiles.*

Alfred   All questions in the world! This is what don't have me in one ah, England madhouse.

Maria   How long you been in England, Mr Morrissss?

Alfred (*rubbing head*)   Last count? . . . Forty-five years, three months, and two weeks.

Maria   When you last count?

Alfred   This morning.

Maria   So you English then!

Alfred (*flash of vexation*)   Don't you ever call me that!

Maria   Oh. OK.

Alfred   How long you been thieving English jobs, Ms Polish?

She raises her eyes.

Maria   I been here year and half months. But I go home soon for holiday? I miss my home.

Alfred   That never changes, no matter how long you here.

Maria (*very gently*)   May I give you trick for chest?

She waits for permission.

Put real ginger from shop on corner in pot of hot water with lemon and um, how you say? (*She says it in Polish first.*) Like pepper . . .

Alfred   What you talking about, child? That is an old West Indian remedy. What all you people in the cold know about ginger and clove?

Maria   I don't know where come from. I just use with my father.

Alfred   Well, I'm not your father, and when you quoting West Indian tings with me . . .

Maria *suddenly jumps up.*

Maria   Oh!

Alfred   What?

She looks at her watch.

Maria   I am due next job?

Alfred   You've only been here a few minutes.

Maria   They tell me come, Johnstone Avenue, client will attack you with stick, you leave immediate, claim full hour . . . Next client booked thirty minutes after attack.

Alfred   They knew I would attack you?

Maria (*throws away*)   Yes. Other lady say no, but for full hour pay is worth risk – and I need money . . .

Alfred (*ignoring*)   What cleaning could you possibly do in an hour?

Maria   All new job start with hour, then, if both happy, increase. (*Beat.*) You want increase Mr A. Morris?

Alfred *looks up at her. And stares for a while.*

Alfred (*almost reluctantly*)   I don't need no increase of nothing . . . but if you passing the chemist or even the ginger shop you could bring these back with you – if you dare.

He takes the prescription from his pocket and hands it to her, along with a fiver.

Maria *smiles and exits.* **Alfred** *smiles before pulling a hard face again.*

Lights.

Scene Three

A few weeks later. **Alfred** *is by a drawer. He pulls out a letter and slips it in his pocket as secretly as he can.* **Gemma** *is walking around.*

Gemma   Three weeks and the place looking better already, boy . . . Look like Polish workin' hard . . .

Alfred   That's what you paying her for, innit?

Gemma   Innit. What's your leg doing out of bandage? It's suppose to be on for another week.

Alfred   Think I rely on dem man dere? I remembered a therapy my mother use to tell me about and bam, the leg fix. Nothing a little ginger rub won't cure. Anyway, what you doing here again?

Gemma *doesn't reply to that.*

Gemma   Dad . . . can't you forgive Janet? I know she went too far – but calling she husband a white bastard and de child a half-breed wretch, cos she told you to not smoke weed in she house, it's enough to make anyone flip.

Alfred (*to* **Gemma**)   Is not him that say the reason he relate to black people is because his father left his mother when he was in the womb, so he has a natural affinity to us black men? Fucking cheek. I raise two children by myself – he has no affinity with me, I can tell you dat.

Gemma   She wants to come over and apologise.

Beat.

Alfred   Did I ever tell you the story . . .

Gemma (*ignoring*)   Probably. I told her I'd ask you, but . . .

Alfred   Everything I say you've heard before, innit?

Gemma   I really think you should, Dad. Life is too short to be . . .

Alfred   Is it? And what you know about life, child? In fact, (*flips the script*) what is your job, Gemma? What are you doing with your life? Come on, tell me.

Gemma   Umm, bits an' pieces . . . Actually, that's kinda what I want to talk to you about . . .

Alfred   I thought you were talking about your sister and forgiveness?

He coughs and subtly holds his chest. **Gemma** *sees.*

Gemma   What? The agency said Polish tell them you in more pain. You never use to do that, rub your chest and dat.

Alfred (*irritated*)   Don't you have somewhere else to go, someone else to see? Why you always here?

Gemma   Is there a problem with me wanting to see my father?

Alfred   When it is preceded by three years of no-shows, yes. Please. Leave my house.

Beat. **Alfred** *puts a fresh piece of ginger in his mouth.*

Gemma   I know you're gonna get mad, but I want you to just listen to me for a moment. Just hear me out and think about it.

Alfred *doesn't reply.*

Gemma (*carefully*)   I was thinking maybe it's time to diversify your portfolio . . . This house is to big for you, Dad – hear me out – maybe if you sold it, and brought a flat maybe, something a little more manageable in the same area, you could buy another flat as an investment . . . I could live in it for you. Eventually even buy it off you, even.

Alfred   What happen to where you living now? The place you never invite me, the *partner* you never does bring me to see?

Gemma   You haven't met because . . . (*Gives the facts.*) If you must know, my partner's gone away for six months and . . .

well, it's over. I need to be out by the time . . . by the end of
summer.

Alfred   You're not moving back in here?

Gemma   Damn right . . . but I don't want to rent again
and although I've been saving, I don't have enough – so I
figure . . . it's not like you've got the money sitting in the bank
that you could loan me. I mean if you did, I'd pay you back,
right.

Alfred   Pay me back with what, Gemma? What do you
have to offer the world that they will give you the kind of
wages you'd need to pay me back?

Gemma   You don't have to speak to me like that, you
know! Loads of parents are helping their kids out.

Alfred   You're not child, you thirty years old, and you
should have thought about that before you left your husband
and child for some bloody coolie man . . .

Gemma   Kia isn't my child, OK! She's Ronald's (*child*) . . .

Alfred   You denying your own child? Denying me a
grandchild?

Gemma (*well irritated*)   I love her, but I met him with her . . .
Don't be placing that guilt on me . . .

Alfred   Did ever I say that about you?

Gemma (*knows where he's heading*)   Don't do this, Dad . . .

Alfred   You know the rumours – you don't look anything
like me.

Gemma   Why are you doing this?

Alfred   But did I run away from you? Even when your
mother left with she new man, did I reject you? No, I'm the
one that stood here.

Gemma (*slightly losing*)   I'm asking you for help, it's not easy you know . . . but you always do this to me? Why you trying to flip it on me? Why you trying to make us fight?

Alfred   You Indian coolie done use you up, and you want to come to me for help? Where were you when I needed help? Where were you? I tell you where, galivanting in Grenada with a woman that didn't give a rass about you . . . Go there and ask your mother for money na!

Gemma   I would if I could . . . believe me.

Alfred   Then you should. You's an ungrateful bitch . . .

Gemma   You know what, Dad, forget it, just bloody forget it. Fuck, people can't talk to you.

She walks out and slams the front door.

Alfred (*almost to himself*)   Yes, that's all you women in this family know how to do, innit? Walk off. Pussyhole. Don't worry – I don't need none of you. None of you. You hear me? I'm good by myself.

Eventually he sits and switches on the TV, puts the volume to the maximum, although he's not taking any of it in. A soap opera is on.

Oh goodie, my favourite soap.

A key is inserted into the front door and it opens. After a few beats **Maria** *walks into the front room.*

Maria   Oh, is terrible loud.

She takes the remote from him and turns it down.

I saw Gemma run out of house . . . she OK?

He doesn't answer. **Maria** *sneezes as she takes out new pills from the pharmacy.*

Here are your pills. I never see you take these ones.

Alfred (*sharp*)   They put me to sleep, so you wouldn't, would you? Why'd you have to go and tell them that I'm in pain?

Maria   Work they ask, I have to report.

Alfred   Well, next time don't. I don't want anyone knowing my business.

Maria   I try best. But if they ask . . .

Alfred   You tell them to call me. I will tell them all they need to know.

Maria   OK.

She sneezes.

Excuse me.

Alfred (*still in mood*)   Bless you.

Maria   Thank you. I get food.

Alfred *turns his eyes back to the soap. After a few beats he shouts.*

Alfred   How old are your parents, Maria?

Maria   Oh, my mother, how you say, fifty, my father no longer here, but two years older, I think. Why you ask?

Alfred (*makes him smile*)   You speak to her often?

Maria   Every day. If not, she think I die. Tell her how much money we save, how close we am to coming home, opening big business in village.

Alfred (*not really hearing*)   I use to write my mother once a week . . . well once a month. You owe it to your parents, love, no matter what. (*Kisses his teeth.*) Char!

He turns the television volume up again.

Maria *enters the room with his food.*

Maria   What is that sound you make with teeth?

Alfred   An articulation of acute dissatisfaction.

Maria   Of television?

Alfred   How is man suppose to lose himself in the nonsense they does put on?

Maria   If is stupid, and you know is stupid, why watch stupid?

Alfred   What did you call me?

She hands him tablets.

Maria   Here, drink this.

He switches channel to the news.

Now take blood-pressure tablet . . . heart tablets . . . and now the urine tablet.

Alfred *takes a sip of his shake and swallows the many tablets.*

Alfred   It's a toss-up for me you know – die or drink this horrible shit.

TV   The trial of Hussain Khan, one of the attempted bombers of the London night club . . .

Alfred   Should be shot.

Maria   You think?

Alfred   Of course. How doctors can make medicine taste so horrible, I'll never know. If they had to face the bullet they'd soon sweeten it up, I tell you . . .

He switches back to the soap.

No no, no more bad news – back to the soap.

Maria   But you say you no like . . . ?

Alfred   There are many things in life I do that I do not like.

She exits back to the kitchen.

Children for starters. Don't have them, Maria, whatever you do. They're ungrateful bitches . . .

Maria   You know what I think? When was the last time you went home? You need to go back home.

Alfred   You just reach and you telling me to get out you country already?

Maria   Is not my country. I just think you should stop doing what dissatisfy you. Is not good for health. We start with this.

She switches off the television.

Alfred   Don't come in my house and order me about! You not in the Czech Republic now, you know!

Maria   I'm not from Czech . . .

Alfred   Same ting, all you people have tendency to autocratic rule.

Maria   What mean you auto –

Alfred   Don't worry.

Maria   Fine. I won't. But what you say very rude.

Alfred   That you have a tendency to autocratic rule?

Maria   That I Czech. I hate Czech. I look like Czech to you? We not look all the same, you know.

Maria *is upset. He see and calms.*

Alfred (*trying to be warm*)   Sorry . . . you're right. That's how I feel when people call me Jamaican. (*Switching subject.*) How was Brent Cross?

Maria (*suddenly beams with joy*)   Oh, just great. Sooo many beautiful things! When I rich and have house I will spend my whole life there. I want to have big chair in centre room like in John Lewis, and all white furniture from the white store – computers by Apple – curtains from Next – as well as much clothes . . . Then I take all back to Poland and find new rich (*husband*).

She stops herself and switches but **Alfred** *has noticed a moment of sadness in her eyes.*

Maria   You should go there, Mr Morris. Your dissatisfy will fly away.

Alfred   Oh, it's far too deep-seated for that, trust me.

Maria   Is heaven, Mr Morris, it must. Second only to IKEA.

She sneezes again.

Excuse me.

Alfred   That's your third sneeze today. How can you nurse a sick man and you have a cold?

Maria (*her face drops*)   I home help, not nurse.

Alfred   Go in the cupboard over the cooker, you should see a Lemsip, it might be out of date but hey. . . !

Maria   . . . No, no, I'm fine.

Alfred   Are you sure you are OK?

Maria   No, I cold is all.

Alfred   The heating's on.

Maria   Not here . . . in my house . . . where I live. Is very cold in night.

Alfred   Don't watch the pennies and pounds when it comes to your body, that's you engine, you know. Put the heating on . . .

Maria   . . . Is my landlady! Say cost too much gas.

Alfred   But it was minus three last night.

Maria   I have jumper I buy Brent Cross . . .

Alfred (*a little vexed*)   Huh, these English doing they stupidness again . . .

Maria   No, she Polish like me.

Alfred   Really?

Maria   Friend of boyfriend . . . We all live together there.

Alfred   Can't *he* tell her . . . ?

Maria   He do, but she . . . put on for one hour then take off. Is no good.

Alfred   You are paying this woman rent, right?

Maria   Much.

Alfred   Well, tell her again, you're a working woman. You can't be walking around sneezing. You know what?

Maria   Where are you going, Mr Morris?

Alfred (*shouts*)   Alfred, I told you call me Alfred.

Maria   You never did . . .

Alfred   Where is it? When you don't want the damn ting it's always there – when you need it now . . .

Maria   You want help?

Alfred   No, no, no. Ahh, there you are.

He re-enters the room with an old-fashioned one-bar electric heater.

Alfred   Da naaaaaa.

Maria   What is this?

Alfred   Let us call it for argument sake a CLB. Cheap landlord buster.

Maria   What you mean by this?

Alfred   Well, you get your boyfriend to walk into the house carrying this instrument. He politely knocks her door and says, would it be alright if he uses an electric heater in the room as you are coming down with colds and fears both of you won't be able to work for a few days – hence might be a little late with the rent.

Maria   How will this make difference?

Alfred   It'll make her shit sheself. This baby eats more in one hour than the whole central heating system does in a week. She'll grab that heater out of his hand and rush to the thermostat quicker than you can say – I'm a Polish builder.

Maria (*not convinced*)   OK, I try. But I don't think boyfriend will like . . .

Alfred   You're always talking about your boyfriend . . .

Maria   Cos he great man. Big plans for us. He know English! If not for him I no be here . . .

Alfred   It's not good to just follow man plan willy-nilly.

Maria   Oh no, I have own plan – many. I save to go college here. When return home – I have brains as well as money, no longer shit like neighbour think I am for . . .

Alfred   Why your people think you are?

Maria (*changes subject, laughs*)   People think what they want. When you went out I thought maybe you looking for Nat King Cole record to give me cure for cold . . .

Alfred   No Nat today – even he would find it difficult to answer my questions today.

Maria   What questions do they?

Alfred   Are they.

Maria   *Are* they.

Though she can see that he is miles away, deep in thought.

(*Has an idea.*) Come, Alfred, you dissatisfy, I dissatisfy, let us go to heaven.

Alfred   What you dissatisfied about? And go where?

Maria   Today quiet, you are last job of the day. Let us go second heaven – let us go IKEA.

Alfred   More like the sixth ring of hell, you mean.

Maria   I have not been for long time. See new sofa, lie down in bed, imagine you have kitchen made by God . . . Watch the smiles on the thousands of people picking and choosing great new home contents . . .

Alfred   I told you, I don't like being around people.

Maria   Forget the people then. Let us go and . . . buy
something new for your house – you will feel better. This sofa
for instance, old, horrible . . .

Alfred   There's nothing wrong with me – or that sofa, I only
bought it two years ago . . .

Maria   That is old, Alfred. This is London – every year,
everything new, whole house, or you are not living. That is
why you are sad all time.

Alfred   What is it with people and my house today? Sad,
who told you that?

Maria   Just come and watch me dream then.

Alfred   If you want to dream, go dream with your
boyfriend . . .

Maria   I don't want to dream with boyfriend.

Alfred (*flips*)   Well, you're not going to IKEA with me.
I don't just go and idle in centres designed to intoxicate the
simple-minded. I have deeper things on my mind. And I'll
have you know that I am not sad. I'm very happy indeed –
ha-ha-ha-happy – in the confines of my own house, with my
own company and my own old furniture.

Maria   But you don't have to be –

Alfred   I choose to. That's the problem with you white
people wherever you're from, you want to come and tell the
black man how to live he life. Well, I won't have it. You hear
me?

Maria   I sorry I wasn't trying to . . . I lose myself for
moment. Sorry. Umm. I think I finish here for the day. I go
home now.

She gets her things together and presents **Alfred** *with her book to sign.*

She makes for the door, then turns before she leaves.

Maria   Excuse English, but all was trying to say is whether
in chair like you or have pain like me, outside is good.

She leaves. **Alfred** *stares at her, a little ashamed. He then takes a letter from his pocket and stares at it. Then he goes to the tablet drawer and throws all the tablets into the bin – all except the painkillers that are in a big blue packet. He looks at the painkillers and an idea is born.*

He picks up the phone.

Alfred   You, my friend, you all I need. Rubbish urine, rubbish heart rubbish. Maria, come back.

Lights.

In the scene change we hear Nat King Cole's 'Straighten Up and Fly Right'.

Scene Four

Later that evening. We hear the front door open and **Alfred** *is pushed in by* **Maria**. *They are laughing their heads off.*

Maria   I told you, didn't I?

Alfred   What, that I'd be in a queue for three hours?

Maria   *Why* you in queue for three hours, Alfred?

Alfred   Cos the whole world and his stepchild was in there?

Maria   Because you kept going back to warehouse section to buy another thing just as you get to checkout.

Alfred   You were the one that pointed them out to me . . .

Maria   So you could pick up then?

Alfred   I don't shop like that. I have to think about it, then if me spirit tell me, I buy.

Maria   Your spirit told you you needed six tealight candle-holders?

Alfred (*correcting her*)   Glazed porcelain teacup holders.

Maria   A packet of extra large plastic glasses?

Alfred Yes!

Maria A bag of IKEA rubber bands –

Alfred Most important ting to have in a house, rubber bands.

Maria – and a cocktail shaker?

Alfred Man has to be able to shake a good concoction!

Maria I agree, but spirit concern itself with such things?

Alfred Depends on the spirit!

Maria *opens a bag and pulls out a big red throw. She throws it over herself as falls on the sofa.*

Alfred You like your throw?

Maria Oh yes.

He pauses for a moment, almost in reverie.

Alfred It's funny, you know, I saw a man the spit of an old friend of mine in that IKEA – Harold. Use to take us all to every funeral in town. We walk into one in Tottenham one day and Harold do just freeze when he see the widow.

Maria Why he freeze?

Alfred If you'd stop jumping in I'll tell you.

Maria You like my father. You temper soooo funny.

Alfred Anyway, Harold was one unlucky brother. He send for two woman from home and both of dem leave him. But he didn't give up – he dig deep and send for a next woman he just about know from high school – Rosemarie. Nobody knew Rosemarie, all the boys tell him, how you could send for a woman you doe know? But he said 'Ah desperate, boy.'

Maria Ahhh.

Alfred So we all go with him to meet the woman at Portsmouth Harbour. When we see dat woman, *every* man mouth drop. I never see a woman so pretty in my life. All man just shake me hand and say – gwann, big Al.

Maria   Al?

Alfred   I mean Harold.

Maria   Alfred you telling story? What happened?

Alfred   What happened? Nothing.

Maria   Nothing?

Alfred   Harold was so taken by the woman, so 'fraid of this beautiful thing before him, he mash it up.

Maria (*falls out*)   How, he abuse her?

Alfred   Abuse? Who tell you anything about abuse?

*It's as if **Alfred**, having pulled another story from the sky, switches and continues.*

Alfred   He wouldn't service.

Maria   Service?

Alfred (*frustrated*)   Sex, Maria!

Maria   Ah, service. She no have sex toys?

Alfred   Decent women wouldn't do that in those day.

Maria   Sad days.

Alfred   Dey say she really love him, but a woman has she needs! Eventually, she find a next man and bam, she gone . . . But twos-twos she nes man dead and his he funeral in Tottenham we arrive at. When Harold see Rosemarie in she funeral blacks, it was like Portsmouth Harbour all over again.

Maria   He so sweet?

Alfred   When Rosemarie see him, she eyes light up and she come and she hug him and hug him and hug him up you see. From that day forward, we never see Harold again. I hear they married and living somewhere in the Caribbean.

Maria   Ahhh, that is lovely story. Like fairy tale.

Alfred   No, it's not. Harold was the only one of us wid a car, so that was the last funeral I went to. Last time I really went out and had some fun.

Maria   Do you think he service now?

Alfred   That was seven years ago.

Maria   You said five.

Alfred   Five, seven, what's the difference . . .

Maria   You right, they probably too old for that now.

Alfred   What?

Maria   They are old people, what need they of . . .

Alfred   Young lady, there's always a need. The flesh might not be willing but there are prescription drugs for that these days.

Maria   So because you no have Harold you stay in house all time?

Alfred   I don't like going out, Maria, because West Indians are run mouth people . . . Before you know it they telling everyone I have this, I have dat, and they be cleaning their suits for my funeral. I don't have time for that.

Maria (*stares at him, asks directly*)   What is illness you have, Alfred?

Alfred   You ever think about death, Maria?

Maria   Sometimes.

She makes her way towards the gram.

Alfred   You ever wished for death?

Maria   Nearly, but no.

Alfred   That's my illness, Maria. I wish for death.

Maria   Why?

Alfred   The question is, what's a young woman like you is doing thinking about death?

Maria   Only once or twice – everybody does, no?

Alfred   When you asked me for the days off last week but you wanted me to sign. You know where you stood? Right there. Right by Lillie. Now you standing there again.

She doesn't answer. **Alfred** *just stares at her. He spots something.*

Alfred   Come here.

Eventually she does.

Bend over.

She does. He looks at her face.

I haven't seen this before. When did you get this?

Maria (*trying to move away*)   It's nothing. I just . . . The boys stopped me on way home from here on Monday. I had good phone. Wouldn't let go, so they . . . hit me till I did. Is fine now.

Alfred   You wasn't here on Monday . . . Did you call the police?

Maria   What is point?

Alfred (*flushing her out*)   What is the point? I'm going to call them right now.

Maria   No . . . don't.

Alfred   You have to report these things, Maria, or else –

Maria   Please, Alfred. Please do not.

Alfred   No no, I have to. It's very important that we –

Maria   I want no trouble. It wasn't boys, OK? Was accident.

Alfred   What kind of accident does bruise up you head like if you run into a man's fist?

Maria   Alfred, can this we forget . . .

Alfred   No Maria, this is serious tings. What is going on?

Maria   You wouldn't understand.

Alfred   Wouldn't understand?

Maria   No, you don't, can't understand feelings of (*woman*).

Alfred   Maria, nothing in the world insults as much as people thinking I can't understand any or everything . . . What, you and Tomas was fighting? You provoke him or something? You seeing a next man?

Maria   Me! Me . . . provoke?

She grabs her phone from bag and shows **Alfred** *picture text. It is of a naked woman bent over a sofa snapped from behind on camera phone.*

Maria   You want to see provoke? This is provoke? I forward from his phone. Naked woman bent over settee – is landlady.

Alfred   Oh!

Maria   This, Mr Morriss, they do when I go to work. I read you this . . .

Alfred   It's fine . . . the picture gives me all the information I need (*thank you*).

Maria (*ignoring*)   Roughly translate . . . 'You love my beautiful pussy from behind?' Here is it. Next one . . .

Alfred   There really isn't a need to – I quite understand . . .

Maria   'I bend over and open up for you to . . . '

Alfred   Maria!

Maria   When I ask him why, how you say, *bam* in face.

Alfred   Why didn't you talk to me about . . . ? I could have told you (*what to do*).

Maria   What you want me to say? Hello, Mr Alfred, my boyfriend just punch hell from me today? What you then think of Polish people? I prefer lie, OK.

Beat.

Alfred   How often does this (*happen*)?

Maria   Is why I no work last week. I go look for other room to rent. But I cannot afford. I need to get out of there, Alfred, or I will . . .

Alfred   You damn right.

Maria   But where I go?

Alfred   Anywhere. Do you have any friends that live locally?

Maria   No.

Alfred   How about . . .

Maria   I have no one anywhere, OK. Tomas is all I know. Why you think I stay here till late or go to IKEA, or Brent Cross or my Whiteleys in Queensmarket.

Alfred   Way . . . Queens-way . . .

Maria   That's right. That way he and she can finish and maybe he leave me alone.

She breaks down a little.

I don't know what to do. I think as you say, Alfred, it will either go away or I get use to. But it is not. And I cannot go home, all my village expect me to return rich, like everyone else. I can't do it alone and I cannot return with nothing. Why men do this, Alfred? Why men so bad?

Beat.

Alfred   I, I, um, don't know. He probably doesn't mean to . . .

Maria   What that mean? I tell you for sure one of these nights one of us three die for sure. I am father's child, I cannot take. How long you take shit for, eh, Alfred? In house I live?

Alfred (*thinks*)   What time he get home?

Maria   Tonight late. He work east London.

Alfred   OK. Go home and get you tings! Go on, then come right back here.

Maria   What?

Alfred   You move in here till we find you somewhere safe to live.

Maria   Why you do that for me, Alfred – you no know me? No, no, no.

Alfred   I'm not doing it for you I'm doing this for me. Who knows, if it does works out, maybe there's a little something you can help *me* with. A little something you can do for me. Go get your stuff.

Maria   Really?

Alfred   Go get your tings.

She slowly leaves. When she has left he walks up to the gram and places the needle on a record. Out blasts Nat King Cole's 'Lets Face the Music and Dance'.

Alfred   What you think, King?

Nat
   There may be trouble ahead . . .   (*Etc.*)

Act Two

Scene One

Two months later. **Maria** *is dancing to Nat King Cole's 'Orange Coloured Sky'. She is singing along as if performing for* **Alfred**, *who is in his chair. He is looking a lot weaker and more frail than he was, but is still joining in with the song. She sings a couple of lines and he joins in with the refrains. They fall about laughing.*

Alfred Good choice, girl, good choice! I'm exhausted just looking at you.

Maria Come and dance then. You haven't got out that chair in three days.

Alfred Let me tell you – in me young days when I enter the dance hall all the young ladies would bwal 'Fire in the house'.

Maria What that mean, fire?

Alfred It mean I would burn up the dance floor with me hot moves.

He coughs for a little. **Maria** *gets him a drink.*

Maria I can believe it. Tell me a story about you and the dance floor, Alfred.

Alfred Girl, you take me for poppyshow? And before you ask, it's West Indian for puppet show. As in amusement – Punch and Judy. Never mind.

Maria I know Punch and Judy?

Alfred You do?

Maria Yes. I read all about England before I come, you know. Anyway, tell me a story.

He waves her off.

I know, tell me one of when you first come England, I get food out.

He looks at her and smiles.

Alfred   Oh, girl, I done forget most ah dem . . . or more frightening, I don't remember whether they are in fact my stories or other people's! I don't want to eat, Maria. I told you, it hurts.

Maria   I went all way to Shepherd's Bush, you know how many times I had to change bus to get you favourite chicken roti and sorrel juice?

Alfred   Who tell you to go and do that?

Maria   You refuse to drink doctor nutrition shake – you won't take tablet. I think maybe if I get favourite food like mother cook, you don't have to send for girlfriend from Grenada and I get to stay here.

Alfred (*smiles*)   Take out the chicken, just leave the juice in the skin. Let me try that.

Maria   Only if you tell me story. I like your stories, Alfred.

Alfred (*stares at her*)   You making me want to change me mind, girl . . . You like it here, Maria?

Maria   In your house?

Alfred   Yes.

Maria   You save me, Alfred. For two month I sleep properly at night. I warm, you find me social security number and citizenship test booklet to make me better citizen. You make so that Tomas cannot find where I live. You are my angel, I very happy.

Alfred   Don't go too far now.

Maria   I am not going to ask you again!

She leaves for the kitchen.

Alfred   I didn't really want to come to England . . .

Maria   Yeahhh . . .

Alfred   I was very happy tending my goats and writing the odd poem or story while I watch them, but one day I went in search of my friends and it suddenly hit me that all of them had gone to England. So I sold two of my goats – big money that, you know, cos dem was fat – jumped on a boat and, man, by the time I arrived in Puerto Rico via Jamaica and Barbados, I was ready to come home. I had seen so much of the world I couldn't take any more. Like being in an art museum, and you can't take it all in. But I stayed on till England. I had never felt cold like that in my life. I couldn't stop writing home. Each time the chill hit me – I go for me pen. Each time a damp lick – I dash for me paper.

Maria (*off*)   Who were you writing to if all your friends were here?

Alfred   My mother! The only letter I ever got back from her – I don't know who she found to write it – was to tell me how surprised she was to read that I had seen a white man pushing a trash van.

He laughs in remembrance.

Twenty-second of May 1960. Still remember the day. I laughed – I rounded up all we new boys to the cold and we just stood there laughing.

Maria (*off*)   Why you laugh?

Alfred   We had never seen a white man do lowly labour like that. Always thought they were better than us – always acted like they was better than us . . . dem white man. Huh!

Maria *enters with food.*

Maria   I don't like when you talk like that.

Alfred   Is that so, Ms Maria?

Maria   Yes, is so, Mr Alfred.

Alfred   And what you going to do about it?

Maria   Not give you your chicken roti!

Alfred Ha! Girl, you think I give a damn about eating?

Maria Then, when you in pain I make you take tablet.

Alfred To make me feel worse ten minutes later.

Maria Your wife – was she white?

Alfred Why do you ask that?

Maria I just wonder sometimes if she is one that hurt you. So you think all is same . . .

He takes a small bite of the roti and **Maria** *helps him take a sip of the juice.*

Alfred Ummm, nice.

Maria (*looks at him*) Alfred, what is really wrong with you? You lose too much weight and you don't go to doctor? I worry is me, no look after you properly.

Alfred I don't need to go doctor, and you have cured my main illness . . .

Maria Which is?

Alfred Do you know the last time someone asked me anything other than – 'Does this hurt?' – 'Can you loan me some money?' – 'Can you sell you house?' Truth is I can't remember, and then – (*Sings.*) 'Wham! bam! alakazam! Wonderful you came by.'

Maria I said what is wrong with you, Alfred? Not why you enjoy telling me stories.

Alfred If nobody don't care about how you get here, how you suppose to feel? Your journey has been of no consequence – that you have achieved nothing in your life.

Maria You have achieved much. You have big house, two beautiful daughters.

Alfred (*vexed*) Those jinals. They born here born with all the advantage and like me they achieved nothing? One is a born-again nut – the other, think I don't know she's a lesbian. No matter how much I provoke her, you know she won't tell . . .

Maria   Maybe she scared you will –

Alfred   Scared of what? You think I care about ting like that, Maria? Who she want to sleep with is she business. I care that she left she child and she husband. Do what you have to do on the side, but don't, don't ever leave your child. She of all people should know that.

Maria   Alfred, you are doing again. I ask what is matter with you?

He stares at her.

Alfred   Go upstairs under my bed. You'll see two boxes. One is an old shoebox, the other green. Bring both of them down with you. Go.

Maria *gets up and leaves.* **Alfred** *wheels himself to gram.*

She returns. **Alfred** *looks at her. Everything he says is calm and collected, even warm maybe.*

Alfred   Open the white shoebox, you will see the letter the hospital sent to my GP and myself after my last scan. And then the one I sent back.

She opens the box and the letter and begins to read. Her eyes suddenly flash up. Her tone very serious.

Maria   What is this word oso . . . ?

Alfred   Oesophagus.

Maria   What that mean?

Alfred   It means I had a scare with cancer of the throat, Maria, a few years ago. They operated and we thought that was dealt with.

Maria   Other long word?

Alfred   Ah, that, my friend, is Latin for saying they were wrong, it wasn't dealt with and now has spread to my bones.

Maria   Your bones? Why you not go back in for new operation? I see letters come from hospital and doctor all the time, you just put them in bin.

Alfred   Because Maria – it is incurable. The boney tumour is on my pelvis and I am terminal. I asked how long I had – years, months, weeks – they said . . . months, without too many 's's. Maybe three months, top. That was two months ago.

Maria   You have month left?

Alfred   Calm down.

Maria   Do children know?

Alfred   No. No one does. Only you.

Maria   When did you find this out?

Alfred   IKEA day.

Maria   Alfred, oh my God.

Alfred   I need you to be calm, Maria.

Maria   I am calm.

Alfred   OK . . . I worked in a hospital for many years of my life, Maria, I saw grown men die horrible humiliating deaths simply cos they wanted to cling onto this thing we call life. I'd watch them as they shat themselves and had to be changed by their children because nurses were too busy. I'd watch as their eyes began to pop out of their head as the smell of death descended. I'd listen to their children cry and wives plead with doctors to do something, as if they were gods. I would watch as the doctors got into character before having to tell a loved one that they were not the deities they thought they were. I would see the nurse as she put two sugars in a cup of tea regardless of whether the person receiving the news of their mortality took sweeteners or not. I heard as they cried in the night, through the night – fearful, weak, scared. I saw all of this, Maria, and I promised myself, that will never be me.

Maria   So?

Alfred   The last few days I have reached a new threshold of pain, Maria.

Maria   Then take painkiller . . .

She gets up to get them. He stops her with his hand.

Alfred   . . . This, they tell me, is the beginning of the swift descent. I will soon stop being able to use parts of my limbs. I will lose the ability to talk and without the use of *industrial strength* painkillers I will probably lie in excruciating pain till I pass through to the next world.

Maria *stares at him, waiting for him to continue.*

Alfred   That is unless . . .

The door bell rings. **Maria** *looks a little afraid.*

Alfred   Don't open it . . . that is, unless you help me – as I have helped you.

Maria   I do anything for you, Alfred, you know that, how you mean help?

Alfred   I can't go like that, Maria. One ting I 'fraid is pain. I need someone to assist me, Maria. If I asked you to assist, to help me, would you?

Maria   How you mean, help?

Alfred   Not gun or knife or pillow over my face, I ain't brave enough for that, no, no . . .

The bell rings again.

Maria   I can't talk this now, I go answer door, Alfred.

She dashes out of the room and opens the front door. It's **Gemma**.

Gemma   What took you lot so long, if I didn't know better I would say all you was doing something you shouldn't.

Alfred   Who tell you we weren't?

Looks at **Maria**.

Gemma   Isn't it a bit past your working hours?

Alfred   Maria lives here.

Gemma   You're a live-in now?

Alfred   No, she – now – lives – here.

Gemma   What?

Alfred   If you came here more than once every few months you might know. Maria was being abused by her boyfriend – she feared for her life. I told her to come and live here.

Gemma   You did what?

Alfred   Till we get the government to sort her out.

Gemma   Maria, would you excuse us a moment?

Maria   Oh, of course. I go upstairs.

Alfred   No, you stay here. If you have something to say . . .

Gemma (*low as she can go*)   Maria, go upstairs.

Maria   Is OK, Alfred, I go . . . I need to, eh, clear head.

Alfred   Don't you leave now.

She leaves the room.

Gemma   You don't know this girl from Adam, how can you move her into the family house?

Alfred   Because I wanted to.

Gemma   Don't you think that's something you should consult your children about – the one's that are paying . . . ?

Alfred   If you looked at your accounts you'd see that *I* now pay.

Gemma   When I was being punched all over the place, you told me I couldn't move in under no circumstances. But she's . . .

Alfred   That was different. Wasn't it, Gemma?

There is something about the way he said the last sentence that makes **Gemma** *pause and look at him.*

Gemma   And apart from Maria being a total stranger, how is it different?

Alfred   I think the time has come for us to be honest with each other, Gemma.

Gemma   I'm all for that.

Alfred   I know you don't like me. It hurts, but hey, you make children, you don't make dey mind. I'm a straightforward man and I've held this on my chest too long. *I'm* unsure if Maria's boyfriend found letters in her drawer saying 'the way we made love last night – from a Susan, April and Joanna . . . '

Gemma (*shocked*)   Shut up. What are you talking about? . . . He told you that?

Alfred   The strap-on too.

Gemma (*regresses to childhood*)   Da what? That's a lie . . . No, it wasn't a lie . . . it wasn't mine, I was looking after it for a friend.

Alfred   And Kia finding you in bed with a woman – that was a lie too, or was that you *returning* it to said friend?

Gemma   Don't be disgusting.

Alfred   Me?

Gemma   So what, that validates him kicking the shit out of me and you, my father, doing nothing?

Alfred   I don't get involved in man and wife business.

Gemma   And what are you doing now with Maria?!

Alfred   You think he didn't tell me all the nasty things you said about me? You know nothing about me and your mother but you would lie about me in that way? Me, who stood by you all you life . . . through your coke habit and you man troubles and you spend two seconds with your mother and I'm the devil! I could have had a career, Gemma, instead what did I do? I stayed here and looked after you and your sister.

Gemma   What's that got to do with the price of plantain?

Alfred   Before you felt the need to run out and do stupidness, when you was going through this new episode, why you didn't feel you could come and talk to me about it? I'm your father, I'm a man of the world, I could have guided you . . .

Gemma   To where? To what? Have you ever listened to yourself? There's no room to talk to you about anything other than you.

Alfred   Don't talk shit.

Gemma   You've no idea how crushed we are under your bitterness –

Alfred   I provided a home for you, Gemma. A good home.

Gemma   Both your daughters leaving home the day they were sixteen – maybe it was a sign that it wasn't so great!

Alfred   It was sign of your fucking slackness. You sister just wanted to run man and you followed she nasty footsteps! You was a nastiness just looking for an excuse. I wouldn't accept in my house. No way . . .

Gemma   I actually came here to see how you were. Why do you do this to me, Dad? Why?

Alfred   Because I'm disappointed in you . . . Your sister was always stupid, but you, you had brain – and you throw it away. I don't care that you are lesbian, I *care* that you didn't tell me. I had to hear it on road. In the betting shop. Thrown in my face. My favourite child I had to hear from strangers tings that she should have told me to my face . . . when a man throw away he life for his family he wants a return. I don't get nothin', Gemma . . . and I might as well tell you now. When I die, all you will be getting nothing in return from me. Not a bloody cent.

Gemma (*almost cool*)   You're a vindictive, nasty old man.
I don't want nothing from you . . .

Alfred   Good. Now, I have used all the energy I have for
the next three days. I'd like you to leave now please . . .
Thank you.

Gemma *stares at him and exits.*

Lights.

Scene Two

Alfred *is on the sofa, covered with a warm blanket. He has his glasses
on and is reading from a book of Polish poetry. He reads aloud the first
stanza from 'In Black Despair' by Czeslaw Milosz.*

Maria   Is Polish?

Alfred   Czeslaw Milosz . . . Did I say that correctly?

Maria   Yes, you say correct. Is very depressing in English.
You must read in Polish now.

Alfred   I don't know how to read Polish.

Maria   I teach you, like you teach me English.

Alfred   You don't think I look too old for such things?

Maria   This is England. There are drugs for such things?

Alfred (*almost childlike*)   Come on, is your turn. Your turn now.

Maria   OK. Choice is yours. Right hand, left.

Alfred   What's in them?

Maria   Don't you worry about that, Mr Alfred. I left
cleaning Mrs Gerald house early so I could go to internet café
and find.

Alfred   OK. Left.

Maria   I was hoping you'd say that.

She runs out of the room.

Alfred   But I could have said right and you could still have done whatever you choose cos you didn't have anything in your hands.

Maria   Quiet, I'm trying to get myself prepare. OK, where is stereo . . . I've recorded the music and everything. Now don't laugh, I try it in Polish and does not work. So I have to do in English –

Alfred   I promise I won't laugh.

Maria   OK. Ladies and gentlemen present, I present to you the LORD INVADER.

She switches on the music from her phone and enters wearing a 1950s-style hat and jacket that she must have taken from **Alfred***'s wardrobe. It is an old-time calypso rhythm. She sings to* **Alfred** *in her Polish accent.*

Maria
The only ting to stop these hooligans
From causing panic in Great Britain,
The only ting to stop these teddy boys
From causing panic in England,
Well I hope that the government
See they need another kind of punishment,
I say one ting to cool down this crime
Is to bring back the old-time cat-o'nine.

(Chorus.)
So the old-time cat-o'nine beat them bad
And they bound to change they mind,
Send them to Dartmoor with licks like fire
And they bound to surrender.
Bom bom bom.

Alfred *falls about laughing.*

Alfred   Bravo, bravo! Fantastic! Oh my God, it was Lord Invader himself.

Maria   You like?

Alfred   Haaaa. I love . . .

Maria   I was going to sing 'Yellow Bird' – but like this better.

He starts to cough. After a while **Maria** *sees that he is not stopping. She runs into the kitchen and returns with a drink of water . . .*

Alfred   No, no, where the, give me the coconut water . . .

Maria   I don't have any ready.

He takes a sip of the water – it is almost as if it is paining him to swallow. But he settles. His chest, however, is giving him much pain.

Maria   Sorry, I make you laugh too much.

Alfred   Don't be stupid. Where you get that song, girl? I don't hear that since . . . I was a child.

She has returned to the kitchen.

Maria (*off*)   Internet . . . You tell me about teddy boys stories, no? Have whole universe of information.

Alfred   Even old West Indian ting?

Maria (*off*)   Everything, Alfred. What a great time to live in, no?

She re-enters with a coconut. She has made a hole in the top. Without **Alfred** *seeing she finishes breaking the last piece of a painkiller in it. When she arrives in front of* **Alfred** *she pours the water from the coconut into his glass. He drinks it down quite quickly.*

Maria   There you are.

Alfred   Even the coconut water taste crap in this country. Where you get it from, the shop on the corner?

Maria   No, I went to Shepherd's Bush as you tell me.

Alfred   The ting must be off.

Maria   They have long way travelling.

Alfred True, true. Anytime I was sick as a boy – bare coconut water my mother would feed me. Medicine for the soul, she say.

Maria How is pain now?

Alfred Sharp but . . . OK.

Maria Do you want a painkiller? . . .

Alfred I told you, I want me mind, not no drugs.

Maria Except marijuana . . .

Alfred I hate that too. Always did. Figure that is why the black man so behind, take them people drugs and make himself slow and stupid. Didn't have a puff you know till I was sixty-two. Bit like masturbation really.

Maria What?

Alfred Didn't do that till my wife left me when I was about thirty-five. After that, I was addicted!

Maria Maybe you should allow the nurse to come see you, Alfred. I am home help, not nurse, but even I know weed is not good enough pain relief . . .

Alfred Once they see me they will put me straight into a hospice. I know how to look after myself, and all you doing is helping me, OK?

Beat as **Alfred** *looks* **Maria** *straight in the eye.*

Alfred (*straight*) How you feeling? Are you still OK about it?

Maria I scared.

Alfred But you ready?

Maria *nods. Beat.*

Maria If you are.

Alfred *smiles.*

Maria *takes off jacket and hat and stands next to Lillie.* **Alfred** *takes out a book from under the sofa and reads from it.*

Alfred   OK. Go, turn the heating down so the temperature in the room is at nine degrees. Go on.

Maria *slowly goes to the thermostat and turns the heating down.*

Alfred   OK, while we wait for that – bring the green box, get the two rubber bands and the plastic bag. You've made sure that the bands are strong enough?

She goes to the kitchen and returns with the cocktail shaker and big IKEA plastic cups. Then she goes to the drawer and takes out the rubber bands and plastic bag.

Make sure when me children see me, they see me like this, yeah? Don't take the bag off.

Maria   Won't they ask who bought the rubber bands?

Alfred   You show them the IKEA receipt. Don't be scared, Maria, I have written everything down. It's not illegal to commit suicide in this country – all you'll be doing is finding me. So that my body doesn't sit here for weeks rotting. My only remembrance. Alfred Morris died alone, like a rotten fruit.

Maria   But is there law for watching?

Alfred (*ignoring*)   The water please . . . coconut.

She goes to the kitchen and returns with it.

Very good. Now bring that table a bit closer to me.

She does. **Alfred** *opens the green box that has been placed on the table. It is filled with the barbiturate painkillers he has not been taking.*

We don't move this table from this moment forward, OK?

Maria   You very smart, Alfred. I first think you no take painkillers cos you like macho man. But you just save up. How much you have there?

Alfred   About three months' supply.

Maria   How much you need?

Alfred Two months'. OK. I am now going to place the contents of the capsules into the water, shake, into the cup and drink it . . .

He imitates doing it but drinks the water.

Maria How long till you sleep?

Alfred Not long at all. But this will help, reduces air . . .

He places the plastic bag over his head and affixes it with the rubber bands.

And then I sleep.

He throws his head back as if having just died. After a few beats **Maria** *runs up and pulls the bag off his head.*

Alfred (*flips*) What are you doing? I told you not to do that.

Maria (*flips right back*) . . . Is rehearsal, Alfred. You don't have to pretend to die.

Alfred Are you going to freak out like this on the day?

Maria No . . .

Alfred . . . Cos if so you need to tell me now, Maria. I need everything to be perfect and if you can't . . .

Maria I said I will do, so I will, Alfred, OK. It's just you pretend too long.

Alfred It's going to be a bit longer than that when we go for real.

Maria That is then, not now.

Alfred Fine . . . legally you're fine, Maria. Go right now and get the copy of the letter you posted for me to the solicitor – here's the book. It is all there.

Maria I don't want to read the book, Alfred . . . Anyway, I ask Ms Donoghue, legal woman I clean for.

Alfred You told her about . . . ?

Maria   No, I ask as if plot in soap opera previous night. Ask if this could happen . . . She tell me maybe, but is difficult after how, she say, Doctor Shipson . . .

Alfred   Shipman.

Maria   Yes. She say most people who do this go Switzerland . . .

Alfred   Why I leaving one cold place to go to a next cold place to dead? No sir . . .

Maria (*thinks*)   You no want to see your home before you go, Alfred?

Alfred   I thought about it, but I don't have nobody home, Maria. No one that would want to see me anyway.

Maria   When was the last time you saw the sea of home?

Alfred   Twelve, fifteen years ago.

Maria   Alfred . . . I have idea. Take me home with you before you go.

Alfred   Pardon?

Maria   All the stories you tell me, you could show me . . .

Alfred   What?

Maria (*excited at new idea*)   I always want to go to Caribbean. Let's go home together. I have money, I save four hundred pounds – you no have to worry about pay . . .

Alfred   I'm not worried about the money.

Maria   Then good, let's go?

Alfred   This isn't a trip to IKEA you know . . . I'm a sick man . . .

Maria   We go for one week. You sleep all the way. If pain, then you take killer – not as if you haven't got many spare! I see home of my Alfred, we come back, you say goodbye happy in heart. What could be better?

Alfred *thinks.*

Maria   Let we go home, Alfred.

Alfred   That's what me wife always use to say. 'Let we go home, Alfred, this country, we . . . Let we go home, boy.' I came home one morning after a long night out, got into the bed. When I woke there was a note. Many years later I thought I saw her from afar once at a funeral – I was too . . . I didn't know how to approach, I just froze . . . They tell me she moved to Grenada about five years . . .

Maria   Why she leave you, Alfred?

Alfred *(looks at her)*   I was Tomas, Maria.

Maria   I think so.

Alfred   Men did things back then without thinking, that today they should not even think about. I don't think I could see her, Maria, just the thought of it frightens me.

Maria   What do people go home for, Alfred?

Alfred   Family, sea, memories –

Maria   – and peace.

Beat.

Alfred   I think I need to sleep now.

Maria   OK. I take you upstairs.

Lights.

Scene Three

Maria *enters the room nervously, followed by* **Gemma***, who seems quite annoyed.*

Maria   Please, you must be very quiet, Gemma . . .

Gemma   I'm not whispering. You're lucky I even walked back into this place.

Maria   Please, Alfred sleep very deep at this time but if we raise voice, he . . .

Gemma *goes to move the table with the green box on in order to get to sit on the sofa.*

Maria   Nooo, don't touch, I have place ready for you.

Gemma   You have a seat ready for me?

Maria   Yes.

Gemma   There's something you may not know about West Indians, Maria – we're very superstitious people. Telling me you have something prepared for me does very little to soothe my supernatural paranoia.

Maria   What that mean?

Gemma   It means I'll stay standing, thank you.

Maria   Would you like tea? I have pot pre –

Gemma *stares at her.*

Maria *pours out two cups. She puts two large sugars in and hands* **Gemma** *the cup.* **Gemma** *takes sip.*

Gemma   Thank you. Bloody hell – what you put in here, the whole of Tate and Lyle?

Maria   Sorry, I think everyone have sweet tooth like me.

She places it on the table.

Gemma   So, what?

Maria (*pops into her mind*)   Do you know if Alfred sent for your mother, Gemma?

Gemma   Pardon?

Maria   Did he send for her from Grenada, or meet here?

Gemma   I have no idea.

Maria   You don't know?

Gemma   That's what I said, innit? Why you wanna know that anyway?

Maria   I think your father send.

Gemma   And the point of that is – ?

Maria   Oh no, just pop in my head. Do you know what village was father born in?

Gemma   Umm, no. What's with all these questions? What is this, some kind ah Polish 419? If you trying to thieve my father's identity, the devil's already done that alright.

She stands. **Maria** *tries to quieten her.*

Maria   There are many things we don't know about our parents, isn't it, Gemma? I knew my father's village because he lived in the same place all of his life. I knew his father's father's name because he lived there before him. I was his star child – only child. The first thing to go was his mind. They knew all along, but he ordered my mother not to tell me. I knew he was ill, but I left. Months later he was wandering around the house peeing himself – and there was I in London mopping the shit of others, earning money to make myself great, when I should have been looking after my father. I will never forgive myself.

Gemma *stares at her.*

Maria   Your father will be die within four weeks.

She hands her the GP's letter.

He has terminal cancer that has spread, and now he is on road to die. He kill me if I tell you, but I must.

Gemma's *knees give way.* **Maria** *dashes to catch her. She places her in a chair.*

Gemma   Oh my God . . .

Maria   Here, have tea . . . sugar will help. He doesn't tell you because he wishes to punish you with it . . .

Gemma   How come he told *you* . . . ? When did you find out?

Maria   By chance . . . Gemma, we could give him his wish and just let him die or we could do something really special . . .

Gemma   Like?

Maria   You ever see, know of your mother?

Gemma (*looks at her*)   I saw her for the first time since she left us, five years ago. She'd moved back to Grenada. I flew there to see her. Why?

Maria   What is name?

Gemma   Rosemarie.

Maria   Huh! I think so. The dream from Portsmouth! The vision at the funeral . . . I think it is very important that your father sees Rosemarie before he dies.

Gemma   How's he gonna do that? You said . . .

Maria   We fly him to Grenada. I have two tickets reserved already to leave on Monday. I have told your father that I will go with him to see the sea, to see where he grow . . . but I think if *you* were to go – take him, Gemma, to see your mother, spend days with him listening to his stories . . . He never says it, but I know every time he looks at me he see Rosemarie, every good deed he does for me is for her. He has never got over what he did to her . . .

Gemma   He shouldn't. She attempted suicide twice over that –

Maria   And it haunts him. We are children, Gemma. We should always stay out of the world of our parents. We don't, we cannot understand . . . I just think to be with you – will make his heart light.

Having regained her composure **Gemma** *stands again. She exhales.*

Gemma   Right . . . So four weeks, you say?

Maria   At most.

Gemma   Can he handle the flight?

Maria   If he can't, he'll die with family? Is a lot better than dying alone.

Gemma   You think he would let me . . . take him?

Maria   Does he need to know?

Lights.

Scene Four

Alfred *is on the sofa in the front room. He is looking a little agitated. And much weaker. There are three suitcases around the room. After a few beats* **Maria** *runs in and takes off her coat.*

Maria   Hey!

Alfred   Where you been? You do say the cab coming at eleven? Is ten-to now, you know.

Maria   Is OK, is OK. Look what I's found!

She holds out an expensive-looking silver tub of polish.

Alfred   What is that?

Maria   I have been looking for everywhere – great bargain for Lillie. Special polish for special wood. I have only been dusting her, not really *cleaning* her – with this, she will look as she did the day you buy . . .

Alfred   What are you doing?

Maria   Polishing Lillie . . . Do you know how long I've been waiting to do this?

Alfred   Where's your case . . . I doe see you bring it down yet?

Maria   Alfred, stop worrying. I'm ready. Look at this . . . doesn't she look better already?

Alfred She does.

Maria What shall we put on to say goodbye to the house? Nat? Billy? How about the new Louis Armstrong I find you in old shop?

Alfred We always playing my music, Maria. Don't you have anything you want to play?

She thinks.

Maria Well, I was going ask if . . . While shopping the other day I find old classic – my favourite when child.

Alfred Put it on, put it on.

Maria You sure? Is not really your type music, Alfred.

Alfred I am a man of wide and varied taste, young lady. Put the damn ting on.

Maria *runs to corner and pulls out a seven-inch single from bag and places it on the new shining Lillie. Out plays 'Like a Virgin' by Madonna.*

Maria *is dancing around the room singing along.* **Alfred** *is waving his arms in the air, singing with the chorus.*

Alfred That's right, the house needs some new music!

Enter **Gemma**. *When* **Alfred** *sees her, he stops.* **Maria** *turns the music off.*

Gemma (*first to* **Alfred**) Hi, Dad.

Alfred *looks around, immediately suspicious.*

Gemma The car's here.

Alfred What car? Maria, what's going on?

Beat as the girls look at each other.

Maria I was going to tell you at airport, Alfred.

Alfred Tell me what?

Maria I no get visa to travel . . . They no let me travel with you, Alfred. Polish Embassy (*too slow*).

Alfred So what?

Maria (*pleading almost*) This trip is too important, Alfred . . .
I ask Gemma to go with you cos . . .

Alfred Are you crazy?

Gemma Dad . . .

Alfred The whole idea, Maria, was that I go to show *you*
where I was born, you where I went school, where I met my
first love – you the one that shows me love . . .

Gemma I'd like to know those things too . . .

Alfred Of course she'd like to know, now there's a free
flight to the Caribbean. She had thirty years to know – is now
she go take an interest? Well, you lie, I'm not going anywhere
with her and that's that.

Maria Alfred . . .

Alfred (*suddenly realises*) You haven't (*told her*) . . .

Maria *No!*

Gemma What? What haven't you?

Maria Nothing . . . to affect you.

Beat.

(*Firm.*) Gemma, may I have moment with father? If you do
not go, Alfred, then I cannot help any further . . . It is what
I feel in my heart you need and it is my gift to you after you
have . . . saved me. We put too much into this for it not to
happen now.

Alfred (*almost with sadness*) Maria, she not going to want to
hear my stories, she hates me. I don't want to be surrounded
by hate at this time . . . She's not going to be interested.

Maria Then you tell me all when you come back! I tell you
now, no more secret . . . I ask Gemma because I want her to
take you see Rosemarie.

He looks up at her. How does she know the name?

Gemma   She wants to see you, Dad.

Alfred   Oh, she does, does she? What make you think I want to see her?

Maria   Every story you tell me is about Rosemarie.

He doesn't reply. Cab horn blows twice.

That is cab, Alfred. What are you going to do?

Alfred   I don't need no kiss-me-arse charity from any of you.

Gemma (*straight*)   But it's not for you, is it? It's for me.

He looks at her. The horn goes again.

Maria   I buy you mobile phone so you can call me every day. From beach, from sea . . . from little rum shack at the bottom of hill in Calliste.

She places it on his lap and goes to leave the room.

I go speak with cab man. Hold on minute.

Beat, beat, beat.

Alfred (*eventually*)   You spoken to her?

Gemma   She's not well herself, actually.

Alfred   Really? (*Then he shuts back down.*)

Maria *re-enters.* **Gemma** *and* **Alfred** *have not moved.*

Maria   Cab man say he won't wait for much longer. What you do, Alfred? This time tomorrow you could be home, in sun. And I will be here waiting for you when you get back. Ready to take our next trip. How many people can plan like that, huh?

He understands what she means and eventually stretches his arms in the air for her to help him get up.

She indicates to **Gemma** *to get the wheelchair. She does.*

Maria   When you arrive, send Gemma to buy SIM and you call me every day. OK?

Lights.

Scene Five

Maria *is sitting on the sofa, reading. She has the blanket wrapped around her. She speaks to herself.*

Maria   Thirty. Thirty members of British Parliament, no cabinet . . . Queen is the constitutional head of the United Kingdom . . . Tim Henman no longer play tennis . . . When do British children get pocket money? When they want it, no?

She turns to the back of the book and adds up her score.

Oh. Once a week . . . Eight out of ten. Yesssss.

She flings the book down and dashes to Lillie. She puts on the Sex Pistols' 'Anarchy in the UK'. She sings with it at the top of her voice.

The doorbell rings.

Maria   Oh.

She switches off the music, dashes to the door. **Alfred** *and* **Gemma** *enter, carrying suitcases.*

Gemma   What kind of mad music you playing, gal?

Maria   History of Britain I learn . . . Oh my God, this so heavy. What you have inside – Alfred body? Sorry, not good joke. How was it?

She gives **Gemma** *a big kiss on the lips.*

Gemma   Don't worry.

Maria   I no worry. Use to watch *Big Black Booty 4* DVD with Tomas. Always wondered what it's like to kiss gay black woman.

Gemma   Who, you or Tomas?

Maria   Both. Was painful?

Gemma   No. So beautiful and peaceful and we all just cried all the time.

Beat.

Maria   Alfred, I miss you so much. So boring in big old house by self. How you cope before I here?

Alfred   Ask me that again? . . . See you kept the place just as we left it.

Maria   Of course. Here, let me take off your jacket. You look great. Is this Alfred I see before me?

Alfred   No, is Lord Invader. (*Sings.*) 'With he old-time cat-o'nine!' Should ah see me yesterday, is the plane that mash me up, I was looking fifteen years younger, today I feel only five.

Gemma *re-enters with final suitcase.*

Gemma   Dad, I'm just gonna pop to Janet's, yeah. We'll be back tonight.

Alfred   Good, good. Later then.

Gemma   You OK, innit, Maria?

Maria   I more than OK. Alfred back.

Gemma   Later.

She leaves.

Maria   So, tell me allll about it . . .

Alfred   You know everything, I called you every day. Tell me what have *you* been doing?

Maria   Well, I finish first citizen test booklet as I said . . .

Alfred   You don't need to do that, only the new EC.

Maria (*excited*)   I love it . . . I sit and test myself as if in exam conditions. I study now for test two. Now you back, is easy. Enough me. Tell me different story from phone!

Alfred   As you done know, Janet flew out here . . .

Maria (*defensive*)   Is not my idea, is Gemma. They both wanted to take you, I say only Gemma.

Alfred   Oh, Maria, it was so beautiful . . . the sea . . . I forget the colour of de sea my modder use to bath me in, girl . . .

Maria (*treads gently*)   And wife?

Alfred (*smiles*)   God can be cruel sometimes you know. How he could give people such beauty knowing that lesser mortals have to look on dat every day . . . She and she new husband would wheel me down to the beach every morning, just as the sun come up and when I put my foot in the water – oh gwad, gal, I feel as if I healing on the spot. I don't lie Maria, I – feel – better. I don't know as if maybe this thing on me bones is getting smaller or less or going away.

Maria   That's great, Alfred . . .

Alfred   I know, who could believe it? I was going down, down, down, Maria, and now I feel I could climb a coconut tree, jump from the top of a bunk bed, swing and bust a big six . . .

Maria   Maybe we should go your doctor? Have them check . . .

Alfred   I was thinking that –

Maria   Oh Alfred, you make me so happy. I told you going home would create miracle. I felt it in my heart . . .

Alfred   As you know, I went on the internet. Sent you an email. I mean, what a wonderful invention. What a wonderful time to be alive. Everything is moving so fast – I could die today, and tomorrow them fine a cure . . . for everything.

Maria   Exactly. I call the doctor tomorrow and we go see him. Go to hospital – they tell us everything OK . . .

Alfred   You know, as I was flying back looking out on the clouds I thought how many people live years after doctors say they go dead. Years. Thing suddenly go in remission. BAM! You back. You don't even know why.

Maria   Let me get you some coconut water? I went out and got some yesterday especially.

Alfred   Dem stale ole ting that you fill up with painkiller. I bought fresh, just fall from the tree before we fly, coconut girl.

Maria   Where are they?

Alfred   Top of that bag there . . . I've been unfair to me children, Maria. Hey, so they both dunce, they didn't achieve nothin, is not every child can be Dawkins and Hawkins is it? How I could expect them not to search for they modder?

Maria   Is right.

Alfred   Is the sea bath release me, gal, like magic touch me soul . . . How was Lillie? She miss me?

Maria   No, cos I play her loud every day. New kinds of music. Even had the neighbours banging one night . . .

Alfred   Good. Them bitches. Keep them up, man . . . Oh girl, what is life? All these years I held in my heart what I had done to that woman and, you know, she had set me free years ago? The moment she saw me she said, 'Hello big Al,' and I knew she had forgiven me. All the nights of . . . of running next woman . . . bringing next woman in me own house to have dominion on her . . . all the days of spending all she money so she had nothing . . . and all of the nights after she had gone, nights of realising what I had done – they all just disappeared and I felt like a man released from a weight greater than himself. In front of my children she forgave me. And for a singular moment, we could have been anywhere, anywhere in the world, but we were a family.

Maria *gives him the water.* **Alfred** *drinks it down in a gulp.*

Maria   My word, you *are* better, Alfred, that would have taken you an hour!

Alfred   Go get me will for me, please, Maria.

Maria   Your will?

Alfred   From the side of the bag there.

Maria   What you want will for?

Alfred   I had a solicitor draw it up in Grenada. I want this house sold, Maria – what do you think?

Maria   I have no thoughts, if you think it is right.

Alfred   Good. And when it's sold I'm going to split fifty-fifty you and Gemma. Janet husband rich, she don't need nothin.

Maria   Oh Alfred, I don't want half of house, I am not your child.

Alfred   Who's going to look after you when I'm gone?

Maria   I look after myself.

Alfred   Let me tell you something. I come to this country with nothing and work like a dog. You come to this country and you working like a dog. You's the rightful inheritor. Not them that squander it.

Maria   If you want to leave me something when you die, which of course we know now will be a long time away now, leave me Lillie. That's all I want.

Alfred (*looks at her*)   I was in the air flying, looking down at the clouds, and I thought, thank God I didn't take my life before this glorious moment . . .

Maria   Life is good, eh, Alfred?

Alfred   But it will never be better than this moment right now.

Maria   Of course it will. Give you a few months, you get strong, back on your feet, you go home again . . .

Alfred   Even if they found a cure tomorrow, I will never feel happier than I feel right now, never.

Maria   What are you saying?

Alfred (*smiling*)   I'm saying, I couldn't wait to get home, Maria.

He smiles, walks and sits on the sofa near the table with the green box.
Maria *stands next to Lillie. She knows what he means.*

Maria   But you just said how (*happy you are*) . . .

Alfred   Exactly . . . I'm ready, child. I'm ready for the next ride.

Maria (*beginning to get scared*)   But you said, Alfred . . . you feel as if it is getting better – it could be going . . .

Alfred (*calm and almost joyous*)   Don't back out on me now, Maria, now's when I really need you.

He opens the box and sees that the capsules are not there.

(*Flips.*) Where are they?

Maria   I threw them away.

Alfred   You did what?

Maria   You sounded so happy I didn't think you'd want to do it any more.

Alfred   Maria, what have you done? You have destroyed the best moment of my life . . . Why would you have me stay here? Why would you do this to me?

He almost sounds like he's screaming from his soul.

Why, Maria, why?

Maria *suddenly darts to a corner and pulls all the drugs out and places them back in the box.*

Maria   *There*, there you are! OK?

Alfred *calms down. Never taking his eyes off her, he eventually smiles.*
Maria *stares at him for a while. Still he doesn't take his eyes off her, but is smiling with his whole face. Eventually* **Maria** *walks to the thermostat and turns it down.*

Alfred   Thank you, Maria.

Maria   Can we at least not wait till the doctors confirm that it is still . . .

Alfred, *not taking his eyes off her, just smiles.*

Maria   You once said that Nat and Lillie had answers to every question in the world. What should I play to give me answer to stop this?

Alfred   This might be the only one I don't think it has an answer for . . .

He breaks the seal on the capsules and pours capsule after capsule into the shaker.

Maria (*starts to cry*)   Don't, Alfred, please don't.

When **Alfred** *is done, he looks at* **Maria** *with so much love in his eyes.*

Alfred   I tell you what to put on. Track three, side two.

Slowly she does. It begins to play – Nat King Cole's 'Let There Be Love'.

Alfred (*while the song is playing*)   Ms Polish. You have made me a very happy man.

He pours the water from shaker into the large cup and drinks it slowly but deliberately. When he is done he leans back in his seat and exhales a long breath. Then, with a sudden jerk **Alfred** *leans forward.*

Alfred   Shall we?

He stands and holds out his arms to dance. **Maria** *stretches out her arms and they ballroom-dance around the room. 'Let There Be Love' continues to play. On the last beats of the song* **Maria** *spins* **Alfred** *back into the chair.*

Nat
Hmmm umm . . . love
Hmmm umm . . . love.

Alfred *lets out a long sigh and leans his head gently to the side. With the biggest smile on his face, he passes to the next world.*

Maria *kneels and places her head on his lap and places his hand on her face.*

Nat
   Let there be love.

Lights

Methuen Drama Student Editions

Jean Anouilh *Antigone* • John Arden *Serjeant Musgrave's Dance*
Alan Ayckbourn *Confusions* • Aphra Behn *The Rover* • Edward Bond
Lear • *Saved* • Bertolt Brecht *The Caucasian Chalk Circle* • *Fear and
Misery in the Third Reich* • *The Good Person of Szechwan* • *Life of Galileo* •
Mother Courage and her Children • *The Resistible Rise of Arturo Ui* • *The
Threepenny Opera* • Anton Chekhov *The Cherry Orchard* • *The Seagull* •
Three Sisters • *Uncle Vanya* • Caryl Churchill *Serious Money* • *Top Girls*
• Shelagh Delaney *A Taste of Honey* • Euripides *Elektra* • *Medea*•
Dario Fo *Accidental Death of an Anarchist* • Michael Frayn *Copenhagen*
• John Galsworthy *Strife* • Nikolai Gogol *The Government Inspector* •
Robert Holman *Across Oka* • Henrik Ibsen *A Doll's House* • *Ghosts*•
Hedda Gabler • Charlotte Keatley *My Mother Said I Never Should* •
Bernard Kops *Dreams of Anne Frank* • Federico García Lorca *Blood
Wedding* • *Doña Rosita the Spinster* (bilingual edition) •*The House of
Bernarda Alba* • (bilingual edition) • *Yerma* (bilingual edition) • David
Mamet *Glengarry Glen Ross* • *Oleanna* • Patrick Marber *Closer* • John
Marston *Malcontent* • Martin McDonagh *The Lieutenant of Inishmore* •
Joe Orton *Loot* • Luigi Pirandello *Six Characters in Search of an Author*
• Mark Ravenhill *Shopping and F***ing* • Willy Russell *Blood Brothers*
• *Educating Rita* • Sophocles *Antigone* • *Oedipus the King* • Wole
Soyinka *Death and the King's Horseman* • Shelagh Stephenson *The
Memory of Water* • August Strindberg *Miss Julie* • J. M. Synge *The
Playboy of the Western World* • Theatre Workshop *Oh What a Lovely
War* Timberlake Wertenbaker *Our Country's Good* • Arnold Wesker
The Merchant • Oscar Wilde *The Importance of Being Earnest* •
Tennessee Williams *A Streetcar Named Desire* • *The Glass Menagerie*

Methuen Drama Modern Classics

Jean Anouilh *Antigone* • Brendan Behan *The Hostage* • Robert Bolt *A Man for All Seasons* • Edward Bond *Saved* • Bertolt Brecht *The Caucasian Chalk Circle* • *Fear and Misery in the Third Reich* • *The Good Person of Szechwan* • *Life of Galileo* • *The Messingkauf Dialogues* • *Mother Courage and Her Children* • *Mr Puntila and His Man Matti* • *The Resistible Rise of Arturo Ui* • *Rise and Fall of the City of Mahagonny* • *The Threepenny Opera* • Jim Cartwright *Road* • *Two & Bed* (due 2009) • Caryl Churchill *Serious Money* • *Top Girls* • Noël Coward *Blithe Spirit* • *Hay Fever* • *Present Laughter* • *Private Lives* • *The Vortex* • Shelagh Delaney *A Taste of Honey* • Dario Fo *Accidental Death of an Anarchist* • Michael Frayn *Copenhagen* (due 2009) • Lorraine Hansberry *A Raisin in the Sun* (due 2009) • Jonathan Harvey *Beautiful Thing* • David Mamet *Glengarry Glen Ross* • *Oleanna* • *Speed-the-Plow* • Patrick Marber *Closer* • *Dealer's Choice* (due 2009) • Percy Mtwa, Mbongeni Ngema, Barney Simon *Woza Albert!* (due 2009) • Joe Orton *Entertaining Mr Sloane* • *Loot* • *What the Butler Saw* • Mark Ravenhill *Shopping and F***ing* • Willy Russell • *Blood Brothers* (due 2009) • *Educating Rita* (due 2009) • *Stags and Hens* (due 2009) • Jean-Paul Sartre *Crime Passionnel* • Wole Soyinka • *Death and the King's Horseman* • Theatre Workshop *Oh, What a Lovely War* • Frank Wedekind • *Spring Awakening* (due 2009) • Timberlake Wertenbaker *Our Country's Good*

Methuen Drama Contemporary Dramatists
include

John Arden (two volumes)
Arden & D'Arcy
Peter Barnes (three volumes)
Sebastian Barry
Dermot Bolger
Edward Bond (eight volumes)
Howard Brenton
   (two volumes)
Richard Cameron
Jim Cartwright
Caryl Churchill (two volumes)
Sarah Daniels (two volumes)
Nick Darke
David Edgar (three volumes)
David Eldridge
Ben Elton
Dario Fo (two volumes)
Michael Frayn (three volumes)
David Greig
John Godber (four volumes)
Paul Godfrey
John Guare
Lee Hall (two volumes)
Peter Handke
Jonathan Harvey
   (two volumes)
Declan Hughes
Terry Johnson (three volumes)
Sarah Kane
Barrie Keeffe
Bernard-Marie Koltès
   (two volumes)
Franz Xaver Kroetz
David Lan
Bryony Lavery
Deborah Levy
Doug Lucie

David Mamet (four volumes)
Martin McDonagh
Duncan McLean
Anthony Minghella
   (two volumes)
Tom Murphy (six volumes)
Phyllis Nagy
Anthony Neilsen (two volumes)
Philip Osment
Gary Owen
Louise Page
Stewart Parker (two volumes)
Joe Penhall (two volumes)
Stephen Poliakoff
   (three volumes)
David Rabe (two volumes)
Mark Ravenhill (two volumes)
Christina Reid
Philip Ridley
Willy Russell
Eric-Emmanuel Schmitt
Ntozake Shange
Sam Shepard (two volumes)
Wole Soyinka (two volumes)
Simon Stephens (two volumes)
Shelagh Stephenson
David Storey (three volumes)
Sue Townsend
Judy Upton
Michel Vinaver
   (two volumes)
Arnold Wesker (two volumes)
Michael Wilcox
Roy Williams (three volumes)
Snoo Wilson (two volumes)
David Wood (two volumes)
Victoria Wood